THE LIFE CYCLE IN WESTERN EUROPE,
*c.*1300–*c.*1500

MANCHESTER
1824

Manchester University Press

MANCHESTER MEDIEVAL STUDIES

SERIES EDITOR Dr S. H. Rigby

SERIES ADVISORS Professor John Hatcher
Professor J. H. Moran Cruz

The study of medieval Europe is being transformed as old orthodoxies are challenged, new methods embraced and fresh fields of inquiry opened up. The adoption of inter-disciplinary perspectives and the challenge of economic, social and cultural theory are forcing medievalists to ask new questions and to see familiar topics in a fresh light.

The aim of this series is to combine the scholarship traditionally associated with medieval studies with an awareness of more recent issues and approaches in a form accessible to the non-specialist reader.

ALREADY PUBLISHED IN THE SERIES

The commercialisation of English society, 1000–1500
Richard H. Britnell

Reform and the papacy in the eleventh century
Kathleeen G. Cushing

Picturing women in late medieval and Renaissance art
Christa Grössinger

The politics of carnival
Christopher Humphrey

Medieval law in context
Anthony Musson

Medieval maidens
Kim M. Phillips

Chaucer in context
S. H. Rigby

MANCHESTER MEDIEVAL STUDIES

THE LIFE CYCLE
IN WESTERN EUROPE,
c.1300–*c*.1500

Deborah Youngs

Manchester University Press

Manchester and New York

distributed exclusively in the USA by Palgrave

The right of Deborah Youngs to be identified as the author of this work has been asserted by her
in accordance with the Copyright, Designs and Patents Act 1988

Published by Manchester University Press
Oxford Road, Manchester M13 9NR, UK
and Room 400, 175 Fifth Avenue, New York, NY 10010, USA
www.manchesteruniversitypress.co.uk

Distributed exclusively in the USA
by Palgrave, 175 Fifth Avenue, New York, NY 10010, USA

Distributed exclusively in Canada
by UBC Press, University of British Columbia, 2029 West Mall,
Vancouver, BC, Canada V6T 1Z2

British Library Cataloguing-in-Publication Data
A catalogue record for this book is available from the British Library

Library of Congress Cataloging-in-Publication Data applied for

ISBN 0 7190 5915 1 *hardback*
EAN   978 0 7190 5915 5

ISBN 0 7190 5916 X *paperback*
EAN   978 0 7190 5916 2

First published 2006

15 14 13 12 11 10 09 08 07 06   10 9 8 7 6 5 4 3 2 1

Typeset in Monotype Bulmer
by Koinonia, Manchester
Printed in Great Britain
by Bell & Bain, Glasgow

To
Mam, Dad,
Alison and Melanie

CONTENTS

ACKNOWLEDGEMENTS

Writing a book on this subject has inevitably made me conscious of the broad range of life's experiences that have formed its content. Academically, the book has its genesis in a module I taught when I was first employed at the University of Wales, Swansea. I would like to extend my thanks to the students who took the module and to my colleagues for their interest and support over the last six years. In particular, Ralph Griffiths, who read and commented on part of the text, has been a constant source of information and inspiration. I am grateful to both Nicholas Orme and Joel Rosenthal for their helpful remarks on early drafts of chapters, and I have greatly benefited from the help of Alex Clarke, Leighton James and Ifor Rowlands. Needless to say, all errors still remaining in the text are my own.

The material on the life cycle has grown thick and fast since I began writing this book with conferences in 2005 likely to produce many more publications. My regular requests for interlibrary loans grew even while the book-writing was supposedly coming to an end. There is still much to be read and said, but life is short and a line has to be drawn somewhere. On that note, I am thankful to Manchester University Press for allowing me the extra time to consider some of the latest research. My family, who have seen far less of me recently than they would have liked, will be relieved that I wasn't given any more. My dedication to them is a 'thank you' for tolerating my absences and for providing welcome distractions. Friends and fellow runners were equally adept at highlighting that there was life outside the book. 3M Gorseinon Road Runners, especially Louise, have shown me that intellectual frustration can be balanced with the physical pain and exhaustion of cross-country running!

Finally, I have been fortunate in having the support of two people whose faith in my work has never faltered. Alex Marsh has been a source of strength for nearly half my life. I have greatly appreciated both his patience and his critical eye. James Thomas deserves the last word (for once) because his invaluable friendship, encouragement and advice have steered me through many a low point. I hope they will think this book worth all their effort.

1

Introduction

Dear sister,
At the age of fifteen years, in the week that you and I were wed, you asked me to be indulgent to your youth and to your small and ignorant service, until you had seen and learned more ... And know, dear sister, that all that I know you have done since we were wed until now and all that you shall do hereafter with good intent, was and is to my liking, pleases me, and has well pleased me. For your youth excuses your unwisdom and will still excuse you in all things as long as all you do is with good intent and not displeasing to me. And know that I am pleased rather than displeased that you tend rose-trees and care for violets, and make chaplets, and dance and sing; nor would I have you cease to do so among our friends and equals, and it is good and seemly to pass the time of our youth [written c.1392].[1]

I N these opening lines from his letter of instruction, the ménagier (or householder) of Paris considers the age of the recipient in ways familiar to the present day. Her age is noted in chronological years (fifteen) indicating that the ménagier not only knew the girl's age, but considered it an important aspect of her identity. Attached to the age was the quality of 'youth', which was associated with certain well-known characteristics: immaturity and lack of knowledge. The letter continues to be sensitive to the issue of age, repeating the girl's need for instruction and referring to behaviour considered typical of her years: tending flowers, dancing and singing. As in the twenty-first century, age in medieval society appears partly determined by calendar years, partly by social and biological development. However, aspects of this correspondence are not so acceptable to the modern mind: the ménagier was a middle-aged husband writing to his new, young wife. While a fifteen-year-old may dream of marriage in modern

1

Europe, and have sexual relationships, perhaps even children, society at large does not consider her 'ready' to take this particular step in her life cycle. The age of consent, like the age of majority and criminal responsibility, is culturally determined and reflects a society's particular views about age.

The ménagier's letter raises issues that are central to this study of age and the life cycle in Western Europe between about 1300 and 1500. This book asks whether medieval society felt the need to measure age. What attitudes were expressed on the ageing process and the achievement of a particular stage of life? To what extent, and how, did age form part of a person's identity? What role did age play in the organisation and government of society? These and similar questions have attracted increasing scholarly attention. In studies focusing on the medieval period, three approaches have proved fruitful. The first, and most easily defined, has been the study of specific age groups. Childhood has led the way and continues to receive the greatest attention: studies are now available on the medieval children of Britain, France, Germany, Italy, Spain and Scandinavia.[2] Academic research has its own cycles, and since the 1990s there has been a growing literature on adolescence, youth and old age.[3] A second, smaller, set of studies has focused on theories of ageing and literary representations of the entire life cycle. Issues considered include philosophical discussions of the life span, fertility and the division of life into a series of fixed stages.[4] A third approach uses the category of age as a tool of analysis: in other words, how a person's age may determine access to power and employment patterns and define status. Certain actions and roles are shown to be characteristic of specific stages of the life cycle. This analysis has been employed effectively in discussions of female workers, English peasant and aristocratic societies, the Venetian nobility, Venetian rape cases and Florentine sodomy trials and in a range of studies on the family.[5] To a greater or lesser degree, all approaches demonstrate the view articulated by Peter Laslett in 1995: 'Together with gender, ethnicity and class, aging is one of the four dimensions of individual and social experience'.[6]

A considerable body of literature is, therefore, accumulating on the subject of age. To date, however, no general overview of the whole medieval life cycle has been considered. One of the key aims of this book is to offer a synthesis of the main findings of current research on age. It is intended as an outline survey and consequently the scope of the book is deliberately broad: it covers two centuries, considers the large land mass of Western Europe with its diverse languages, customs and cultures, and ranges across the social spectrum. Such an ambitious task has its practical limitations, and the constraints of time and space have made it necessary to be selective. Plans to cover Jewish and Muslim life cycles had to be changed, and the book will focus solely on the Christian West.[7] The balance of the study has been largely influenced by the availability of the material, and partly by personal interest. Most attention has been accorded studies on England, France and northern Italy because these areas have the most developed bibliographies on life's stages. But I have also drawn upon comparative material from the Low Countries, Germany, Spain, Scandinavia, Scotland, Ireland and Wales. The coverage inevitably reflects the fragmentary nature of the evidence for the period, and it has to be underlined that sources for a study of age and age groups in the Middle Ages are not in abundance. Particularly frustrating are materials for children, adolescents and the elderly. As later chapters will indicate, their marginalisation in life is reflected in their invisibility in many admin-istrative and legal records. As with all medieval sources, there is also a heavy male bias to the records, and we know far more about the life cycle of the nobility than about that of the peasantry. Nevertheless, the research undertaken on age-related issues has revealed the breadth of material available if the net is cast sufficiently wide. A second major aim of this book is to demonstrate just how extensive that range can be. Examples featured in this study are drawn from manorial accounts, tax assessments, spiritual writings, didactic literature, romances, elegies, art and architecture. Many sources are already well known, but their value to life cycle studies remains unexplored. I have, therefore, incorporated quotations from a number of primary sources in order to highlight the range of possible materials that can be used to tease out medieval perspectives on age.

The main thrust of this book is that age formed an essential part of a person's identity in late medieval Europe. A key question is whether it did so in specifically 'late medieval' ways. To age means to experience physical and psychological changes, for example in body size, skin elasticity, hair colour and memory recall. While these are common to all humans, how that process is understood varies across cultures, and shifts with historical time. In modern-day Britain, age is calculated as the number of years passed since birth, and it is widely used as an identifier on passports, employment records and criminal files, among other official documents. It is common to divide life into stages and label particular ages with terms such as 'baby', 'child', 'adolescent', 'adult' and 'elderly'. Yet in other cultures, chronological age and age divisions do not assume such signi-ficance. The Inca civilisation bemused the sixteenth-century Spanish conquistadores in this attitude towards time. According to Bernabé Cobo

(1582–1657) the Incas 'did not count their age in years; neither did they measure the duration of their acts in years … there was never an Indian who knew his age, and there are hardly any today who know how many years old they are'.[8] Modern researchers, with feelings of a similar culture gap, have sometimes argued that medieval society did not employ age divisions nor recognise distinctive phases of life. The best-known example is Philippe Ariès's *L'enfant et la vie familiale sous l'Ancien Régime*, published in 1960 (translated into English as *Centuries of childhood* in 1962). He claimed controversially that childhood was not considered a distinctive period of life before the seventeenth century. What was lacking in the medieval period was an awareness of childhood as an age group distinguishable from adulthood with its own special needs and characteristics. Instead, the young were quickly integrated into society; in work and in image they were treated as miniature adults. Adolescence has been considered an even later development, not emerging fully until the end of the nineteenth century with the introduction of prolonged schooling and the delay in entering the workforce. The related idea of 'youth culture' is similarly seen as a modern invention, dating to the mid-twentieth century. Finally, modern sociologists assert that old age has not always been considered a distinct life stage. In pre-industrial society, it is argued, adulthood simply flowed into old age with no institutional markers.[9]

This book is not intended as solely another debunking of modern assumptions about the Middle Ages. Even though these views can still hold sway in the popular imagination,[10] researchers of the medieval period have sufficiently undermined the claims that the modern world invented or exclusively defined childhood and youth. As Chapter 2 will discuss, theories of ageing appear in a range of medieval literature, as does the concept of life stages. They demonstrate the tendency to group people together on the basis of age and to employ terms to denote childhood, adolescence, youth, adulthood and old age. The use of the phrase 'life cycle' in this book reflects the medieval view of life as a series of fixed stages, which everyone passes through. It is the case that medieval society may have understood these terms to refer to different chronological ages or reflect different qualities from those understood by modern society. What is interesting, and what this book will consider, is the extent of that deviation, and the question of continuity and change between the medieval and later periods.

It is not a modern imposition, therefore, to divide the main body of this book into the following life stages: infancy, boyhood and girlhood, adolescence and youth, adulthood, old age. While these groups are treated separately, it is with the conviction that they can be understood only in relation to other stages of the life cycle. Each chapter has three broad aims. The first is to examine the qualities medieval society thought natural or typical to a particular age group. Age formed part of a person's physical description and carried with it certain assumptions or 'age expectations' about an individual's behaviour and capabilities. A broad range of literature can reveal how medieval society expected a child, adolescent or adult to act, and how people were treated according to their age. As has been shown, the ménagier had not expected his fifteen-year-old wife to act with maturity. Nevertheless, age qualities (like those associated with femininity and masculinity) could also become detached from the actual ages of the person: a forty-year-old could act 'childishly'; a young child might have 'old' characteristics. As such the existence of age stereotypes and potential age discrimination will feature in several of the chapters.

A second aim is to consider the entrance and exit points to key stages of life. Ageing is a constantly changing experience. Unlike belonging to an ethnic group or a gender, which is generally a permanent state of affairs, membership of a particular age group is not something that can continue throughout life. Each stage is transitory; individuals, in the words of Giovanni Levi and Jean-Claude Schmitt, 'simply travel though it'.[11] Life for late medieval people was punctuated with milestones of varying degrees of significance: birth, starting work, marriage, parenthood, widowhood, inheritance, leaving home, becoming knighted, becoming a master crafts-man, withdrawing from work, death. In some cases rituals marked the point of transition. Arnold Van Gennep and Victor Turner have taught us to see these rites of passage as a tripartite schema: a person is separated from one stage, and experiences a transitional or liminal period, before becoming fully integrated into the next life stage.[12] While this study will not apply that model rigidly to every situation, it does accept the basic premise that the purposes of rites of passage were to smooth over transition and declare publicly the new state of being. While they were tailored to specific situations, there are interesting features common to the rituals operating in the late Middle Ages. In the process of moving from one state to another, there was an underlying sense of graduating from a lesser to a better state of being. In the case of baptism or churching, it was the change from an unclean to a clean state; a parallel may be drawn with university initiation rites, which declared a transformation from beast to civilised person. Socially, the rites publicised that a person (usually male) had shown himself able to serve a community, be that as a knight or a guildsman. The

5

process of integration was celebrated at a communal level, spiritually through the ceremony of the Mass (available for baptism, marriage, churching, knighthood and death) and by the more earthy feasting, which occurred at virtually all public events.

The third aim is to consider the changing opportunities and possibilities for people as they progressed through life. What doors opened and which others closed as people aged? Age operated as a means to organise roles and responsibilities in both the family and political society, and it acted as a form of social control. At one level this would involve controlling a person's behaviour by ensuring that he or she conform to age-appropriate behaviour. This might be done directly through censure (scolding a youth for acting childishly), or indirectly through public scorn (an old person ridiculed for acting inappropriately for her or his age). At a more official level, society could prohibit, permit or compel individuals towards a series of activities and situations on the basis of their chronological age (payment of taxation, inheritance, marriage, official positions). This tracked their development into maturity and full social status. In so doing, age inequalities became ingrained in the structure of medieval society. Access to social roles and political power was linked to a person's age, his or her life stage and the assumptions made about both. Subsequent chapters will show that children had no formal access to power; those in their teens had greater, but still limited, roles. The ruling (adult) bodies of fifteenth-century Florence, for example, excluded from government boys (*fanciulli*), young men (*giovanni*), the commoners and women. Each group was said to possess specific characteristics that marked them out as unworthy for rule. In the case of boys, they were prone to violence as seen in their rock, fist and truncheon fights at Carnival, and their habit of dismembering the bodies of executed criminals. The *giovanni* mocked the political affairs of their fathers, leading to fears of political upheaval. Collectively these groups were deemed to lack the gravity, reason and controlled sexuality that government demanded.[13]

What this example also highlights is that adult commoners and adult women were considered on a par with the immature young male elite. While the book takes age as its primary focus, it is does not assume that age can be treated as an isolated variable and that everyone in medieval Europe experienced the ageing process in the same way. The broad scope of the book permits difference to be explored via the key variables of status, gender, space and time. It considers whether there are points in a person's life where age mattered more than other variables like gender or class (or vice versa). More commonly, age will be discussed in terms of its interaction with other variables. In the case of social status, chapters will consider the extent to which social rank influenced life expectancy, the methods and goals of upbringing, marriage patterns and funerary memorialisation. Gender will feature prominently throughout the book, reflecting the current wealth of new research. It will be shown that at almost every stage of the life cycle, gender differences are apparent. Upbringing played an important part in shaping gender roles, and the pressure to conform to expected masculine and feminine characteristics increased as a person grew older. Gender influenced the experience of adolescence, the age of marriage and the attitudes one could expect in old age. At the same time, I do not want to give the impression that men and women travelled two separate paths. Children in particular shared experiences that were not gender-specific (or indeed class-specific), and the period of adolescence brought opprobrium on both male and female.

The study ranges across Western Europe, and general comments will be made about the Christian West as a whole. The unifying force of the Christian church, the influence of Roman law, the mobility of the elite, the development of the universities, the spread of classical ideas and the popularity of vernacular romances, among others, all contributed to unifying Western culture. It should not be surprising to read, therefore, that attitudes towards ageing and the experience of growing up were similar across the continent. Nevertheless, Western Europe was not a single entity, and we would expect to see differences in relation to customary practices and regional laws. A number of studies have drawn attention to divergences between northern and southern Europe in terms of marriage patterns, family formation, opportunities for women and attitudes towards death and its rituals.[14] Regional and detailed local studies have indicated further diversity between neighbouring, or at least nearby, settlements. This study cannot pick out every tone of Europe's rich canvas, but it will endeavour to show some of the colour of local variation.

A final consideration is time. The period chosen for this study is the fourteenth and fifteenth centuries, a period often called the 'later' Middle Ages and one traditionally associated with crisis, upheaval and socio-economic change. The list of trials and tribulations is well known. From the late thirteenth century, a cooling down of the economy exacerbated the strains placed on a burgeoning European population. When climate change in the early fourteenth century brought cold, wet weather and damaged harvest, many Europeans began to suffer from food shortages and high food prices. A series of devastating crop failures led to widespread famine, and between 1315 and 1322 an area of around 400,000 square miles of northern Europe was afflicted by a 'great hunger'. In Ypres in 1316, one-tenth of the population (over 3,000 people) died. A weakened population succumbed to tuberculosis, influenza and typhus. Yet none was as devastating as the plague, which first appeared in Europe in 1348. The death toll makes it Europe's greatest natural disaster. The most recent assessment of the impact of the Black Death during the years 1348–50 suggests that as much as 60 per cent of Europe's population may have been killed. Recurrent plague attacks occurred in virtually every subsequent generation in the fourteenth and fifteenth centuries. At the same time Europe experienced warfare to an extent not seen since the Viking invasions. War zones dotted Europe, and the major conflict known as the Hundred Years War (1337–1453) drew in at least thirty different countries at its height.[15]

As Chapter 2 will indicate, these factors had a considerable impact on life expectancy and age profiles, in both the short and medium terms. More difficult to assess is whether developments in society brought about changes in perceptions of ageing or the experience of the stages of life. There is good reason to argue that continuity characterises the later Middle Ages in relation to age. Not only do attitudes towards ageing appear comparable in say 1300, 1400 and 1500, but they share features with those expressed in times before and since. Readers will themselves note many points of similarity between the late medieval and modern worlds. Exasperation with the noisiness of children, the follies of youth, and the view that people can be 'past it' will all seem familiar. Such transhistorical affinity can spring from the role that nature plays in influencing behaviour. In her work on medieval childhood, Shulamith Shahar has criticised the focus on the social construction of age and promoted the 'immutable and universal' biological factors involved in caring for children; nurture and care are needed in order for the child to survive. While she goes further than most in her support of biological influence, there is an important point here concerning the role that basic human emotions play in history.[16] Nevertheless, the fourteenth and fifteenth centuries did witness some important developments that had an impact on the experience of ageing. The establishment of foundling hospitals, an increase in hospital places for the old, and a growing number of schools and apprenticeships had the potential to alter the quality of life. Opportunities and experiences could vary from one generation to the next: (re)marriage patterns and employment prospects for young people fluctuated with plague attacks and the changing socio-economic climate. Each chapter will draw attention to the degree of continuity and change for a phase of the life cycle.

In looking at age in the context of a developing medieval Europe, this book examines the considerable potential of using age as a tool of analysis. In the late twentieth century, class and gender came to be seen as significant variables in the study of medieval people, and they continue to be applied to a wide range of texts and debates. It is hoped that this book will establish that age and the life cycle warrant a similar prominence in historical and literary analyses.

Notes

1   The full Old French text can be found in Brereton and Ferrier (eds), *Le ménagier de Paris*; the quoted lines are on p. 1. I have adopted the translation of Amt (ed.), *Women's lives*, pp. 317–18.

2   E.g. Arnold, *Kind und Gesellschaft*; Alexandre-Bidon and Closson, *L'enfant à l'ombre*; Nicholas, *Domestic*; Shahar, *Childhood*; Beer, *Eltern und Kinder*; Hanawalt, *Growing up*; Haas, *The Renaissance man and his children*; Alexandre-Bidon and Lett, *Children*; Orme, *Medieval children*.

3   E.g. Eisenbichler (ed.), *The premodern teenager*; Phillips, *Medieval maidens*; Karras, *From boys to men*; Goldberg and Riddy (eds), *Youth*; Minois, *History of old age*; Rosenthal, *Old age*; Shahar, *Growing old*.

4   Burrow, *The ages of man*; Sears, *The ages of man*; Goodich, *From birth to old age*; Biller, *The measure of multitude*.

5   E.g. Goldberg, *Women, work and life cycle*; Bennett, *Women in the medieval English countryside*; Harris, *English aristocratic women*; Chojnacki, *Women and men*; Ruggiero, *The boundaries of eros*; Rocke, *Forbidden friendships*.

6   Kertzer and Laslett, *Aging in the past*, p. 4.

7   Interest has grown in the development of Jewish children and adolescents. See e.g. Marcus, *Rituals of childhood*.

8   Bernabé Cobo, *History of the Inca empire*, pp. 252–3.

9   Ariès, *Centuries of childhood*. To John Gillis, in *Youth and history*, the period 1870–1900 discovered adolescence, with 1900–50 'the era of adolescence'. See Hall and Jefferson (eds), *Youth subcultures*, p. 1; Hareven, 'The last stage', p. 205.

10   E.g. Jeanette Winterson writing in the *Guardian* in 2001: 'The nineteenth century invented childhood, so that it could sentimentalise its own brutality. Throughout history, kids have always been little adults, expected to contribute to the family economy and usually to marry very young. What we call progress – keeping kids at school, letting them doss at home, giving them money, removing responsibility – has not produced happier, stable individuals who make good spouses and parents'. (*Guardian*, 15 May 2001, p. 9).

11   Levi and Schmitt (eds), *A history of young people*, p. 3.

12   Van Gennep, *The rites of passage*; Turner, *The ritual process*, especially ch. 3. See also the following historical study, which came out after I had written this book: Nicola F. McDonald and W. M. Ormerod (eds), *Rites of passage. Cultures of transformation in the fourteenth century* (Woodbridge, 2004).

13 Trexler, *Public life*, p. 367.
14 E.g. Smith, 'The people of Tuscany'; Kittell, 'Testaments of two cities'; Cohn, 'The place of the dead', pp. 17–43.
15 The literature on these topics is vast. For a thorough assessment of the Black Death and an extensive bibliography see Benedictow, *The Black Death*. See too Jordan, *The great famine*. For a brief survey see Griffiths, 'The interaction of war and plague'.
16 Shahar, *Childhood*, pp. 1–2.

2

Age and life expectancy

T HE modern view of the Middle Ages is that life was brutal and short. Later medieval society would probably agree. People's lives were short compared with the eternity that awaited them in the afterlife. They were short too in comparison to those of the Old Testament Patriarchs, who had lived to ripe old ages: Abraham had achieved 170 years, while the infamous Methuselah reached 969. Air pollution and sinful behaviour were among the factors medieval writers blamed for the drop in the life span. Instead, as the Bible told them, man and woman could now hope for three score years and ten. While some successfully achieved their potential, the late Middle Ages were not conducive to long lives. In a period of relatively poor sanitation and medical care, increased warfare, famine and endemic plague, death was an ever-present reality at any age. It was not uncommon for contemporary writers to express the view that life in the 1300s and 1400s was shorter than in previous centuries. Despite reaching his eighties, the French prelate Gilles le Muisit (1272–1353) believed that people did not live as long as they had done in his youth. The Florentine Giovanni Morelli (1372–1444) had compared present and past members of his family tree and reckoned that forty years of life in the twelfth and thirteenth centuries were equivalent to only twenty-five or thirty in his own time.[1] These views raise three interlinked issues with which this chapter is concerned. First, the knowledge medieval people had of their own ages: was Morelli unusual in having data about present and past ages? Second, the attitudes towards age and the ageing process: how far did 'age' as a concept matter to medieval people? Third, the tricky issue of life expectancy: how far were medieval people able to achieve three score years and ten, and what were the factors preventing or assisting that process?

Chronological age

It is a common assumption that people in medieval society did not know and did not invest much importance in knowing their age. Historical evidence does go some way in supporting the claim. It only takes a glance at various legal and administrative documents to realise that there was no systematic recording of ages. Records of mortality, such as the coroners' rolls of England or the Books of the Dead of Florence, rarely mention ages, almost never for adults. Few autobiographers and biographers saw the birth date as integral to their work; their starting point was their subject's public or spiritual birth. Ignorance is found even in the higher reaches of society. No one knows precisely when Henry V (d.1417), one of England's most famous kings, was born: maybe 1386, maybe 1387. When King Louis XII of France (c.1462–1515) tried to annul his marriage on the basis that the union had been forced on him when he was under the age of consent, his case faltered on the grounds that no one knew with certainty when he was born. Witnesses to the king's case offered a range of ages from eleven to thirteen and others simply fell back on what they remembered about the king's height and build.[2]

Nevertheless, as that last case illustrates, exact age could matter in certain circumstances. In Western Europe between about 1300 and 1500 there was a growing interest among sections of the population in the issue of chronological age. Part of the impetus came from the top, as growing government bureaucracies, particularly urban authorities, amassed information on the populations under their control. From the thirteenth century, Venice had a special statistical office to collect information on the population, undertaking an early census of the city in 1338, and population censuses are later recorded in Dresden (1430), Ypres (1431), Basle (1454) and Strasbourg (1470). More significantly, baptismal records appear in Italy, Spain and German-speaking cities from the last decades of the fourteenth century – Barcelona (1359), Siena (1381), Münster (1403) and Florence (1450) – before spreading to England and France in the early sixteenth century.[3] Their introduction can be partly attributed to the desire for greater precision in the matter of age. In the early fourteenth century the Florentine communal government, which had hitherto accepted a rough estimate, now insisted that all its subjects know and record their age. Behind the order lay financial and political concerns: a person's birth date and age would decide the tax burden, military service and entry to high office. Of particular significance was the Florentine taxation system (known as the *catasto*), which made those living in the city conscious of the ages of eighteen and sixty, the entrance and exit ages for paying taxation. The growing frequency of official questioning about age does appear to have made Florentines more aware of their ages. David Herlihy and Christiane Klapisch-Zuber have noted a marked improvement in the accuracy of ages offered in the *catasto* of 1470 compared with that of 1427.[4] In other cities the collecting of data was related to specific or abnormal events rather than a long-term policy. In Barcelona in 1457, plague attacks forced city fathers to order reports on the number of daily baptisms and burials in each parish. It was hoped that the information, showing the 'real' rather than the feared mortality rate, would calm citizens and persuade them not to flee the city.[5]

Medieval society also used chronological age as a way to control the development of the person, regulating his or her full entry into society. As subsequent chapters will detail, the Church set age threshold levels in relation to marriage, confession, communion and taking Holy Orders. In the cities of Florence and Venice, minimum age levels were set to enter the main government offices. Candidates were asked to provide proofs of age, which were systematically recorded from the early fifteenth century, suggesting a growing concern over age-qualification for office.[6] Across Europe, laws and customs relating to inheritance promoted an awareness of the age of majority. Depending on the tenure of land, the minimum age of inheritance could be fourteen (common for copyholders) or twenty-one (if holding by knight's service). Under- age heirs would not be able to take control of their inheritances, but would become wards. Their assigned guardians administered the lands, directed their education and could organise their marriage. It was therefore important that the age of an heir was known. In England and Wales proof-of-age inquisitions required several witnesses to come before a jury to offer evidence on the birth date of the subject.[7] Individuals, therefore, could face a number of age thresholds throughout their lives, determined by the societies they lived within. In late medieval Castile, civil codes directed the gradual achievement of adulthood: seven was the minimum age for betrothal; ten and a half was the minimum age for discerning right from wrong; twelve and fourteen were the ages for marriage; seventeen was the earliest age to practise law; and twenty was the minimum age to be a judge.[8]

Yet it was not simply a top-down imposition. Society as a whole was becoming more eager to note birth dates in personal records. In Florence, Leon Battista Alberti (1404-72) believed that 'as soon as the child is born one should note in the family records and secret books, the hour, day, month, year as well as place of birth'.[9] That a number of Florentine citizens did so can be seen in surviving family memoirs (*ricordanze*), where the listing of the births and baptisms of their children are recorded alongside public and private events. While primarily a family record, the memoirs could have a public function too as the Florentine government accepted the books as proof of age. In France, birth dates were recorded in *livres de raison*, and in England, from the late fifteenth century, merchants and gentry recorded their children's births into commonplace books. The London merchant Richard Hill listed the hours and dates of the births of his seven children as well as their godparents and baptismal gifts.[10] An alternative was to record births in devotional works. The birth date of Margaret Beaufort (1443–1509), mother to the English king Henry VII, was written into her mother's book of hours. When Margaret later inherited the book she had her chaplain note down key family events, including the birth dates of nearly all her grandchildren.[11] Further examples are to be found in liturgical manuscripts, particularly those stored in the churches where the individuals had been baptised. Examples can be found in the testimonies produced in proof-of-age cases in both Wales and England. In eleven English cases recorded between 1399 and 1405, witnesses from Essex, Dorset, Wiltshire, Somerset, Bedford, Derbyshire, Lincolnshire, Northumberland and Yorkshire mention seeing the subject's name and birth date written in books kept in the parish church. The most favoured was the missal, in which five births were recorded; two others were in martyrologies, one in a psalter, and two in an unnamed 'book'.[12] The noting of the birth appears to have been part of the process of etching a potential heir's birth and age on to a community's memory. To this end, neighbours could receive gifts from the child's parents or be invited to celebratory meals at the time of birth or baptism.[13]

There is no evidence that these birth dates were annually celebrated, but scattered references do indicate that age milestones among the elite were marked. In 1362 King Edward III invited leading English nobles and French noble hostages to a ceremonial hunt in his forests and parks to celebrate his fiftieth birthday. It is also known that Alfonso, brother of Queen Isabella of Castile, received a poem on 14 November 1467 from Gómez Manrique 'in honour of his fourteenth birthday'. Lower down in society, recorded birthday celebrations are noticeable by their absence. The word 'birthday' was known in Middle English, but it was not in common usage. Nicholas Orme has suggested that because the entrance books of Winchester College noted the ages of the boys in relation to major saint's days or festivals, it is possible that the boys only had a 'rough, seasonal idea of their birthdates'.[14]

Greater accuracy, however, was important in the compilation of horoscopes, where the exact date and preferably the hour of birth was needed. In the later Middle Ages, horoscopes performed an essential function in the prognostication of illness and disease. They could decide when treatment should begin or on what days medicine should be taken. The horoscopes made for the French king Charles V (*reg.* 1364–80) and his children were compiled precisely in case a physician needed them. It is from surviving manuscripts from the end of the fourteenth century, and largely from the fifteenth century, that horoscopes feature in greater numbers. They became very fashionable among Europe's elite; in 1500, for example, Antonius Gazius assembled a casebook of horoscopes of Italian noblemen and women. For most of the later Middle Ages, only a small proportion of Europe's population showed interest in horoscopes. Nevertheless, astrology and horoscopes were spreading through the population.[15] The provincial English gentleman Humphrey Newton (1466–1536) noted the exact hours and dates of birth of all his children in his commonplace book. Given that the manuscript contains astrological material, including a table of the planets, it may well be that Newton was prepared to make his own prognostications.[16]

Chronological age crept into a variety of other records too, indicating its use as a form of description. In a case study of 600 miracle stories across Europe, predominantly from the fourteenth and fifteenth centuries, Ronald Finucane noted that 335 cases specified the person's age.[17] The brass of the young English girl Anne Boleyn (d.1479) gives a very precise date for her death: she died at the age of three years, eleven months and thirteen days.[18] Artists wishing to capture the likeness of themselves or their sitters at certain stages of the life cycle occasionally recorded an age on their work. The fifteenth-century portrait of Margaretha Van Eyck notes both the date of the artwork and her age, thirty-three, at the time of the sitting. Likewise the Nuremberg painter Albrecht Dürer (1471–1528) produced an unusually high number of self-portraits in his teens and early twenties on to which he had someone inscribe his age.[19]

Nevertheless, a greater recording of age did not mean that rough reckoning disappeared. For some, the rounding up or down of age was deliberate. In one of Francesco Petrarch's letters to Giovanni Boccaccio, he made reference to the way the old and the young falsified their ages. While youth pretended to be younger to prolong youthful pleasures, the old increased their age hoping for greater respect.[20] There could be more material gains on offer. Florentine and Venetian males advanced their ages to over thirty and twenty-one respectively in order to be eligible for a government position. Fathers sometimes lied about their daughters' ages in the pressure to get them married. In 1315 the family of Maria of Cyprus-Lusignan managed to convince envoys of King James II of Aragon that Maria was below twenty-five, the upper age limit stipulated by the king. She was, however, over thirty.[21] Massaging ages was also a means to save money. The Florentine *catasto* results of 1427 indicate that male ages were lowered or raised outside the range from eighteen to sixty in order to avoid paying taxation.[22]

For others, a rough guide was all that appeared necessary. It is rare in official records to find people declaring that they did not know their age; they appear to have offered it to officials without hesitation. Authorities too assumed that people knew their ages: at the Abbey of Westminster entrance turned solely on a novice's own testimony concerning his age.[23] Nevertheless, there are numerous official records across Europe where respondents have offered ages in terms of 'around', 'about' or 'and over'. Multiples of ten were popular, with even numbers preferred to odd numbers not divisible by five. A clear example is offered by the Florentine *catasto* of 1427, where 259 people said they were thirty-nine, and 253 said they were forty-one, but 11,200 said they were forty. Preferences changed in relation to the life cycle. In the responses to the 'mouth count' for Reims in 1422, parents appear to have known fairly accurately the ages of their children up to thirteen (girls) or fifteen (boys): the full range of ages is used. Thereafter there is an increased preference for even numbers. For ages sixteen to thirty-two, thirteen times as many people gave their age in even numbers as in odd numbers.[24] Rough reckoning assumed a greater prominence in records where age had nominal value. In the canonisation proceedings for St Yves in 1330, held in Tréguier, three-quarters of those offering their age and profession gave their age as a multiple of ten.[25] Choice of age may also have been made in relation to lucky and unlucky numbers. Seven and nine were deemed particularly unlucky, so an age having a multiple of either was risky.[26]

What still held good in medieval society was a judgement according to physical appearance. Even proof-of-age inquiries continued to record the qualification 'as he appears according to his physical aspect'.[27] The Church overall differed from secular authorities in never demanding proof of a person's age. Candidates presented for the priesthood (with a minimum age of twenty-four) would have their maturity judged on their appearance and mental capacity rather than any written proof. As a result of such attitudes, many ambiguities in calculating ages extended into the early modern period. In England there were no clear guidelines over whether age was calculated in terms of the year a person had just left or the one just beginning. It was not until 1851, and for the census, that age was defined as 'age last birthday'.[28]

How many knew their ages in the medieval period cannot be known. What can be said is that during the fourteenth and fifteenth centuries Western Europeans were living in societies where chronological age was mattering more. Growing bureaucracies and the accompanying amassing of written records provided more reasons to be aware of one's age and birth date. The demands were likely to vary according to where a person lived and his or her occupation: a Florentine merchant would have more need to know his age than a peasant in a village in Aragon. Nevertheless, even though knowledge was patchy and not always precise, a wide cross-section of society would recognise the significance of ages such as eighteen and sixty for financial reasons, and fourteen or twenty-one for inheritance. Chronological age mattered to medieval society as an identifier and a form of control; age was a measured quality. But, as shown above, absolute accuracy (outside astrology) mattered less than the cultural meaning given to each age: a person might be old enough to inherit, old enough to marry or old enough to pay taxes.

Theories of ageing

Chronological age was merely one way of signifying age, and only one indicator of a person's capabilities. In modern theories of ageing individuals may be described in terms of having a physiological age, a social or cultural age, or a functional age.[29] While medieval society did not use these terms, they similarly saw age as a scientific category (like weight or speed) which formed part of the physical description of a person. This point is forcefully made in the sheer range of material on the ageing process available in the later Middle Ages. Theoretical discussions on issues ranging from the life span and fertility to the different stages of life were produced by university scholars, physicians and moral and social commentators. There is little that is distinctively 'late medieval' about them, for they were based on the accumulative wisdom of several centuries: a combination of classical and Arabic moral and natural philosophy together with Christian theological writings. Of particular significance was the work of Aristotle (d.322 BCE), including his treatises collectively known as *On animals*, and the *Liber canonis* ('Canon of medicine') by the Arabic physician Avicenna (980–1037). The great programme of translation and synthesis which took place in the eleventh to thirteenth centuries meant that by 1300 anthologies of essential classical quotations on the life span were readily available in schools and universities. For example, Engelbert of Admont (*c*.1250–1331) gathered together an impressive collection of classical quotations from writers like Seneca and Cicero, which discussed the division of ages and the stages of childhood, adolescence and youth.[30]

These commentaries were written in the world of the educated elite, and it is possible to argue with Georges Minois that these theories of life were merely 'intellectuals' games' with a limited readership.[31] Nevertheless, during the fourteenth and fifteenth centuries discussions on the ageing process, increasingly in the vernacular, became available to a broader literary public. Ideas about particular age groups and their attributes provided the framework for a wide range of popular preaching and entertainment. Friars used them for pedagogical purposes, employing the ageing process as a metaphor for the development of the soul. On a similar spiritual theme, the life cycle was a useful device in morality plays where the transience of human life was highlighted. As later chapters will show, poets like Dante, Chaucer, Boccaccio and Charles d'Orléans used age in romances and ballads to mark the passage of time, to add character to protagonists and to employ and explore age stereotypes. Visually, the various stages of life were employed on church and secular buildings, tapestries, manuscript illuminations and stained-glass windows. Examples are found in the stained glass of Canterbury Cathedral, the fourteenth-century frescos of the Eremitani in Padua and the fifteenth-century marble floor of the duomo in Siena. Images of life's stages also became, according to Elizabeth Sears, 'part of the stock in trade of the late medieval house decorator'. Two walls of a room in the castle of Sargans in Switzerland, for example, were painted in about 1470 with images of the different ages of life.[32]

The ideas expressed in these works can be roughly grouped into two linked subjects of interest. The first was the physiological process of ageing, which philosophical and medical texts described as progressive and irreversible. In discussions on the organisation and functions of the human body, emphasis was placed on its composition of the four basic elements: fire (hot and dry), water (cold and wet), earth (cold and dry) and air (hot and wet). In addition, the body's survival depended on the four bodily fluids or humours: blood, phlegm, yellow bile and black bile. Together they formed a person's complexion, and their balance was essential to the maintenance of good health. What determined the length of life was the combination and retention of heat and moisture. Following the arguments of Aristotle and Galen (d.*c*.201), ageing was shown to be the result of a gradual loss of vital energy as the body's moisture dried and its heat wasted away. Arabic scientists compared life to an oil lamp, which would gradually burn itself out as the heat consumed the body's moisture.[33] The logic of this argument meant that the young would naturally have more heat and moisture than the old, who would be defined as cold and dry.

How much moisture and heat each body had, and the time it took to dissipate, depended on a number of variables. Most importantly, texts stressed individuality, as each person had her or his own complexion and humoural balance, which rendered a personal life span. All, however, were affected by two further variables. The first was gender. Males, even in the womb, possessed more natural heat than females and did not lose it so quickly. By the age of puberty, women had cooled to the extent that their bodies were unable to dry up superfluous moisture, and regular monthly blood flows were necessary to get rid of excess fluid and waste. Throughout their adult lives women were characterised as colder and moister than men, and consequently less perfect and weaker. They were not uncommonly compared to children in terms of their immature, incomplete bodies.[34] This affected their life span. The traditional Aristotelian view stated that, with less heat, women progressed more speedily through life than men, ageing more quickly and dying earlier. It appeared to be proven by reproduction. Women became capable of reproduction around twelve to fourteen at the onset of their menses, but would stop reproducing in their forties. Conversely it was believed that men would not be able to reproduce until twenty-one, yet could generate in their sixties, possibly later.[35] By the later Middle Ages, however, a challenge to that view came in the work of Albertus Magnus (d.1280), who may well have been influenced by personal observations of long-lived women in the religious community of Cologne. For Albertus, women's greater longevity was the result of the purifying power of menstruation, their lighter work load and their less frequent sexual activity.[36] Whichever view was preferred, both ultimately rested on a woman's perceived biological and physical weaknesses.

While individuals could do little to alter their sex, they did have some control over the 'drying' process. A second variable was what medieval society labelled the 'non-naturals' and what the modern world might call 'life style' or living standards: environment, air, exercise, food and drink. Following Avicenna, late medieval writers noted that those living in high places would be healthy and strong, and those living in moist regions were likely to live longer, while those in hot, dry regions would see old age at thirty. Good health meant keeping the body's elements and humours in balance, and avoiding anything that quickened the loss of moisture. Women would age more quickly if they had many children; men would significantly reduce their life span if they over-indulged in sex because the emission of seed weakened the body.[37] It was, therefore, logical for Michele Savonarola (from Padua, c.1385–c.1466/68) to recommend that women breast-feed their babies because this would reduce the number of pregnancies and add length to life: every birth was seen as a body beating.[38] This and other advice could be found in guides to healthy living, which grew in number in the later Middle Ages. Their popularity was not in small part due to the claims by medieval physicians and philosophers that, should due care and attention be taken, ages in the region of 100 could be reached.[39]

A second focus of interest was the stages of life. In describing the changes along life's journey, the majority of writers and media divided the progress into a set of fixed stages. This type of schema – often going by the name of 'ages of man' or 'ages of life' – had been inherited from antiquity, where Aristotle had divided life into the three stages of youth, maturity and old age. By the later Middle Ages the number of stages ranged from three to twelve, with some preference for seven among English writings and ten in German-speaking areas.[40] Of particular influence was the work of Isidore of Seville (d.636), whose Latin dictionary, the *Etymologiarum*, described the etymology and characteristics of six stages. In this he established some of the most commonly used conceptual terms for discussing life's stages and the age limits applied to each: *infantia* (up to age seven), *pueritia* (up to fourteen), *adolescentia* (up to twenty-eight), *iuventus* (up to fifty), *aetus senioris* or *gravitas* (up to seventy) and *senectus* (until death).[41]

In trying to understand the nature and number of life's stages, medieval philosophers were working towards a greater goal: the desire to link the human life cycle to other numerical schemata in the universe. The idea of a single law governing the planets, the seasons and the human body had been a feature of ancient texts, but it achieved greater importance in the hands of Christian writers and preachers: their 'ages of man' literature promoted the essential unity of God and nature.[42] This is illustrated in the fourteenth-century psalter owned by Englishman Robert de Lisle (d.1343), where ten stages of life are drawn to form a wheel. At the hub lies God with the inscription 'I see everything at once and govern by reason'.[43] The selection of particular numbers was a deliberate attempt to link the human life cycle with other universal bodies and timeframes: seven brought to mind the seven planets, the seven deadly sins or the seven days of the week; four linked the cycle to the four elements of life, the four seasons, the four evangelists or the four corners of the world. The canonical hours were a favoured timeframe. A fifteenth-century English lyric saw life as a day, with death occurring at night. The poet describes his birth in the morning, his dubbing as a knight at midday, his crowning as a king at nones and his decline at evensong.[44]

In other words, while the essential motor of life was change, underlying everything was the constancy and immutable presence of God. In providing an explanation for change and a framework for life, this could bring comfort to many who could see no other pattern to life, especially in a period of social and political upheaval. Nor did it matter, therefore, that these theories of ageing were ancient and had originated in societies unlike those of later medieval Europe: what mattered was that God's plan remained the same. Ageing in the medieval world was presented ahistorically and as a universal event, whose stages everyone went through in the same order.

Similarly predictable were the qualities of each life stage: each 'age' was believed to exhibit a specific set of characteristics. As later chapters will show, age formed part of the physical description of the person and carried with it certain assumptions, or 'age expectations', about an individual's behaviour and capabilities. In the words of Dante: 'some manners and some kinds of behaviour are more reasonable at one age than another'.[45] As a result, to behave in ways suitable for an age group other than one's own was considered a deviation that was treated suspiciously and often harshly. The old should not try to act as though they were young, the young should not shoulder responsibilities suitable for the more mature. One example would be the case of children who showed early signs of piety, a quality deemed natural in the old. While some preachers and moral writers approved of early piety, others appeared less tolerant of wise boys than of naughty boys; the latter were at least acting according to age type. There was a danger, as the medieval proverb stated, that young saints would end up old devils. There were serious health ramifications too: premature development would use up vital moisture and therefore shorten the life span. Desiderius Erasmus (1466–1536) noted in his *Adagia* (1500) that it was a common belief that boys wise before their time would not live long and would lose their wits when they entered adulthood.[46]

Each person, therefore, should 'keep' to their age group, but that did not mean that all ages were equal. Theories concerning age were based on the assumption that everything in nature grows, sustains itself and then decays. Dante described this ascent and descent as an arc with a climb in youth to maturity at its apex, and a downward move to old age and death. A good illustration of the movement is the wall painting surrounding the arched entrance-way in Longthorpe tower near Peterborough (decorated c.1330), where the early stages of life climb up the left-hand side and the later stages decline on the right. An alternative was to present life as a wheel, which allowed analogies with the wheel of fortune and the upward and downward turns of life.[47]

Each stage marked a phase in an individual's physiological, psychological, social and spiritual development. As Christine de Pizan (c.1365–c.1430) wrote, 'The difference in age ensures a difference in their attitudes and social positions'.[48] On the upward motion of the arc or wheel, childhood and adolescence were characterised by the gradual acquisition of maturity, power and substance. The development was reflected in age terminology: Isidore of Seville explained how the term *infantia,* which was given to those in their first years of life, derived from the child's inability to speak as the teeth had yet to develop fully.[49] As shall be shown in Chapter 3, attitudes towards the undeveloped young meant that children had few legal responsibilities. At the other end of life's cycle, on the downward turn of the wheel of life, elderly individuals were characterised as losing their physical and mental capacity, and thereby their substance and power. Age was hierarchical, a point reflected clearly in artwork of the period: whatever the real relative sizes of an adolescent boy and a mature man, the latter would always be represented as taller because of the power he had accumulated in life.[50] The pinnacle of a person's life was achieved when the bodily humours were in balance and where physical capabilities were matched by mental capacity; Aristotle called it 'the ideal moral mean'. While the peak would differ according to the individual, perfection would ultimately be reached in adulthood. The concept of a 'perfect age' was widespread in medieval literature and became attached to the mid-thirties. As Chapter 6 will discuss, adulthood was therefore the aspiration, the top of the arc or wheel, the goal that children were moving towards and the old were moving away from.[51] It was only natural, therefore, that society was ruled by 'adults'.

The 'ages of man' literature, as Mary Dove and others have so clearly shown, almost exclusively considered the male life cycle. Issues of social power chart a masculine public and active life; the majority of artwork presents images of male (and overwhelmingly aristocratic) characters with swords aloft or crowned as kings. Only a very few examples can be found of female life cycles, and they emphasise the different trajectory of life expected for women. One is the pseudo-scientific *Secretum secretorum,* where the four seasons are described in relation to female development. Spring is represented as a young, beautiful woman admired by onlookers; a richly clothed bride represents summer; a mature woman past youth, and usually described as 'old', symbolises autumn; and a decrepit old woman signifies winter. In other words the women's experience is solely defined by her physical appearance and biological function. It charts the growing maturity of the women's sexuality before the loss of beauty marks her decline. In this way a woman will always age socially more quickly than the male because while he can still enjoy his perfect age (in his thirties and forties), she is already in the autumn of her life.[52]

As the issue of gender illustrates, medieval society believed that certain individuals would pass through life's stages more speedily than others. In the fourteenth and fifteenth centuries a few writers thought that life was generally moving more quickly than in times past. Michele Savonarola believed that the young were experiencing life's stages sooner than they had 200 years earlier: three-year-olds were as astute as five- or six-year-olds; five-year-olds behaved like children of seven and eight; and youths married much earlier.[53] Similarly, when Count Gaston Phébus was writing his hunting manual (c.1387–89) he observed that seven-year-olds were better able to gain and retain knowledge than had been the case for twelve-year-olds when he was young.[54] That these appear well-worn, timeless phrases should not undermine but indeed enhance the point that medieval society subscribed to the idea of age timetables.

Life expectancy

So far this chapter has shown that age theory and classification were found in a wide range of late medieval writings. In the fourteenth and fifteenth centuries these ideas circulated in the vernacular at the same time as the growing bureaucracies of Church, state and urban governments fuelled the need for individuals to know their own age. But what medieval society was not interested in doing was testing theory by gathering and using statistics to calculate birth rates, mortality rates and life expectancy. Medieval society did not regularly produce, either intentionally or as a by-product, the large data-sets of 'age' figures that evidence demographic studies in the early modern and modern periods. Add to that the rough-reckoning calculations and the fragmentary nature of the surviving documentation, and it is clear that the simple question 'how long could a person expect to live in the later Middle Ages?' turns out to be one of the hardest to answer. Nevertheless, demographic historians and archaeologists have made ingenious attempts to turn material such as tax assessments, hearth surveys, manor court rolls, monastic records and skeletal remains into approximate figures for mortality rates and life expectancy. While the difficulties and pitfalls of these calculations render them 'high-risk operations', they offer our only rough guides to the length and quality of life expected in the later Middle Ages.[55]

For a large percentage of Europe's population, life ended not long after it had begun. Infant mortality was appallingly high in the later Middle Ages, and all the evidence points to birth and infancy being the most dangerous times of the entire life course. Estimates from written records suggest an infant mortality rate (infant usually meaning the under-sevens) in the region of twenty to thirty per cent.[56] These figures should be set in the context of a wide under-reporting of young children, especially neonatals, whom society saw little reason to commit to record. Archaeological material confirms the high mortality rates even while it too is an imperfect source and under-records children: infant bones disintegrate quickly and are more likely to be disturbed than those of adults. Given this, the small cemetery of Fröson, Jämtland (territorially in Norway), which served the surrounding peasant population between 1050 and 1350, is humbling: half of the total cemetery population had died before the age of seven.[57] This may well reflect a number of crisis years relating to population pressures at that time. Other parts of Europe record high infant mortality rates following on from periods of plague or famine. In the parish of St Peter's, Reims, the crisis years of 1420–21 saw the mortality rate of the under-sevens rocket to around fifty per cent.[58]

Death struck across the social spectrum. Higher standards of living and better access to nursing care may have saved some children, but the wealthy were not immune to infant deaths. Between 1330 and 1479 around a third of children born to England's ducal families died before reaching their fifth birthday.[59] Tragedy could hit those who otherwise appeared omnipotent: Edward I of England, conqueror of the Welsh and Hammer of the Scots, saw seven of his sixteen children die before they reached the age of seven. A more significant factor may have been gender, because boys appear more vulnerable than girls in their early years. James Grubb's sample of the children of memoir writers in the Veneto suggests that over twice as many males as females died in their first month. The disparity began to reduce only after the age of three, and girls continued to have the advantage until twenty.[60] These figures have to be viewed with caution as memoir writers may have felt less need to record their daughters' than their sons' deaths. Nevertheless, while the data from the late medieval period is slim, the greater vulnerability of boys has support from the much richer records of late Tudor England.[61]

Infants are the most vulnerable people in any period, but there were particular reasons why the rate was so high in late medieval society. Infants had to survive the traumas of birth in a society with little obstetrical medical support. They were the most susceptible to malnutrition and starvation during periods of famine, while their underdeveloped immune systems came under attack from disease and infection. The urban death registers produced by the grain office of Florence, which Ann Carmichael has studied for the years 1385–1458, list some of the prominent killers of children. Diseases causing diarrhoea such as 'worms' and the dysentery-like *pondi* mainly attacked children, while newly-borns were susceptible to the *mal maestro* ('master disease'), which appears to have been akin to tetanus or sepsis.[62] There were no effective medicines or vaccines to immunise the child, and perhaps the only slim chance of immunity came from breast-feeding, which twenty-first-century medical studies have suggested offers some protection against certain diseases. With this in mind, Ole Jørgen Benedictow has argued that infant mortality in medieval Norway increased as the belief spread that a woman's first milk (colostrum) was injurious to babies' health in the first few days or weeks of life. The decision to feed newly-borns sour cream, butter or cream porridge instead of mother's milk may have proved harmful to the baby's digestion.[63] The question of if, and how far, this may have affected other children in Western Europe awaits further research.

A far greater killer of children was plague. Chroniclers across Europe agree that, while the Black Death of 1348–49 hit a broad cross-section of society, children were the major victims of plague in the later fourteenth century and fifteenth century. In Paris, Jean de Venette, a Carmelite friar writing around 1359–60, thought that 'the young were more likely to die than the elderly, and did so in such numbers that burials could hardly take place'. In England, Spain and France the plagues of 1361–62 and 1369 were believed to target infants and young men; the *Anonimalle chronicle* (from northern England) labelled the 1361–62 attack 'the plague of children' ('la mortalite des enfauntz'). The story is similar in Arles, southern France, in the 1370s and in Mainz, Germany, in the late 1380s. Nor did the situation differ in the fifteenth century. A Parisian journal writer described the plague of 1418 thus: 'And out of four or five hundred dead not a dozen would be old people but all children and youngsters'.[64] While a few doubts have been expressed over these opinions, historical research tends to confirm that, in the century following the Black Death, plague had become a child's disease. Remarkable figures have emerged from the records of the Dominican cemetery in Siena. Whereas in 1348 only a small proportion of plague mortalities were of children, by 1383 children comprised eighty-eight per cent of plague victims. Similar evidence is recorded for Pisa (1374) and Florence (1423–24), while even in Ghent, where plague deaths were lower, the outbreaks of 1368–71 drove child mortality rates to 'catastrophic proportions'. Children additionally suffered in plague years because epidemics disrupted normal sanitary care and food delivery, leaving them open to greater risk of other infections. During epidemic years in Florence, around two-thirds of all deaths were of children.[65]

It was, therefore, a very fortunate section of society who survived their infancy. Once they had done so, the chances of living a long life improved notably. Death rates declined in late childhood, and there are some indications from data collected for fifteenth-century Pistoia and Florence that the ages between seven and fourteen saw the lowest mortality rates of the life course.[66] It is the improvement in survival that has led demo-graphers to estimate medieval life expectancy from a point later in life when the hazards of childhood had passed. The fragmentary nature of the surviving evidence has meant that figures can be estimated only for certain social groups. Yet they do show some uniformity. Information gathered for London's merchants, and peasant societies in the midlands and south-east of England suggests that, on reaching twenty, men could expect an average life expectancy in the early fifties. Similarly, in fifteenth-century Florence, Verona, Vicenza and Padua, men who reached twenty-five could expect another thirty years of life.[67] While this is below the Biblical three-score years and ten, such estimates belie the notion that all of medieval society died young. Several studies show that a substantial minority exceeded expectations. Joel Rosenthal's study of 434 secular peers summoned to the English parliament between 1350 and 1500 indicates that thirty-one per cent lived beyond sixty years.[68]

The causes of adult deaths were various. Instead of the twenty-first-century concerns of cancer, heart disease and AIDS, there were fears of plague, famine, malnutrition, tuberculosis and, in the fifteenth century, sweating sickness. Reaching maturity also brought a new set of factors that helped to determine the quality and length of life. Those in their twenties to fifties were the most active in society, whether that meant working in the fields, fighting on the battlefield, travelling on business, having children or managing a household. They were placing their bodies in high-risk situa-tions, and mobility could open them up to new infections. Getting older took its own toll on the body, and skeletal evidence shows high rates of osteoarthritis, as well as problems of heart and lung disease. Some of the toils can be seen on the skeleton of Sir Hugh Hastyngs, a Norfolk landowner who died in 1347 before reaching his fortieth birthday. He was suffering from osteoarthritis, probably the result of weapon bearing and physical damage during his military activities; his teeth had been eroded by coarse foods, and several teeth were missing, the likely consequence of a blow to the mouth.[69]

The variables of social status, wealth and gender had roles to play. Among the peasantry of the English manor of Halesowen divisions of wealth appear to have translated into life expectancy. Whereas at twenty the more substantial tenants could expect a further thirty years of life, poorer tenants could only hope for just over twenty and the destitute cottagers a mere ten.[70] Nevertheless, the evidence does not suggest that the life expectancy of the wealthier peasantry was out of line with those in the upper echelons of society. This may well have been because peasant survivors of the fourteenth-century crises enjoyed a better standard of living than their pre-plague forebears, who suffered the effects of an overcrowded landscape. The English peasantry benefited from better housing conditions and improved diet; increasing amounts of beans, dairy produce, fish and particularly meat added necessary protein, vitamins and minerals. It appears that the Halesowen peasants lived an average of five to seven years longer in the second half of the fourteenth century than their predecessors had achieved in the first half. Christopher Dyer has suggested that the improvements 'had more influence on the lives of the peasantry than the ravages of epidemics'.[71] On the other hand, a surfeit of food and more comfortable surroundings did not necessarily lead to long life. Monastic communities in fifteenth-century England, easily among the best-fed – and probably overfed – groups in the country, struggled to reach the life expectancies of England's peasant communities (see below). Late medieval writers would not have been surprised at this outcome, as their health regimens often preached that over-indulgence would lower life expectancy. A few even praised the peasant diet as a way to strengthen the young body.[72]

At the highest levels of society other factors conspired to show that greater wealth and status did not axiomatically bring long life. For aristocratic men, trained for war and politically prominent, death by violence was not uncommon. The increased warfare of the fourteenth and fifteenth centuries provided plenty of opportunities for battle. The proportion of England's secular peerage who succumbed to violent deaths grew substantially across the period, fuelled by the continuing war with

France (1337–1453) and the 'Wars of the Roses' in the mid- to late fifteenth century. While under four per cent of peers born before 1325 died from violence, over twenty per cent of peers born in the years 1351–75 died violently; for cohorts born between 1401 and 1450, the figure rose above thirty-five per cent. For the majority, it was a young death, as just over three-quarters died before they were fifty, a third of these in their twenties.[73] Nor was this peculiar to England. In 1354, the Count of Flanders commented that wars had so depleted the numbers of men that numerous noblewomen were unable to find a husband and were turning to religion.[74] Death in battle is also suggested by Marie-Thérèse Lorcin as one reason why noble testators in the Lyonnais between 1300 and 1500 mention an average of only eighty-five sons for every hundred daughters.[75]

These last examples introduce another variable: gender. Among ducal families in England between 1330 and 1479, life expectancy at birth has been calculated at only twenty-four for men and thirty-three for women. By age twenty, the differential had increased to ten years, underlining the better life expectancy for women among the elite. This example has been used by David Herlihy in an influential and regularly cited essay to suggest that women in general enjoyed longer lives than men in the later Middle Ages. Some circumstantial evidence does lend weight to this theory. As mentioned above, boys appear more prone than girls to infant death, and chroniclers believed that they were more susceptible to plague. In France Guy de Chauliac wrote how 'a multitude of boys and a few women were attacked'. From Florence and Arezzo burial records offer some support to the chroniclers' views, although the difference is not acute; in Arezzo in 1390, fifty-eight per cent of plague burials were of males.[76] Improved living standards, especially to diet, in the later Middle Ages may have particularly advantaged women, who had hitherto suffered from severe anaemia and related diseases. Yet the evidence remains inconclusive, and the imaginative suggestion that the introduction of iron cooking pots in the twelfth and thirteenth centuries significantly increased iron intake flounders on the fact that most pots at that time were made out of copper.[77]

If we move out of the shadows of Herlihy's essay and below the level of the aristocracy, the evidence does not point to greater female longevity. The commoners of the Lyonnais show a very different balance of the sexes from their noble contemporaries: non-noble wills mention 113.5 sons for every 100 daughters.[78] Archaeological excavations in Scandinavian cemeteries have habitually found that men lived longer than women in the medieval period. On two sites in Svendborg, Denmark, for example, the average age of death was thirty-three for men and twenty-eight for women.

Similarly, at York, excavations have found that whereas over half of women were dead by their mid-thirties, only a little over a third of men did not make it to forty.[79] These examples show women having a worse life expectancy during their early adult years, and it may well be that men and women out-performed each other at different stages of life. In Pistoia, women under sixteen and over sixty-one had a better life expectancy than men, but those in the intervening years did not. Why might women have suffered particularly during their adult years? A traditional explanation has been the travails of pregnancy and childbirth, but studies have moved away from this in favour of more social causes. One suggestion is that women were commonly the carers of the sick and therefore exposed to more infection than men.[80] The evidence, as it stands, is too fragmentary and ambiguous (given the under-reporting of females) to prove that either sex had the greater life expectancy during the later Middle Ages. But what is important to note is that, despite cultural expectation, women were not obviously weaker than men. Female skeletons do not exhibit any more signs of malnutrition than the men buried alongside them.

The discussion so far has ranged across the fourteenth and fifteenth centuries, but mortality rates clearly fluctuated throughout the period. Not surprisingly the plague had a primary place in shortening life. For English landowners, life expectancy dropped by nearly ten years from the start to the mid-fourteenth century. In Florence, life expectancy in the last quarter of the fourteenth century was virtually half (just under twenty) of what it had been in 1300 (forty years).[81] There is some evidence of recovery in the fifteenth century. The inhabitants of Aalst (Flanders) and Périgueux (France), and of various English towns from 1450, witnessed lengthening life expectancies.[82] Nevertheless, the results were not uniform, and some groups fared worse during the course of the fifteenth century. Life expectancy decreased at two monastic communities in England: Christ Church, Canterbury, and the Abbey of Westminster. At the abbey, for example, life expectancy at the end of the fifteenth century had dropped by ten to eleven years (to under forty years) from its level at the beginning of the century.[83] Both communities suffered high mortality rates because their location within centres of high population increased the risk of infection: in Christ Church, deaths reached crisis point seventeen times during 1395–1505. Beyond the cloister walls, plague attacks and high death rates were hitting other groups in England. In fourteenth-century London fewer than a fifth of orphans had died before they came of age (twenty-one), but by the fifteenth century a third did not reach their majority.[84]

What these studies all underline is that life expectancy varied considerably across time and place. This was particularly so with the growing localised attacks of the plague in the fifteenth century. Searching for patterns is not easy because of the fragmentary nature of the material. There are variables which are almost impossible to consider for the medieval period. Mary Dobson's research has shown large variations in the levels of mortality across the geographical contours of southern England in the seventeenth and eighteenth centuries. Ratios of baptism to burial have been linked to patterns of natural drainage, settlement size, relief, manufacturing status, nature of traffic and distance from London. Analysis of the data suggests that the crude death rates of the chalk down-lands and uplands of Kent, Essex and east Sussex were much lower than those of low-lying marshlands such as Romney Marsh in Kent.[85] The available medieval evidence does not permit such comparisons to be made, but growing knowledge of regional differences suggests that similar levels of diversity could be found.

Age profiles

Given the figures discussed so far, how might later medieval society have appeared in terms of age profiles? If it conformed to the traditional features of pre-industrial European society then the largest age groups would be those of children and adolescents, with progressively smaller proportions of people in the higher age brackets. Diagrammatically this would render a pyramid shape.[86]

In 1300, high birth rates and low life expectancy combined to see Europe awash with children and young people. Some parts of Europe had half of their populations under twenty-one, with a third under fourteen.[87] During the next two centuries, there were examples of prolific late medieval families, which would have bolstered the younger cohorts of society. For periods covering the fourteenth and fifteenth centuries, couples in Limoges, Arras and Florence produced an average of just over nine children. In the aftermath of the great famine and the Black Death, it has been suggested, miniature 'baby booms' helped restore some popula-tion loss, which would have pulled the average age of society down further.[88] A few contemporaries believed that recovery was under way soon after the 1347–49 plague. In France, Jean de Venette wrote that 'everywhere women conceived more readily than usual. None proved barren, on the contrary there were pregnant women wherever you looked. Several gave birth to twins, and some to living triplets'.[89] In some Italian cities large families meant that the young continued to form a significant proportion of the population. In fifteenth-century Florence, Pistoia and Arezzo well over a third of the population was fourteen and under.[90] For comparison, this figure is close to the proportion of young people found in the 'young' countries of twenty-first century Africa.

Yet the picture is not consistent across Europe. Other towns and villages had comparatively smaller proportions of young in the century following the Black Death. In the parish of St Peter's in Reims in 1422 and in Verona in 1425, only around a quarter of the population was aged fourteen and under.[91] Instead, these areas, like several other Western European towns, exhibited signs of an ageing population. In the 1420s, the proportion of over-sixties in Arezzo, Florence, Pistoia and Verona reached between fourteen and sixteen per cent.[92] Such high figures compare most readily with the percentage of elderly people found in twenty-first century Europe. Why was this? One potential explanation, as witnessed in the world at the end of the twentieth century, is that life expectancy was lengthening and the elderly were living longer lives. There is some evidence from Périgueux that the median age of death among its male taxpayers was lower in the early fifteenth century (around sixty) than it had been in the early fourteenth century (occurring in the early forties).[93] Yet life expectancy in the early fifteenth century did not improve across Western Europe to the extent that it significantly increased the number of people over sixty. More likely, the proportion of the elderly had increased because the number of younger people had fallen. Despite examples of large families, it appears that the number of children declined in Western Europe from the mid-fourteenth to mid-fifteenth century. In pre-plague Halesowen, thirteen per cent of tenants had died childless, but from 1350 to 1400 the figure tripled to thirty-nine per cent. Similarly, between 1340 and 1420, testamentary evidence of commoners in the Lyonnais indicates a fall in the number of infants per testator, with a high percentage without living children.[94] One possible reason for this is that birth rates were suppressed in some way, which may have stemmed from low fertility (relating to diet), contraception or late marriages. It is telling that evidence from England, France and the Italian states indicates that wealthier households – with rich diets and early marriages for women – had larger numbers of children than the poorer households. In Pistoia, the wealthiest households in both the countryside and the city of the region had twice as many children as their poorer neighbours. This contributed to a much younger age profile among the wealthy of Europe: half of Florence's poor were twenty-five or under, whereas half the rich were seventeen or younger.[95]

A second and more significant factor was the high infant mortality rates, which have been discussed above. To Jacques Rossiaud it was the selective mortality of the plague that caused French towns to 'buckle under the weight of the elderly'.[96] In villages too, signs of an ageing population can be found in the growing numbers of isolated, old people found after each recurrence of plague. In 1433, plague had left only thirteen hearths remaining in the community of Baigorri (Navarre): two of the heads were over seventy, nine were between fifty and seventy, and only two were under fifty.[97]

Death was not the only reason why certain communities lost their youth and came to appear elderly. Land available as a result of the population collapse encouraged some to seek their fortunes away from their natal communities; towns and cities proved a draw for the young. This appears particularly to have been the case among young women, who were attracted in significant numbers to towns such as Pistoia, Nuremberg and Ypres. In Reims, the proportion of those in their teens and twenties was augmented by significant numbers of domestic servants. In contrast, the population of the rural English manor of Halesowen appears to have aged in the second half of the fourteenth century. Those in their twenties and thirties had formed two-thirds of tenantry in 1350, but comprised only around a third in 1393.[98] Either death or opportunity had knocked.

By the early fifteenth century, therefore, the age profiles of some European towns and cities were not looking very pyramid-like. Pierre Desportes's age distribution diagram for Reims is similar to the more 'bee-hive' profile of modern Britain and France: relatively small groups of the old and young, with the main age group in the adult years. The age distribution diagrams generated by the Tuscan *catasto* data also show a distorted pyramid. Here, however, it is the adult age group (twenty to fifty-nine) that suffers, 'crushed between a plethora of old people and a swarm of little children'.[99] Age profiles clearly differed across Europe and from town to village. Age distributions were skewed by localised attacks of the plague hitting particular age cohorts, while settlements lost and gained their attractiveness among the young. Nevertheless, the limited evidence collected so far suggests that, while Western Europe was home to significant numbers of children and adolescents, the century after the Black Death witnessed an ageing society.

For some social groups, a high proportion of elderly people continued into the late fifteenth century. Russell's study of 3,400 English landholding adults shows a steady rise in the proportion of the over-sixties from the late fourteenth century to the end of the fifteenth century.[100] However, as Europe's population showed signs of recovery in the later fifteenth century, the pendulum appears to have swung back in favour of the young. Testamentary evidence from the Lyonnais suggests a 'baby boom' beginning around 1460–80: the number without children decreased and the number of infants per testator was the highest for the period 1300–1501. Contemporaries began noticing signs of growth. A German chronicler in 1483 wrote, 'within these twenty years there had not been any real pestilence; and seldom is there a couple but they have eight, nine or ten children'.[101] In Verona in 1502, the percentage of those over sixty had virtually halved since 1425. The balance had shifted in favour of the young, with thirty-five per cent aged fourteen or below. This resulted in a lowering of the average and median ages for Verona. While in 1425 the average age was just under thirty for men and nearly thirty-two for women, in 1502 the average age for both men and women had dropped to under twenty-six.[102] That the biggest increases were among those aged five to nineteen suggests that the city was attracting more young – and long-lived – people than it had managed previously.

Conclusion

Giovanni Morelli was not unusual in knowing the ages of his ancestors, or considering them an issue worthy of discussion. Chronological age had a variety of uses in the fourteenth and fifteenth centuries: as a form of description, an entry into power and a means of control. Morelli's Florentine society was particularly conscious of noting birth dates and policing the age thresholds of taxation and official duties. As a result the demographic data is richer for this city than for any other in Western Europe. Yet even here precision was not highly valued, and medieval society recognised the limitations of judging a person solely by the number of years accumulated. To society at large it mattered more that a person was able to carry out her or his job or appeared sufficiently mature to inherit.

Nevertheless, medieval society did make assumptions about a person that were based on her or his stage of life and incorporated them into its laws and customs. Individuals were expected to go through life in a predicted order, exhibiting the appropriate behaviour (including vices) for each age. Some may have reached stages earlier than most, and others might be 'late developers', but both scenarios presupposed a known timetable of life events accepted by the general society. Gender, geography and life style could influence the timing of the stages, but in highly foreseeable way. The expectations and predictability of life are clearly visible in intellectual and moral discussions of the ages of man. The attitudes expressed are close to what has been termed a 'life cycle theory' of age, an approach that lost favour in the latter part of the twentieth century. The criticisms made by sociologists of 'life cycle theory' are a useful summary of all the reasons why medieval society promoted the idea of the ages of man: they were a series of fixed, inflexible stages that were universal, ahistorical and asocial.[103] Human development was linked more closely to God's plan than to social changes and conditioning.

At the same time, medieval society knew that life was precarious and that the wheel of fortune could turn at any time. The uncertainty needs underlining. Not only were life expectancy lower and the death rate higher in the later medieval period than in the modern world – or indeed the early modern world – but they fluctuated considerably.[104] Research has tried to chart some of these changes and estimate crude life expectancies. The results are not wholly satisfactory, but it is possible to make the following tentative remarks. At birth the odds of living to and through one's twenties were slim. The greatest hurdle was childhood, and late medieval society could expect around a third of all children to die in infancy. Early adulthood had its own dangers: cemeteries around Europe were filled with a substantial number of those in their thirties. Such low expectations for life would have made some towns and villages in Western Europe appear 'young' in their demographic profile. Nevertheless, it is too simplistic to say that life was short for all in the Middle Ages. Once early adulthood had been reached, there was a strong chance of seeing another two or three decades of life. Age-specific plague attacks, low birth rates and the mobility of the young all contributed to the old achieving a statistical prominence in late medieval society. In short, late medieval Europe was home to both young and old.

Notes

1 Guenée, *Between Church and State*, p. 86; Herlihy and Klapisch-Zuber, *Tuscans*, p. 85; Pleij, *Dreaming of Cockaigne*, p. 185.
2 Allmand, *Henry V*, p. 7; Hale, *Renaissance Europe*, pp. 15–16.
3 Minois, *History of old age*, p. 212; Ariès, *Centuries of childhood*, p. 14.
4 Herlihy and Klapisch-Zuber, *Tuscans*, pp. 163–4.
5 Smith, 'Barcelona "bills of mortality"'.
6 Herlihy and Klapisch-Zuber, *Tuscans*, p. 159; Law, 'Age qualification'; Chojnacki, *Women and men*, p. 239.
7 E.g. Walker, 'Proof of age'; Smith, 'Proofs of age'; Bedell, 'Memory and proof of age'.
8 Boswell, *The kindness of strangers*, p. 33.

9   Alberti, *I libri*, p. 123.

10 Dyboski (ed.), *Songs, carols and other miscellaneous poems*, pp. xiii–xiv.

11 Jones and Underwood, *The king's mother*, pp. 32 and 34; Brooke, *The medieval idea of marriage*, pp. 34–6.

12 Smith, 'Proofs of age'; Kirby (ed.), *Calendar of inquisitions post mortem*, vol. 18: *1–6 Henry IV: 1399–1405*, nos 309, 311, 530, 854, 858, 886, 990, 996 and 997.

13 Walker, 'Proof of age', p. 316.

14 Martin (ed.), *Knighton's chronicle*, p. 185; Boase, *The troubadour revival*, p. 111; Orme, *Medieval children*, pp. 46–8.

15 Carey, *Courting disaster*, particularly pp. 118–26.

16 His commonplace book is in the Bodleian Library, Oxford: MS Lat. Misc.c.66, fos 1, 75, 89–90, 122.

17 Finucane, *The rescue of innocents*, p. 8.

18 Orme, *Medieval children*, p. 44, fig. 16.

19 Ariès, *Centuries of childhood*, p. 14; Ames-Lewis, *The intellectual life*, ch. 10.

20 Petrarch, *Letters of old age*, vol. 1, p. 263.

21 Sablonier, 'The Aragonese royal family', p. 212.

22 Herlihy and Klapisch-Zuber, *Tuscans*, pp. 138–68.

23 Harvey, *Living and dying*, p. 121.

24 Herlihy and Klapisch-Zuber, *Tuscans*, p. 161 and fig. 6.3; Desportes, 'La population de Reims', p. 497.

25 Minois, *History of old age*, pp. 171–2.

26 Petrarch, *Letters of old age*, vol. 1, pp. 266–7.

27 Walker, 'Proof of age', p. 312. In Périgueux in 1301, Stève de Périer was described at his marriage as 'plus de 25 ans comme il apparaît d'après l'aspect de son corps': Higounet-Nadal, *Périgueux*, p. 282.

28 Harvey, *Living and dying*, p. 119; Thomas, 'Age and authority', p. 206, fn. 5.

29 E.g. Pilcher, *Age and generation*, pp. 3–4 and references therein.

30 Biller, *The measure of multitude*, p. 264; Goodich, *From birth to old age*, p. 4.

31 Minois, *History of old age*, p. 5.

32 Sears, *The ages of man*, p. 136.

33 Grmk, *On ageing*, pp. 8–9.

34 Cadden, *Meanings of sex difference*, pp. 180–1.

35 Biller, *The measure of multitude*, pp. 257–9.

36 Herlihy, 'Life expectancies', pp. 1–11; Biller, *The measure of multitude*, p. 289.

37 *Ibid.*, pp. 260–1.

38 Bell, *How to do it*, p. 128.

39 Biller, *The measure of multitude*, p. 263; Shahar, *Growing old*, p. 61; Rawcliffe, *Medicine and society*, p. 3.

40 Dove, *The perfect age*, p. 11; Goodich, *From birth to old age*, p. 61; Grössinger, *Picturing women*, p. 139.

41 Lindsay (ed.), *Isidori Hispalensis episcopi*, vol. 2, book XI.ii.

42 Burrow, *The ages of man*, p. 2; Goodich, *From birth to old age*, pp. 15, 69.

43 Burrow, *The ages of man*, p. 45. Dove, *The perfect age*, ch. 10.

44 Brown (ed.), *Religious lyrics*, no. 147, pp. 230–2.

45 Dante's *Il convivio*, p. 220.

46 Burrow, *The ages of man*, pp. 146–9.

47 Dante's *Il convivio*, p. 47; Dove, *The perfect age*, ch. 9.

48 Christine de Pisan, *Treasure*, p. 162.

49 Lindsay (ed.), *Isidori Hispalensis episcopi*, vol. 2, book XI.ii, lines 10–12.

50 Burrow, *The ages of man*, p. 24; Pastoureau, 'Emblems of youth', p. 229.

51 Dove, *The perfect age*, p. 7.

52 *Ibid.*, ch. 3. Grössinger, *Picturing women*, p. 139; Phillips, 'Maidenhood'; Burrow, *The ages of man*, p. 30. See the Middle English versions of the *Secreta secretorum* gathered together in Manzalaoui (ed.), *Secreta secretorum*.

53 Bell, *How to do it*, pp. 153–4.

54 Phébus, *The hunting book*, pp. 36–7.

55 The phrase is Christiane Klapisch-Zuber's in 'Plague and family life', p. 126.

56 Shahar, *Childhood*, p. 35; Grubb, *Provincial families*, p. 58.

57 Benedictow, 'Demography', p. 122.

58 Desportes, 'La population de Reims', p. 499.

59 Russell, *British medieval population*, p. 180, table 8.2; Hollingsworth, 'A demographic study', p. 360, table 5.

60 Seventeen per cent of boys, compared with seven per cent of girls, died in their first month: Grubb, *Provincial families*, p. 60.

61 Wrigley and Schofield, *The population history of England*, pp. 248–9.

62 Carmichael, *Plague and the poor*, pp. 41–9, 91–3.

63 Benedictow, 'The milky way', p. 25.

64 Horrox (ed.), *The Black Death*, no. 7; Galbraith (ed.), *The anonimalle chronicle*, p. 50; Goodich, *Violence and miracle*, p. 90; Shirley (trans.), *A Parisian journal*, p. 132.

65 Cohn, 'The Black Death', p. 734; Nicholas, *Domestic*, p. 151; Carmichael, *Plague and the poor*, p. 93; Benedictow, *The Black Death*, p. 263.

66 Herlihy, *Medieval and Renaissance Pistoia*, pp. 86–7. The Florentine dowry fund shows that girls aged eight to twelve had the lowest death rates: Morrison, Kirshner and Molho, 'Epidemics in Renaissance Florence', p. 531.

67 Poos, *A rural society*, p. 119; Howell, *Land, family and inheritance*, pp. 225–6; Thrupp, *The merchants of medieval London*, p. 194; Grubb, *Provincial families*, p. 59. For similar statistics for France see Dupâquier (ed.), *Histoire de la population*, vol. 1, p. 353; Vovelle, *La mort*, p. 97.

68 Rosenthal, 'Mediaeval longevity', p. 288. Other studies showing significant numbers of those over sixty are Carmichael, 'The health status of Florentines', p. 42; Moss, 'Death in fifteenth-century Tottenham'.

69 Rawcliffe, *Medicine and society*, p. 3.

70 Razi, *Life*, p. 43.

71 *Ibid.*, p. 130. Dyer, *Standards of living*, p. 182.

72 Bell, *How to do it*, p. 154.

73 A sharp contrast can be made in life span with those peers who died non-violent deaths (or 'natural' deaths): only forty-three per cent died before they were fifty. See Rosenthal, 'Mediaeval longevity', pp. 289–90.

74　Herlihy, 'Life expectancies', p. 11.

75　Lorcin, *Vivre et mourir*, pp. 20–1.

76　Herlihy, 'Life expectancies', pp. 1–11; Hatcher, *Plague*, p. 65; Cohn, *The Black Death transformed*, pp. 210–11; Carmichael, *Plague and the poor*, p. 91 and graph 4–1. Note that twentieth-century cases of plague show young men to be more susceptible than young women, but it is questionable how similar this is to the fourteenth-century plagues: Bolton, 'The world upside down', p. 37.

77　Bullough and Campbell, 'Female longevity', pp. 317–25; criticisms in Biller, *The measure of multitude*, pp. 293–5.

78　Lorcin, *Vivre et mourir*, pp. 20–1.

79　Ottaway, *Archaeology in British towns*, pp. 206–7; Schofield and Vince, *Medieval towns*, pp. 198–200; Daniell, *Death and burial*, p. 133.

80　Sawyer, *Medieval Scandinavia*, pp. 41–2.

81　Russell, *British medieval population*, p. 186, table 8.11; Herlihy, *The Black Death*, p. 43.

82　Nicholas, *Medieval Flanders*, p. 367; Dupâquier (ed.), *Histoire de la population*, vol. 1, pp. 350–1. For lower death rates in England after 1450 see Loschky and Childers, 'Early English mortality', p. 95.

83　Harvey, *Living and dying*, pp. 127–9; Hatcher, 'Mortality in the fifteenth century'.

84　Hanawalt, *Growing up*, p. 57.

85　Dobson, *Contours of death*, in particular part II.

86　Pilcher, *Age and generation*, p. 9.

87　Goodich, *From birth to old age*, p. 6.

88　Klapisch-Zuber, 'Plague and family life', p. 135; Delmaire, 'Le livre de famille des Le Borgne', p. 305; Genicot 'Crisis', p. 675.

89　Horrox (ed.), *The Black Death*, p. 57.

90　Herlihy and Klapisch-Zuber, *Tuscans*, p. 186, table 6.6.

91　Desportes, 'La population de Reims', table IX, p. 497; Herlihy, 'The population of Verona', p. 101, table 1.

92　Klapisch, 'Fiscalité et démographie', p. 1,324, table III.

93　Dupâquier (ed.), *Histoire de la population*, vol. 1, pp. 350–1.

94　Razi, *Life*, pp. 86–7, 143–4; Lorcin, *Vivre et mourir*, p. 14; Howell, *Land, family and inheritance*, p. 235; Hatcher, *Plague*, p. 27; Bolton, 'The world upside down', p. 36; Blockmans, 'The formation of a political union', p. 73; Herlihy and Klapisch-Zuber, *Tuscans*, pp. 44–6, 69, 91.

95　Herlihy, *Medieval and Renaissance Pistoia*, pp. 97–9; Razi, *Life*, pp. 86, 144.

96　Rossiaud, 'Crises et consolidations', p. 487: 'les effets des mortalites sélectives pouvaient faire ployer la ville sous le poids des vieux'. For an increasingly elderly population see Dupâquier (ed.), *Histoire de la population*, vol. 1, p. 361.

97　Minois, *History of old age*, pp. 210–11.

98　Herlihy, *Medieval and Renaissance Pistoia*, p. 83; Desportes, 'La population de Reims', pp. 487, 498; Razi, *Life*, p. 150.

99　Desportes, 'La population de Reims', p. 498; Herlihy, *The Black Death*, p. 43; Herlihy and Klapisch-Zuber, *Tuscans*, p. 183. Razi's diagram for late fourteenth-century Halesowen shows a similar ageing population: *Life*, p. 151.

100 Russell, *British medieval population*, pp. 180–6.
101 Lorcin, *Vivre et mourir*, pp. 13–14, 20; Helleiner, 'The population of Europe', p. 24; Dupâquier (ed.), *Histoire de la population*, vol. 1, pp. 371–2.
102 Herlihy, 'The population of Verona', pp. 101 and 113.
103 Pilcher, *Age and generation*, p. 18.
104 Houlbrooke, *Death*, p. 6.

3

Infancy

THE first years of life were arguably the most dramatic of the medieval life cycle. They were a period of rapid physical and psychological growth, and were the most susceptible to death; here the wonders, messiness and precariousness of life converged. There is a substantial body of evidence to demonstrate that medieval society recognised these early years as a distinctive stage in the life cycle. Law codes and admin- istrative records distinguish the young from the rest of society with a number of terms and ideas. While there were far fewer words to describe children in medieval Europe than in the modern world, age-specific terminology was in use. Gravediggers in Florence in 1400 did not use the Latin terms *infans*, *puer* and *puella* for anyone over the age of nine; the French used *enfant* for boys under twelve and girls under seven. In Middle English literature, the words 'child' and, to a lesser extent, 'infant' were in widespread use by the late fourteenth century. While both could have a general use, like the modern-day 'girl' or 'kid', they were more specifically applied to cover the ages up to puberty, with 'infaunt' becoming used in the fifteenth century for a baby or young child. In addition, the adjectives and adverbs 'childish', 'child-like', 'childishly' and 'infantile' were found in a wide range of European vernacular literatures, suggesting that a specific set of behaviours and qualities had become attached to the age group. Several writers took their points of reference from 'ages of man' literature, in which the rapid growth of the young led to sub-divisions in the age group. Infancy, the first stage, was said to last until two or four, but most commonly seven; it was followed by a later stage of childhood lasting until the early teens. In following that division, this chapter considers the earliest or infant years, and Chapter 4 focuses on later childhood, although it will become evident – especially in the section on play – that the division is necessarily a fluid one.[1]

The dynamics of medieval infancy cannot be recovered from first-hand accounts. Following the writings of Isidore of Seville, infancy was defined as the age 'which cannot speak' and, true to their nature, the under-sevens are silent in historical documents. Children as a whole, if we extend the group up to fourteen, have left virtually nothing on the written record. This is why, as David Herlihy has observed, 'of all the social groups which formed societies of the past, children … remain for historians the most elusive, the most obscure'.[2] Their silence speaks of the position of children in society, their public roles, the value placed on their opinions and their ability to express themselves in written and pictorial form. Above all it reflects the dominance of adults in children's lives and in the historical record. In reading this chapter and the next, therefore, it is important to recognise the adult-centric nature of the evidence, which can render the child passive. The challenge of much modern research is to uncover the experiences and evaluate the agency of the young in an adult world.

Qualities

Qualities said to distinguish childhood, and more specifically infancy, from other age groups are a contradictory mix of incapacity, evil, naivety, innocence and hope. One highly negative view, dominant in German writings, focused on physical and psychological weaknesses: infancy is placed firmly at the bottom of the life course.[3] According to medical writings, the infant's ill-formed, incapacitated body suffered an excess of water and heat, which left it in a constant state of flux. It made the infant incapable of controlling the body and reliant on older people or walking frames for support and transport. In addition, lacking teeth, or well-formed teeth, the infant was unable to speak properly and used 'baby-talk'. Vapours from the heated waters hampered the infant's reasoning capacities and he or she was deemed incapable of making rational decisions. Florence's commune defined 'infanti' as those children under seven 'who did not have the intellectual capacity to distinguish their needs'.[4]

A wide range of literary and visual sources supported the view of the hapless infant. The newly-born in the English morality play *Mundus and infans* is named Dalliance, a term for baby-talk. He is given bright clothing and food and told to obey, and does nothing else; he is solely a passive recipient of care. Likewise in the Scottish poem *Ratis raving* the infant just eats and sleeps, with little to distinguish it from animals, apart from an ability to laugh and cry. When children do act, they are often considered untrustworthy. Miracle stories provide examples of young children not being believed because they were assumed to be speaking childish words, misinterpreting reality or overreacting to unfamiliar situations.[5] Tantrums and ignorance were traced back to the view that babies were born tainted with 'original sin'. Those who followed the writings of St Augustine emphasised the domination of sin and evil in the child's early years.[6] Thus when praise was showered on children it was often because they showed qualities beyond those expected for their years. Helene Kottanner, nurse to the baby son of Queen Elizabeth of Hungary (1409–1442), marvelled at the maturity of the baby king when he was twelve weeks old, for she said he had the strength of a one-year-old. The king could hold up his head and bawl loudly, abilities that were obviously not considered possible at three months.[7] On similar lines, friends and family of the Marcello family of Venice commented variously that the child Valerio (d.1461) was an 'adult-like child' or a 'manlike boy', who 'exceeded his years' and possessed a body, intelligence and virtue that were more befitting old age than infancy.[8]

A belief in the incapacity of infants was reflected in law, where children were accorded few rights and responsibilities. Legal codes based on Roman law and south German law decreed that children under seven were not responsible for their actions. In England's countryside, if a child (usually under twelve) committed an offence the parent was charged and fined, and if a villager sued a child the case was delayed until the child came of age. Similarly, in Wales in 1354, the case of theft against Gwerful, the daughter of David Pentan, was acquitted because she was under twelve. Laws did not compel infants to do anything, but they excluded them from many responsibilities, including taking up an inheritance, getting married, paying taxes, receiving a knighthood and acting in government and other official positions. While understandable to modern eyes, this still means that in terms of power and juridical standing, infants lacked the rights of full adulthood.[9]

On the other hand, Europe's laws reflected a seemingly more positive attribute of infancy and childhood: innocence. This state was achieved at the ceremony of baptism (see below) and was a quality that adults lacked. Dante spelt it out in his *Paradiso*: 'For faith and innocence are in the heart of children only; both aside are cast before a beard upon the cheeks may start'.[10] Children neither had the knowledge nor had been corrupted by life to be malicious; they were generous of spirit, playful and light-hearted. Proverbs of the period underlined these common assumptions in the sayings 'as meek as a child', 'as merry as a child' and the several variations on the theme that children love an apple more than a castle.[11] A child's innocent nature is seen too in late medieval artwork, which increasingly produced life-like portrayals of a wriggling Christ child needing the support of his mother, while trying to catch a bird, grab his mother's veil or look to see what gifts are brought.[12] What these works additionally reveal is the holiness associated with innocence. Clerical writers drew attention to Christ's pronouncement: 'In truth I tell you, whoever does not receive the Kingdom of God as a little child will not enter there' (Mark 10:15). In this context, to act like a child was praiseworthy, and artists commonly used the infant's form to depict the soul as it left the body to travel to heaven. The idealisation of the innocent child received impetus as Mary's pregnancy and the birth of Christ achieved a central importance to Christian worship in the later Middle Ages. The Nativity developed into a detailed narrative; by the fifteenth century the custom of placing the infant Jesus on the altar at Christmas was widespread in Florence.[13] The cult of the baby Jesus was supported and promoted by Europe's visionaries as several holy women saw 'union with God [as] the embrace of a naked baby'. Agnes of Montepulciano (d.1317) had visions of the Christ child whom she held in her arms, while St Ida of Louvain (d.1330) described giving Jesus a bath and delighting in the exuberant way he splashed himself and all around in water.[14] A close association was therefore made between the child, innocence and Christianity, and thereby hope for the human soul.

Medieval society had few qualms about manipulating this innocence in order to evoke sympathy. France in 1448–49 suffered a spate of child kidnappings as gangs stole and mutilated young victims, turning them into beggars to provoke pity from passers-by.[15] In late medieval literature the abuse or death of a child was an important narrative device to heighten pathos. An important reference point was the Biblical tale of the Holy Innocents, where King Herod ordered the deaths of all infants under the age of two. The episode was graphically described in various media, where – in contrast to the twenty-first-century West – there was little compunction over showing infants being killed. In the carved screen on the life of Christ in the cathedral of Notre-Dame de Paris (made 1300–50) a sword plunges down to sever the right arm of one child as another's bloody body lies at a mother's feet. Childhood innocence, and its emblematic association with Christianity, was heavily exploited in creating negative stereotypes of the Jew. Accusations of child ritual murder against Jews had developed in the twelfth century and grew rapidly in the fourteenth and fifteenth centuries, appearing in high-profile murder cases, popular literature and graphic woodcuts. In Trent in 1475, the death of the two-year-old Christian boy Simon resulted in the arrest of eighteen Jews. A new development in this period was the link made between child-like innocence and the host, the wafer consecrated by priests at Mass and held to be the body of Christ. In the altarpiece of Jaime Serra (c.1400) in the monastery of Sijena near Huesca (Spain) a Jewish man drives a knife through a bleeding host, while Christ is shown as a baby in a barrel of boiling water.[16] These stories have two common features: the child as helpless victim, and the notion that to abuse a child is to abuse innocence.

A child is born

What of children themselves? From reading a selection of medieval sources, one might be forgiven for thinking that children were not welcomed in the Middle Ages. Religious orders who praised chastity, and saw sex as sinful, depicted children as part of the archetypal joyless marriage. There are high-profile cases of religious women who happily left their children in order to pursue a religious life; Angela da Foligno (c.1248–1309) thanked God that her children as well as mother and husband had died in a recent epidemic. Intellectuals like Eustache Deschamps (1346–1406) viewed children as nothing but crying, stench and a troublesome burden to their parents.[17] These groups dominate the literary output of the later Middle Ages, but they do not present the majority view on children. While numbers of children appear to have contracted in the later fourteenth and early fifteenth centuries, there appears no ground for thinking that parents wanted to be childless. Whether out of a wish to have descendants or more workers, out of a civic or Christian duty, or simply out of a desire for family life, most medieval couples 'wanted swarms of children'. Plague attacks do not appear to have diminished the desire for offspring, and after each onslaught there were noticeable increases in the birth rate.[18]

Infertility was not meekly or gladly accepted, but deeply distressing to those concerned. From every corner of society – medical writers, midwives, family, neighbours, the Church – advice on improving fertility was directed at the beleaguered couple. Most was directed to the mother, suggesting that this was where the blame lay, while giving her the responsibility to rectify the situation. Prayer was essential, particularly to St Margaret, the popular patron saint for childless women, and to St Elizabeth, who had miraculously produced children in old age. A pilgrimage might be the answer: one site of particular power was Our Lady of Chartres, which contained the chemise the Virgin was said to have worn at the Annunciation when she conceived Christ. Votive offerings were made, numerous fertility devices were recommended, and certain foods and drink were linked with improving fertility. Advice manuals covered the sex act itself, and virtually all general works on medicine devoted significant space to sterility. Michele Savanorola advised husbands during intercourse to shoot the semen out in one go and stay blocking the entrance to avoid air getting in, while the Ferrarese physician Matteo Palmieri advised women not to sneeze in case they ejected the semen back out again.[19]

Significantly, much of this literature assumed that male children were desired. Small figures of male children were placed in the trousseaus of Florentine women. Advice on engineering a boy included eating the testicles of a cock, drinking malmsey wine, or avoiding foods, like fish or fruit, which would cool the sperm and turn the seed female.[20] The desire for a boy is not surprising in the context of a late medieval society where males had priority in inheritance, would carry the family name, would perpetuate the lineage, and could further the family's ambitions on the battlefield, in the Church or in government. Christine de Pizan wrote in her *Book of fortune's transformation* (1403) that her own father had 'wished for a male child who could be his heir and inherit his riches'. While Christine felt herself loved, she could not inherit and, more annoyingly for her, suffered through a 'lack of learning'.[21]

Once pregnancy was announced the developing infant began to have a place in society. Conventional scientific wisdom believed that humans, like all animals, started as a seed, which developed into a lump of blood known as a foetus. Nourished by the mother's menstrual blood, the foetus went through a series of developmental stages as it slowly took human form. Only when the infant's body was evenly shaped and looked human did life and the soul infuse the body. In Aristotelian terms this was the move from a vegetative existence to a 'sensitive' soul and finally into a rational human.[22] It was said to take forty-six days for boys, but ninety days for girls as they lacked the heat and strength to form as quickly. In the outside world, the child's sex was already being guessed at: if it lay mainly on the mother's right side it was a boy; on the left, a girl. It was loved in the womb. The Florentine Giovanni Morelli recalled his delight at his wife's pregnancy and how he had felt 'his [son's] movements in his mother's stomach which I diligently sought out with my hand, awaiting his birth with the greatest pleasure'.[23]

Birth would usually take place at home. Among the wealthy, the importance of the event translated into elaborate birthing chambers. Christine de Pizan described the chamber of one Parisian merchant's wife as hung from floor to ceiling with tapestries, an ornamented dresser covered with golden dishes, gold carpets, a large bed covered with fine linen and a bedspread of gold tissue.[24] The newly-born would first experience an exclusively female world. Usually only in special circumstances, such as the urgent need of a priest, were men allowed into the chamber. In 1442, all male servants and courtiers were excluded from the lying-in chamber of Margaret of Anjou, the wife of Henry VI of England.[25] The main supervisor was the midwife, an important figure who in late medieval Nuremberg could earn as much as a craftsman or journeyman.[26] Fathers, however, would often arrange and lead the celebrations following a successful birth. At lower levels of society this might mean buying a round of drinks, or inviting people for a meal. A wealthier example is that of Manno Petrucci, in 1430, who distributed confections to celebrate the birth of his daughter as well as arranging a large feast. What this example further shows is that despite a cultural preference for boys, girls were not necessarily treated as a disappointment and their births ignored.[27]

After the birth, the umbilical cord was tied, the child washed, and the limbs straightened and wrapped in swaddling clothes. These may appear to us to mummify the baby, constricting the movements, but contemporaries saw swaddling as assisting the correct development of the child's limbs as well as providing useful armour against draught-induced chills and accidents.[28] Armour was needed, for the separation of mother and child was a traumatic event and, as Chapter 2 has indicated, infant mortality was high. Death at birth was particularly feared because the newly-born was clothed in original sin and had not become incorporated into the community of the blessed. This liminal position on earth had a spiritual equivalent. By 1300, a baby dying in sin was believed to pass into Limbo, a place where she or he would not experience the full physical horrors of Hell, yet remained barred from Heaven and the presence of God. It was a hefty spiritual punishment, and caused Dante to describe Limbo as full of 'sighs which kept the air forever trembling'. Preachers and religious writers were more forthright, leaving parents in no doubt of the consequences: Robert Mannyng of Brunne wrote in his *Handlyng sin* (1303) that the unbaptised child was damned.[29]

Help however was at hand in the ritual of baptism, an act that would wash away the original sin from the child, placing him or her in a state of grace: a rebirth. By 1300 the ritual was undertaken as soon as possible; in Florence, virtually all children were baptised within three days of their birth.[30] Where time was pressing, the ritual was dramatically truncated. There are tales of people running to the nearby church to secure baptism if they felt the child's life was in danger, which may also reflect the idea that a baptised child had a better chance of survival. In Vienne (France) local belief held that a stillborn baby could even be revived at the moment of baptism.[31] Such was the importance of baptism that the Church not only allowed, but actively encouraged, the laity to perform the rite in emergencies. In John Myrc's *Instructions for a parish priest* midwives were advised to baptise a dying child, even if it had only partially emerged or needed to be cut out of a dying mother. In Paris in 1311, the local synod declared that every vill should have midwives skilled in the art of baptism, while in Meaux (just outside Paris) midwives were tested on their knowledge at the bishop's court, earning themselves a certificate on successful completion.[32]

If the baby seemed healthy, the baptism ceremony was undertaken at a more leisurely pace. The rite still retained its central religious purpose, but time allowed for a public celebration of the birth and welcoming of the child into the local community. As a result, baptisms in the Veneto took place, where possible, on a Sunday, the holiest day and a time when most people were available.[33] Among the elite, this was a lavish ceremony, with princely babies of late medieval France enveloped in white satin or velvet and ermine.[34] The communal occasion was a time of drinking, feasting and present giving; in England, pots of wine were taken to the church as part of the celebration. The ceremony began with the baby being taken to the local church in the arms of one of the elected godparents, of which there could be several. From the Church's point of view, godparents were chosen to be the child's spiritual guardians: a second set of parents for the 'rebirth' marked by baptism. But families often used the opportunity to form alliances, patronage and clientage bonds. In Montaillou, Pierre Maury served as godparent to many children, welcoming the invitations to attend baptisms and consolidate friendships. To what extent godparents played a continuous role in the lives of their godchildren is debatable, but the one major role that they did play was during the baptism ceremony.[35]

The regimented and highly symbolic ritual began at the church door, indicating that the infant was on the threshold of Christian society. The baptismal party would be met by a priest who asked the child's sex and name, and the identities of the godparents. The child was then blessed and exorcised of evil, which allowed entry into the church. The next stage of the ritual took place at the font, where the infant would be immersed or sprinkled with water, warmed especially for the event.[36] The priest placed salt in the infant's mouth, which represented the reception of wisdom, and rubbed oil on the chest and back, before the godparents lifted the newly baptised child. The final stage of this spiritual journey was towards the altar, where the godparents made a profession of faith on behalf of the child, who was now a fully fledged member of the Christian community.

The baptism ceremony was also the arena where a child would formally receive a name. Naming practices differed across Europe. In England and areas of France it was common for children, especially sons, to be named after godparents, and any deviation from the norm could occasion surprise. For England, there is some evidence to suggest that godparents were chosen for their names, which would explain why siblings could share the same first name.[37] In contrast, in the northern states of Italy, it was the father who chose the child's name irrespective of the godparents. During the fourteenth century, an increasing preference was shown for saints' names. In Vicenza, Giovanni was the first choice for boys throughout the fifteenth century, while Caterina and Lucia held top two positions for girls in 1450–1505.[38] Other families in Europe similarly chose saints' names, partly in the hope that the saint would act as special guardian to their namesake. St Dorothea von Montau, for example, was named after St Dorothy of Cappadocia and was baptised on the latter's saint's day (6 February).[39] Another strategy in Tuscany was to choose the name of a recently deceased relative. Gregorio Dati and his second wife Betta named their first daughter in memory of Dati's first wife, and a second daughter after Betta's mother.[40] Naming practices in both southern and northern Europe reflect the greater value placed on the male. Sons, who would perpetuate the family name and lineage, had names chosen from a limited range. In fourteenth- and fifteenth-century Arras and Lyons, Jean was never toppled as the first choice, and there are indications, shared by England and Italy, of a narrowing in the range of boys' names during the same period. Family tradition served to limit choices. In the Tann family of Salzburg, the name Eckhart was used in every generation (sometimes for two or more sons) from 1127 to 1398.[41] Daughters on the other hand, who would marry into another line, were named with various, often exotic-sounding, names. Even among the English peasantry could be found names like Tibia and Strangia.[42]

Child-parent relations

Who brought up baby? Among the noble and gentry families of Europe it was common for the infant to be given to a nurse in the same way as all the routine tasks of the household were performed by hired servants.[43] Nurses were a status symbol, demonstrating that a mother could afford not to endure the daily and nightly chore of breast-feeding. There were practical reasons too. Noble life styles demanded a high degree of mobility, and young children would commonly await their parents at home. In the larger households, the children were cared for in specially assigned nurseries, possibly the only child-defined space (if we discount Limbo) of the period. Hiring wet-nurses was an equally widespread practice among the merchants of Florence, who similarly saw it as a mark of status, although here most of the infants were sent outside the family home, usually into the countryside. This was an early break from the natural family: most babies left within the first month of birth, with many taken to nurses living over fifteen kilometres from the parents' houses.[44]

The practice of wet-nursing has received a fair amount of modern criticism for militating against close child–parent relations. The baby may have found it difficult to forge bonds with anyone. In Florence, infants remained on average only ten months with the same nurse. Gherardo, son of Guidini of Florence, stayed with his mother for five weeks after his birth in 1385 before being sent consecutively to three wet-nurses for periods of six, nine and three months.[45] Contemporary writers could be scathing about the practice: not only were nurses criticised for neglectful and drunken behaviour, but their milk could transmit inappropriate character to the child. Francesco Barbaro in his treatise *On wifely duties* begged Florentine noblewomen to breast-feed their children. Milk from a nurse, always of a lower social class, could lead to degeneration in the infant.[46] Yet there is no indication that the infants concerned were simply given to anyone. Great care was taken to find a suitable nurse, and Florence buzzed with advice and gossip on the availability of good women. The practice does not appear to have caused greater infant mortality. Indeed, a period away from the city in plague years probably increased their chances of survival.[47] In the English royal household a nurse's food was checked to ensure that she would produce good-quality milk, and a physician was on hand to advise about appropriate feeding methods.[48] Nor did a wet-nurse prevent child–parent contact. Christine de Pizan described the ideal aristocratic mother as one who saw her children daily, and checked on their behaviour and the discipline they were receiving.[49] It should finally be noted that nurses were always confined to a small section of Western Europe and were more popular in some areas than others. In the cities of London, Ghent and Nuremberg, and in the rural district of Montaillou, wet-nurses were not commonly used and were called upon only as a last resort. When wet-nursing did occur, most infants would not be 'put out', but nursed in the parent's household.[50]

For most of Europe's infants, therefore, early care was based in the home and provided by their natural family. During the later Middle Ages the dominant discourse decreed that babies were women's work. Mothers were defined as nurturers and the safeguards of their children's welfare, and a range of literature suggests that this continued to be the case, for both male and female children, until they reached the age of seven.[51] A mother's love was believed to be instantaneous. Francesco Barbaro wrote how nature had 'instilled in women an incredible love and affection for their offspring', while Christine de Pizan wrote how a mother 'who has given birth forgets the pain and labour as soon as she hears her child cry'.[52] Other literature emphasised a gender division of labour. In *The ballad of the tyrannical husband* (from fifteenth-century England) the husband goes out to work in the fields all day and the wife is confined to household duties, including the sole care of the children both day and night.[53] In folk literature, didactic works and mystery plays, fathers are never given nurturing roles and can often be portrayed as incompetent in the ways of childcare.[54] Instead the primary role of the father was as educator, moral adviser and disciplinarian. As Dante wrote in his *Convivio*, 'So as a child clings to the mother's breast as soon as it is born, likewise as soon as some light appears in his mind he ought to turn to the correction of his father, and his father should give him instruction'.[55] This situation often arose only in later childhood. Thus the primacy of the mother in an infant's life led Barbara Hanawalt to claim that a father's death 'may not have been as important as the mother's would have been'.[56]

Nevertheless, while this labour division held good at a general level, we should be cautious in assuming too sharp a distinction between parental roles. Mothers did not merely feed and clean, but helped to counsel and guide their children. They had a particularly important role in the early religious education of their children, teaching prayers and taking them to church. Joan of Arc, for example, learnt her Pater Noster, Credo and Ave Maria from her mother.[57] On the other hand, the image of fathers was changing in the later Middle Ages as the developing cult of St Joseph showed him enjoying family life and performing a 'mothering' role. Fifteenth-century Nativity paintings show Joseph spoon-feeding Christ, preparing his bath and cutting swaddling clothes from his own garments (the *Josefshosen*, which survive as a relic in Aachen Cathedral).[58] Fathers may never have become househusbands, but they had the opportunity to bond with their children from an early age. The Florentine humanist Gianozzo Manetti wrote that fathers love their children immediately at birth and revel in the knowledge that they have produced children from their own flesh and of the same nature. The love of the father was clearly believed to be intense, as Alberti noted: 'Who would believe, except by the experience of his own feelings, how great and intense is the love of a father toward his children ... I am sure that no love is more unshakeable, more constant, more complete, or more vast than the love which a father bears to his children'.[59] How much time fathers spent with their children varied across social groups. Peasant children saw their fathers on a regular basis, or at least fathers appeared nearby when their children succumbed to accidents.[60] When, at higher levels in society, business dragged fathers away for often extended periods of time, their thoughts could still be on their offspring. King Edward I of England is not known to history as sweet-tempered and compassionate, but he appears to have had a soft spot for his children. While away on military campaign, in 1306, he reproached the woman in charge of his children for failing to send news on their welfare. He wanted to know 'how they are growing and if at play they are lively and cheerful and well behaved'.[61] Children also saw enough of their fathers to miss them. In Florence, Clarice de' Medici wrote to her husband Lorenzo saying that their three-year-old son was wandering around the house asking when his father would be home.[62] Nor was attention only lavished on sons. In the Veneto, Bonaventura Bovi had three living sons, but singled out one of his daughters as the 'most honest and modest, most sweet and well-loved' of his children.[63]

It is worth while to record these sentiments because it was once held that medieval parents withheld love and affection from their children. While this idea owes much to modern, negative views of a 'barbaric' Middle Ages, it is also considered the logical defence mechanism against the high probability of infant death.[64] Journal writers often wrote stoically about the deaths of their children. Paliano Falcucci recorded on 27 March 1483 that 'it was pleasing to God, our Lord, to call to himself the above mentioned Antonio, my son'. This is a common form of words in Italian memoirs and reflects the widely held Christian belief, promoted by preachers, that a child was God's gift; what he gave he could take away. There was no cause for complaint.[65] A harsher written response, at least to modern eyes, is found in the lists of offspring found in the commonplace books of Humphrey Newton (Cheshire gentleman) and Richard Hill (London grocer). The names of those children who died were marked with a simple 'mortus est' ('has died') and literally crossed out; there appears little difference between the closing of financial accounts and these living accounts.[66]

Yet we know nothing of the feelings lying behind such actions. Against such laconic responses are the cases of extreme parental anguish at the accidents and deaths befalling their children. In 1468, a butcher from Nuremberg committed suicide on hearing that an accident had killed both his children.[67] Miracle stories are filled with requests to help infants; they dominate the cases noted in the canonisation of Thomas of Hereford in 1320.[68] Parents are shown wanting to save their children: they anxiously pray, search out medicines and ointments, and express profound sorrow.[69] If parents felt no grief for their dead children, then many medieval lyrics and plays would make no sense. Fifteenth-century lyrics on Mary's lament at Christ's crucifixion ask mothers to weep for Christ as they would for their own dead children. Medieval plays on Abraham and Isaac, the Biblical story of a father ordered by God to kill his only son, intentionally manipulate parental sentiments for dramatic effect.[70]

It was during the later Middle Ages that poets from as far afield as Wales, Ireland, Iceland, Castile and Italy began to express grief over their own children's deaths. In them, a stoical acceptance is far from apparent, and they rage against the dying of their loved ones. In Wales, the arrival and regular outbreaks of plague provided the impetus. Ieuan Gethin of Baglan (near Swansea) wept when he saw the pox on his son's arms and was so infuriated with God that he compared him to an Englishman. In Venice in 1461, the death of his eight-year-old son, Valerio, sent Jacopo Antonio Marcello into a deep, long and public display of despair. He described himself as being 'in this perpetual mourning, in this protracted lethargy and constant sorrow, whose eyes are flooded with relentless tears'. Such comments testify to the deep emotional bonds fathers had made with their sons during infancy. This is spelt out by the humanist Giannozzo Manetti who, suffering at the death of his seven-year-old son, Antonino, spoke of how he had enjoyed raising and educating his son in his 'years of helplessness'. The interaction is more beautifully expressed in the final lines of Lewys Glyn Cothi's elegy for his five-year-old son Sion (c.1450s):[71]

> and farewell to games with nuts
> and farewell now to the ball,
> and farewell to loud singing
> and farewell, my cherry friend.
> Down below while I live, Sion, my son.

All the above are examples of extreme grief heightened by poetic licence. It should be noted that Marcello and Manetti were criticised by family and friends for the public spectacles they made of themselves. Both were cautioned against acting in a 'womanish' way and told to act in a manly way like the stoical heroes of ancient tales. Both were told that they should draw comfort from their child's certain happiness resting with God in Heaven.[72] Nevertheless, both Marcello and Manetti argued in response that to be a father was to be human and to grieve was to be human; they were not made of stone. While their work reflects contemporary stylistic fashions, it is important to note that these poets considered paternal love and grief as worthy sentiments.

Was it only for sons? Welsh poets only very briefly mention daughters and more rarely give their names. Miracle stories suggest that parental concern was more focused on their sons' welfare: boys outnumber girls by two to one in cases involving miraculous healing from accidents and illnesses. Nevertheless, grief for daughters could engender comparable emotion; the sentiment appears in literature and in the comments of parents. One of the most eloquent was written by the poet Boccaccio when a friend's granddaughter painfully reminded him of his dead daughter. He recalled her eyes, hair, gestures and chattering, and so 'holding your child in my arms and listening to her prattle, the memory of my own lost little girl has brought to my eyes tears that I conceal from all'.[73]

Upbringing and play

The world of the infant was dominated and regulated by adults. They provided transport, clothing, food and the means for socialisation. Advice on upbringing would, like today, have come from conversations with family and friends. What has survived consists mainly of the works of physicians, theologians and philosophers who were eager to offer parents advice on breast-feeding, teething, washing, coping with a crying infant and dealing with childhood diseases. These can help us to understand what certain sections of medieval society thought was the appropriate way of bringing up children, but cannot of course provide a clear window into actual practices. Parent–child relations belonged to a world where communication was overwhelmingly spoken and private. The frequency of the bathing or the changes of swaddling clothes or the quality of diet is impossible to uncover and would probably alter according to wealth, time available and custom. Stressed, working peasant women had fewer opportunities to change their children than living-in nurses of the aristocratic household.

The overwhelming message from the advice literature was leniency. Stressing the softness and fluidity of the infant's body, writers urged caution in its handling: the child should not be overstrained with exercise or large meals, nor given harsh medical treatments like bleeding.[74] No rigorous daily timetable was imposed; even the feeding of babies 'on demand' was advocated. Close attention was paid to the development of the infant: one view held that children walked at thirteen months, talked at eighteen months and would be weaned at two.[75] The weaning of a child was considered an important turning point, and one that produced a new set of guidelines. Physicians and nurses recognised the delicate digestive system of the newly weaned. Eating the wrong foods could irritate the stomach, leading to diarrhoea and even death. Michele Savonarola recommended that infants should not be given any phlegmatic or viscous foods that would exaggerate the wet, warm humours of the young body. The first food should be softened by soaking in milk, pre-chewed by the feeder or mashed with a spoon.[76]

Some contemporary writers held the view that girls required less food than boys because they were physically less active. Barbara Hanawalt and Christiane Klapisch-Zuber have also suggested that boys received better-quality care and were suckled for longer than girls. However, no firm evidence has been produced to show that girls were poorly fed or cared for less than their brothers. The fourteenth-century house book of a German family, the Cerruti, shows no distinction between the diets of boys and girls. Figures for child accidents and deaths in medieval England show no bias against girls.[77] Pampering clearly went on for both sexes. The popular Florentine preacher Giovanni Dominici (1356–1419) criticised mothers for the time they wasted on combing and curling children's hair and attempting to keep girls' hair blonde. He highlighted the vanity and expense of 'embroidered bonnets, ornamented capes, fancy petticoats, carved cradles, little coloured shoes and fine hose'. He would clearly have disapproved of the chest belonging to one Tuscan noble family, which contained around fifty items of infant clothing.[78]

While care needed to be taken, it was recognised that children could not be shielded from the world, and that socialisation into adulthood would begin as soon as possible.[79] This should be done at the child's pace, taking into account the child's own developing powers. A few writers recommended beginning with images and visual stimulation to teach good behaviour. Physical correction should be done delicately as a common proverb observed: a light blow to a tender branch causes more damage than a deep cut to a mighty tree trunk. Developing motor skills would see a child learn by following parents or the nurse in their daily tasks, gradually being allowed to help. Infants do not appear to have been excluded from adult culture by notions of censorship and protection, and very young children were encouraged to mix with adults at home, in church and in public processions. In Venice, the infant Valerio Marcello followed his father around the house, sometimes clinging to his side, hanging from his neck or jumping on his lap, and would accompany him daily to church.[80] Labouring families often had to take their infants to work, particularly during intensive periods of harvest.[81]

Even while they were in an adult context, however, children were never treated as adults, and it was play rather than work that defined the culture of infancy. Parents themselves actively encouraged play by introducing, directing and supervising the child's earliest games and toys. A string holding a rattle could be tied across the top of the baby's cradle; fathers threw their children into the air before catching them; and the mother or nurse would sing or whistle nursery rhymes, which, as Nicholas Orme articulated, functioned as 'a dialogue between adult and child'.[82] Driving adult participation was the belief that play had physical and educational benefits. Konrad von Megenburg, in his *Yconomica* (1352), recommended running for strengthening legs. Matteo Palmieri in *Della vita civile* ('On civic life', 1439) advocated teaching two-year-olds to read by cutting fruits and pastries into different-shaped letters that could be used as rewards if they guessed correctly.[83] Children's own games could mimic adult life, and in this way play formed important practice for later careers. Toys fed the desire for adulthood: miniature toy banks were given to merchants' children, and hobby horses or toy soldiers to future knights. It was not uncommon for biographers to trace adult roles back to childhood games. St Catherine of Siena (d.1380) is said to have formed a play group of friends who flagellated themselves with knotted ropes.[84] Yet many of the toys simply reflected the parental enjoyment of buying gifts for their children. Giovanni Dominici believed parents were often excessive in purchasing toys, which would cause vanity in children. His bile was directed at 'little wooden horses, attractive symbols, imitation birds, gilded drums and a thousand different kinds of toys', a list that cannot help but sound appealing.[85]

Children, however, were not constantly under the eye of an adult, and both sexes were given a fair amount of unsupervised playing time, often with children of their own age. At her trial, a few of Joan of Arc's witnesses stated that Joan had spent her childhood in church when her parents thought she was 'at the plough, in the fields, or elsewhere'.[86] Miracle stories are fruitful sources for descriptions of young children playing together with their 'age mates' unobserved by adults. Pleas for help were made to the English saint Henry VI after a three-year-old girl was killed while playing under a large stack of firewood 'in the company of other children of that age who were playing by themselves'.[87] As this sadly show, examples of children's 'own time' can often be best gleaned from records of accidents and deaths. While children were not regular victims of serious accidents, they lived in a world free of safety catches and soft furnishings. Peasant children succumbed to the blazing fire of the central hearth, the animals that wandered freely in and out of the open door, and the open wells and mill ponds. A child in the town had high wooden balconies to wander upon and wagon wheels, prowling dogs and runaway horses to dodge in the streets. A large proportion of these accidents befell those between two and five, toddlers who had not long found their feet and were eager to discover the world.[88]

For some infants, accidents happened during a prolonged period of parental absence, as the next two examples show. In fourteenth-century Padua a little girl drowned in a ditch while her mother went to get fire from a neighbour. In fifteenth-century Sweden a mother put her eighteen-month-old son to bed and went to supper in a neighbour's house. Shortly afterwards the child got out of bed and froze to death.[89] While these mothers might be accused of negligence, Hanawalt's reading of coroners' rolls for late medieval England suggests that parents in the poorest families, where every able-bodied person was required to work, often had little choice but to leave their children unattended. Babies were likely to suffer the worst accidents during the busiest parts of their parents' day, and were especially at risk during the intensive agricultural season of May to August. Medieval society did show disapproval of young children being left alone. The coroners' records hint at the censure meted out to those who had left their children 'without a caretaker'. The Church too issued warnings about the dangers to children of cradle fires and scalding; parents of children who accidentally drowned, were burnt or fell to their deaths were required to do penance for their negligence.[90] But the balance between childcare and work was not easy to strike when survival was an issue.

Child's play, therefore, was not always controlled by adults, nor consumed by attempts to mimic them, and much of the culture passed from child to child. A long list of children's games and toys in the Middle Ages has been compiled from a wide range of evidence, including archaeological finds, miracle stories and manuscript illustrations. Medieval children of all ages (and here it is difficult to separate infants from older children) played marbles, flew kites, and enjoyed see-saws and musical chairs. They made their own toys, such as the child in *Ratis raving* who created a sailing ship from broken bread. By exercising imagination, they could transform sticks into horses and hats into helmets.[91] One of the longest lists of children's games and toys is found in a semi-autobiographical poem by Jean Froissart of Hainault (1337-1410). Group games included the seemingly timeless 'Follow the Leader' and 'Hide and Seek'. On his own, Froissart made mud pies, collected shells, played with a spinning top, and blew soap bubbles through a pipe, and he attached thread to a butterfly's wings so that he could make the poor creature fly 'as I pleased'. Froissart's poem appears typical of a small boy of any historical period: the mess, the running around, the cruelty to animals.[92] For other young boys, there was early encouragement in weaponry: in 1492 six bows were given to the five-year-old Prince Arthur, son of Henry VII of England.[93] Nevertheless, medieval parents did try and stop violent behaviour: then as now there are examples of 'toy' weapons being confiscated from children's rooms.[94] Gender differences were becoming apparent even while boys and girls played together. Froissart describes how 'in front of girls' he and the boys would beat each other with their caps. Girls never appear to have been active participants in Froissart's games but, in an imitation of later life, were the passive onlookers as the boys showed off.[95]

Abandonment and infanticide

Not all childhood experiences in the later Middle Ages would be within a loving family, or indeed a family at all. The issue of child abandonment is prominent in a broad range of late medieval writings from church sermons to romance literature. Abandonment took several different forms, and it is clear that children could feel deserted whenever they were displaced from the family home. They included orphans, those placed in minor seminaries or nunneries and those left behind by widowed mothers who remarried. In Florentine society children were considered part of their father's lineage, and it was consequently rare for children to follow their remarried mothers into the home of a new husband. The mother who placed the demands of her own lineage and wealth over that of her children was a figure stigmatised in society. It was a practice that clearly affected the young Giovanni Morelli. Born in 1371, he was barely two when his father died, and his mother shortly afterwards remarried, leaving Morelli and his siblings in the care of grandparents. When he later came to write his family memoir, the lack of a father figure and the loss of his mother through remarriage were prominent grievances.[96]

Morelli, however, was lucky to be taken in by extended family. In

September 1336 a mother left her three-year-old child on the porch of the hostel of the Bishop of Châlons in Paris.[97] She was not unusual. Writers described a Europe where the streets were home to starving and begging abandoned children, whose chances of survival were negligible. In the fifteenth century one Parisian writer mourned: 'In the year 1420 you might see all over Paris here ten there twenty or thirty children, boys and girls, dying of hunger and of cold on rubbish heaps. No one could be so hard of heart as not to be greatly stressed hearing them at night crying "Oh, I am dying of hunger!"'[98] The reasons for abandonment in the fourteenth and fifteenth centuries were similar to those of previous years – parental death, poverty, illegitimacy, disabilities and ill-health – although the economic downturn in this period and the endemic plague may have increased the numbers of children affected. Medieval society extended its sympathy to the abandoned. Canon law texts and manuals for parish priests voiced concerns over the baptism of abandoned children, and were exercised by the potential for accidental incest because family relations would not be known. Secular law occasionally prosecuted: in fourteenth-century Ypres a woman who had abandoned an infant was sentenced to five years' exile. Nevertheless, medieval chroniclers and public opinion at large recognised the plight of parents forced to leave their children, and in doing so they treated abandonment as a fact of life. Legal prohibition was rare, and there were no major campaigns by either Church or State to condemn and prohibit the practice. According to the *Siete partidas* law code of Castile, while parents had a responsibility to rear their offspring, they could be excused on the grounds of poverty. Instead of condemnation, the most common response was to provide help, as exemplified by the foundling hospitals considered below.[99]

For some children their fate was worse: death. Modern historians were once convinced that later medieval Europe was in the grip of widespread infanticide. They believed it was 'woefully common' (Tucker) 'a fact of life' (Trexler), 'a sad reality' (Brissaud) and 'an accepted norm' (Shahar).[100] Yet the evidence to support such views is ambiguous. Take for example the problem of interpreting court records of infanticide accusations and convictions. Overwhelmingly the numbers are low. Barely a handful of cases are found among gaol delivery rolls and coroners' rolls for fourteenth-century England, or the ecclesiastical courts of fifteenth-century London and Canterbury.[101] Hanawalt and Boswell interpret the statistics positively to suggest that infanticide was rare in late medieval England and Europe.[102] However, a low number of cases could equally indicate that infanticide was not considered a serious crime. This is the interpretation preferred by historians of the great profusion of infanticide cases in sixteenth- and seventeenth-century Europe. In the imperial city of Nördlingen only one case of infanticide was prosecuted in the fifteenth century, while penalties in Nuremberg were mild before 1510, the year in which the first execution for infanticide occurred. In this analysis, infrequent court appearances support the view that infanticide only became criminalised in the later sixteenth century.[103] Medieval research can support the sense of leniency: at Canterbury the penalty for child murder was roughly the same as that for committing sexual offences.[104]

Other evidence, however, suggests greater concern. Central to Christian culture was the belief that every human being was precious to God and could be saved. This rendered a higher status to young children than they had received in classical antiquity or in pagan law, both of which had condoned infanticide in certain circumstances. In England, the Christian view was strongly written into synodal legislation. In stark contrast to laws formulated in France, Spain and Tuscany, England's synodal legislation is 'saturated with provisions about child-care and infanticide'. Popular manuals for priests, like the *Memoriale* of 1344, have lengthy sections on penances for those parents guilty of killing their children. At the very least, the evidence points to a society concerned for the child's life.[105] Not that England was alone in condemning offenders; elsewhere in Europe cases also appeared in secular courts. In fifteenth-century France voluntary infanticide was punished by burning or burial alive; in southern Germany the penalty was drowning; and, in Florence in 1407 a woman found guilty of infanticide was led through the streets on a donkey with the corpse of her dead child tied to her neck before being buried alive.[106] Despite the low number of prosecutions, child murder became one of the most feared crimes in fourteenth- and fifteenth-century France, and was singled out for its threat to the social fabric.[107] In Europe at large, society's willingness to blame and the fear of suspicion can be seen in the actions of parents who carried their dead children out of the house to show neighbours as if to deflect any suspicion of foul play.[108]

In addition, infanticide was an action that medieval society believed only the insane, evil or desperate would commit. Women – and it was mainly considered a female crime – were accused of being possessed of a fever or of some external agent, like the devil, or being ashamed at giving birth to illegitimate children.[109] Medieval society's horror of infanticide is seen in the way child murder became an accusation with which to denigrate certain groups in society. Jews, as shown above, were stigmatised as child killers, and the accusation was extended to heretics and witches. It was used in political contexts too: Edward I made the accusation against the Welsh; the French made it against members of the English royal family and the Armagnacs. Nor was it simply enemies and marginal groups who suffered the slur. The accusation was sufficiently powerful to damage the reputation of King Richard III (reg. 1483–85), who has gone down in English history, rightly or wrongly, as the murderer of his nephews, the two young sons and heirs of Edward IV. Despite being boys of ten and twelve, they were infantilised as their innocence and vulnerability became an important political tool. A marginal comment in *The great chronicle of London*, which reads 'mors innocentium' ('the death of innocents'), explicitly links the princes with the Biblical innocents, while Henry VII's bill of attainder against Richard III accused him of the 'shedding of infants' blood'.[110]

Innocence was also an issue in the sensational case of the paedophile and serial killer Gilles de Rais (1404–40), one-time companion in arms to Joan of Arc and Marshal of France. At his trial in 1440, dozens of victims, mainly boys, were described as being sexually assaulted, mutilated, and murdered and their remains buried in Rais's castles, primarily those at Machecoul and Champtocé. On the one hand the trial confirms the strength of parental feeling as parents recounted their suffering and fruitless searching for their lost children. Though they were frightened, and in some cases threatened by the marshal's men, the victims' families continued to voice their suspicions at his involvement; in 1440 the Bishop of Nantes noted the 'strong public rumour' that Rais was sodomising and murdering children.[111] The canonical trial consistently highlighted the victims' innocence, with Rais portrayed as 'a murderer of innocent children'.[112] That the murders were evil was never in doubt: the inhabitants of Marchcoul had first associated the disappearances with the English.[113] Ultimately the civil authorities declared Rais guilty of homicide; he was sentenced to death and executed the following day.

Nevertheless, the trial also reveals differences in the way child murderers were considered then and in the modern West. It took eight years of rumour before the authorities acted. When they did, it was for an unconnected political crisis exacerbated by Rais's storming of the church of Saint Étienne-de-Mermorte and seizure of property belonging to the Duke of Brittany. More significant is the reaction of the courts when Rais and his men finally confessed. Throughout the recording of the ecclesiastical trial, the issue of sodomy appears to disgust the Church more than the child murders; certainly sodomy is condemned in far more lurid detail. After Rais's show of remorse, the Church lifted the sentence of excommunication and allowed his burial within a church. Finally, the trial records show that the victims were children of largely peasant status; a number had gone to the castles of Rais with the intention of begging for alms. Not all children were therefore reported missing.[114] For those who perpetrated the crimes, those who knew and those who suspected, the social status of the children made them appear of less significance.

It is impossible to gauge the extent of abandonment and infanticide in this period of high infant mortality. How many deaths were written off as accidents? Who did murder those erroneously assigned to the Jews or Gilles de Rais?[115] What can be dismissed are pronouncements like this of Lloyd deMause: 'The history of childhood is a nightmare from which we have only recently begun to awake ... the further back in history one goes, the lower level of child care, and the more likely children are to be killed, abandoned, beaten, terrorised and sexually abused'.[116] There is little to suggest that children in medieval Europe were either abandoned or murdered in high numbers. True, there was little sensationalism in reporting infanticide, and abandonment was treated leniently, but this did not amount to an endemic callousness towards children. Both actions were considered wrong. Both were carried out by a minority. Illegitimacy was a problem in many areas of Europe, but it was not an automatic ticket to death, and in areas like the Low Countries, where illegitimacy had little social stigma, infanticide cases were rare.[117] Nor should it be assumed that children with mental or physical disabilities were routinely killed or abandoned. Miracle stories show that the parent's first, perhaps continuous, action was to pray for help.[118] For others there was a limited degree of welfare.

Welfare

What happened to the abandoned, the orphaned or those infants suffering abuse or poverty? A number would spend their days begging on the streets, near wealthy households, relying on private charity. They would not necessarily receive sympathy: to some commentators, begging children could appear as undeserving as begging adults.[119] However, medieval society as a whole did not believe that infants could or should fend for themselves. Weak and vulnerable to disease, they were the only age group where age alone qualified them for help. For this reason, couples and families took in children who they felt were in need. The majority of cases were informal arrangements; examples from Wales and Norway show fathers 'adopting' their illegitimate offspring, and Florentine couples are recorded taking in the orphaned child of relative or friend, or welcoming home children off the streets as an act of charity.[120]

While parents were alive, ruling bodies rarely interfered in a child's upbringing. Both secular and Church authorities thought a child better off within the family unit and acted to promote and ensure family support. By the fourteenth century, church courts in England had the power to order fathers of illegitimate children to contribute to the child's upbringing, fixing amounts in some cases.[121] Instead governments were reactive in their help and stepped in only if the infants had no one else to care for them. There were several courses of possible action. In fifteenth-century Montpellier, the municipality accepted its duty to care for abandoned children by employing nurses to look after them. It became big business in the second half of the century: between 1450 and 1496 the numbers of nurses on the municipality's books grew eight-fold.[122] In addition, several cities had specialist offices or procedures to protect orphans, although it should be noted that they were overwhelmingly children with an inheritance to safeguard. The commune of Florence instituted an office (Ufficiale dei Pupilli) to administer the affairs of orphans, and the child's estate was invested on her or his behalf in state funds overseen by specially appointed officers. In London, city officials decided who would raise the orphans, monitored their fortunes and acted against mistreatment. Similarly, magistrates in Ghent drew up lists of orphans' property and appointed guardians. They tried to ensure that the children's interests were met, and fined guardians who treated children harshly or with neglect. Nevertheless, laws could go only so far, and interference in the guardian–child relationship was kept at a minimum. How much care and attention these orphans actually received is a moot point, and cases of brutality can be found.[123]

For most other children, help largely came from religious institutions, which cared for children as part of their general charitable duties. Hospital statutes in France and England obliged authorities to take responsibility for orphaned children until they reached the age of seven. Infants formed a significant proportion of inmates at the hospitals of Auffredi at La Rochelle, the Hôtel Dieu in Paris, Holy Trinity in Salisbury and St Leonard's, York.[124] A significant development occurred in the fourteenth century, when hospitals dedicated solely to the welfare of abandoned children were established. Although they were absent from the British Isles, during the fourteenth and fifteenth centuries foundling hospitals were established in over a dozen continental European cities including Ulm, Nuremberg, Cologne, Strasbourg, Marseilles, Chartres, Paris, Barcelona,

Valencia, Prato, Rome and Florence.[125] The records of hospitals demonstrate an acute awareness of the child's plight. This is also seen in the surge of donations to foundling hospitals by Roman testators in the last decades of the fourteenth century.[126] It may be that in the wake of the plague, growing numbers of orphaned and abandoned children became more visible in society and specialised hospitals came to be considered a necessity. But the move towards these foundations was also the result of a new, institutionalised way of dealing with society's problems, and reflected changes in methods of charity giving. By the fifteenth century, Florentines were giving less to religious orders and more to those institutions that specialised in social problems, which included the care for the young.[127]

Records of the foundling hospital of the Innocenti in Florence, which opened its doors in 1445, offer an interesting insight into the life of the fifteenth-century foundling. The vast majority of children left at the hospital were babies between three hours and three weeks old. Most had been conceived illegitimately, commonly with slave or servant mothers, while others arrived as a result of parental illness or the remarriage of a widowed mother; very few had been subject to any physical mistreatment. In 1452, for example, Giorgio, a carter, sent his daughter Andrea to the Innocenti because his wife had been taken seriously ill. Her time there was brief: Andrea was one of six per cent of cases in the mid-fifteenth century where children were later reclaimed by their families. She was in a minority, however, for boys were three times more likely than girls to be reclaimed. Infancy was not spent entirely behind institutional walls. The Innocenti placed a high value on family life, and the infant was placed for as long as possible with a 'real' family outside the hospital. The child would finally return to the hospital, aged four or five, for a few years of moral and practical education, before being put up for adoption and very likely apprenticeship. While providing some sort of family life for the infant, this approach could mean a very disrupted childhood.[128] Information gleaned from other hospitals suggests similar problems and procedures. At Santa Creu, Barcelona, the largest group comprised illegitimate children, and babies were shunted back and forth between wet-nurses. However, here, as in the rest of northern Spain, poverty appears to have been a much greater factor in the decision to leave children at hospitals than in the wealthier city of Florence.[129]

The hospitals grew increasingly attractive. In fifteenth-century Genoa the growing number of foundlings precipitated such a serious financial crisis in its hospital that the city government forced pregnant slaves and servants to swear that they would keep and raise their babies.[130] It may well be that the opening of specialised institutions had the inadvertent effect of increasing the numbers of foundlings as there was now a safe place to leave one's child. But it was not completely safe, especially with the growing numbers. In its first years, the death rate at the Innocenti had been around a quarter of the admissions, not much different from and possibly lower than infant mortality in the city in general. Thereafter the death rate began to creep upwards and had more than doubled by 1451. In this environment it does appear that girls were more susceptible to infant mortality, as they accounted for sixty per cent of deaths among children up to one year.[131] It is impossible to know whether those who left children at the hospital knew of the poor chances of survival, but many had little choice and the hospitals might still have been the better option for most.[132] Behind the foundling hospitals lay positive, charitable intentions, and contemporary Florentines were proud of these institutions. The fifteenth-century chronicler Gregorio Dati believed that the foundling hospital was 'a wonderful thing'. Hospitals gave support to abandoned children who might otherwise have died through exposure or attack by prowling animals. Nevertheless, at least the persons who left the child, and those who came across her or him, would directly face the consequences of that action. Boswell offers a more cynical reading of the foundling hospitals: ultimately, what they achieved was the removal of unwanted children from the streets and the view of the passing citizen; they allowed parents, relatives and society to forget.[133] There is, of course, no right view: the tension between personal responsibility and institutional care is an age-old problem. But whichever interpretation is preferred, late medieval society cannot be accused of ignoring the plight of abandoned children, and it directed its charity to a very public issue.

Conclusion

Infants are a difficult age group to research for any period. Their youth and state of dependency means that their quality of life has to be examined through adult-produced literature. For the medieval period, the under-sevens had few chances to reach the written record because they had a largely private existence, were given little responsibility and played no active role in society. These are also some of the qualities that helped to distinguish infants from other age groups. In addition they were seen as weak, vulnerable, lacking self-control, innocent, passive and irrational. Unlike the modern-day images of childhood, the medieval approach allowed no waxing lyrical about the baby's body; the softness, the gurgling, the attempts to crawl were not considered kindly. Nevertheless, the picture emerging of the life of late medieval children suggests a more positive and active existence than the one implied by contemporary images. The under-sevens had considerable freedom of movement and were not confined to classrooms or tested physically and mentally to some set standard. Medieval children did receive love and affection, guidance and care, and their deaths were occasions for grief. Even in an age where life was precarious, infants' lives were felt worth fighting for, and money was often no object in the attempt to keep children alive.

Age alone did not define the infant's life. Infants were considered vulnerable and innocent, but they did not escape society's prejudices. When a black child called Benenguda was abandoned in Barcelona in 1396 she passed through the hands of ten wet-nurses in as many months. This was because 'the child was as black as a cooking pot and no wet nurse wanted to have her'. While local authorities had tried to help the child, they were operating in an Iberian peninsula where ethnic divisions were rife. Castilian law forbade Muslim and Jewish women from suckling Christian children, and vice versa.[134] Gender also influenced the quality of infancy. Boys were seen as a social necessity either for inheritance or a strong pair of hands. They were more culturally valued than girls and may well have received most of the family's attention. Their accidents and deaths dominated miracle stories and poems of consolation, which suggests that they would be mourned more. On the other hand, this does not mean that girls were unwanted, received little care and suffered abuse. Their births were celebrated; they were loved and pampered and could pull at the heart strings of fathers and mothers alike. They too needed to be educated for life, with play and household tasks constructing their gender identity. Where documents record a comparatively small number of female children, the reason is likely to have lain in society's oversight, what Ozment refers to as 'gender prejudice not gendercide'. There is one exception, however, and that is those abandoned to foundling hospitals. In this specific group of infants, there does appear to have been a gender bias because girls were far more likely to be left and to die than boys.[135] Life would alter too with social status and geography. Nurses rather than parents dominated the care of the children belonging to the aristocracy and merchant elite; peasant toddlers had more freedom to roam away from their families. Wet-nursing was popular among the wealthy merchants of Florence but is rarely mentioned in London's records; foundling hospitals appeared in continental cities, but not in the British Isles; and while German literature dwelt on the negatives of childhood, northern Italian writings offered more positive readings. While it is possible to list these differences, evaluating their significance is more difficult; how they might translate into a varying quality of life requires further study.

Did infant lives alter during the later Middle Ages? Certain developments can be traced in the image and lives of infants in the period, but most relate to broader changes in society rather than new concerns for this age group. Developments in art, a growing fear of crime and a more selective method of charity giving resulted in more life-like representations of infants, a growth in literary descriptions of infanticide and new foundling hospitals. Likewise, the importance of Marian worship and the increasing Christo-centric nature of fourteenth- and fifteenth-century religious practices helped to place the Christ child near the centre of Christian worship. It is possible that the onslaught of plague in the fourteenth century and its attack on infants did focus society's minds more firmly on the young. The Welsh grief poems date from the post-plague era, and low numbers of children in Florence led authorities to sense that family life was under threat.[136] Yet none of this necessarily means a new interest in children or that they were more loved in 1500 than in 1300. Despite the obvious upheavals of late medieval society, continuity rather than change underlined the private lives of medieval infants.

Notes

1 Hanawalt, 'Medievalists and the study of children', pp. 447-8; *Middle English Dictionary*, s.v. 'child' and 'infant'; see also note 11 below.

2 Herlihy, *Women, family and society*, p. 215.

3 Schultz, 'Childhood', p. 114.

4 Taddei, 'Puerizia', p. 16.

5 *Mundus and infans*, lines 55-9, in Lester (ed.), *Three late medieval moralities*, p. 114;. Finucane, *The rescue of innocents*, pp. 9-10.

6 Shahar, *Childhood*, p. 14. Herlihy, *Women, family and society*, p. 228.

7 Williamson (trans.), *The memoirs of Helene Kottanner*, p. 44.

8 King, *The death of the child*, p. 7.

9 Nicholas, 'Childhood in medieval Europe', p. 33; Ozment, *Ancestors*, p. 74; Bennett, *Women in the medieval English countryside*, p. 67; Arnold, *Kind und Gesellschaft*, p. 25; Smith, 'Proofs of age', p. 139; Boswell, *The kindness of strangers*, p. 28.

10 Dante, *The divine comedy: Paradise*, canto 27, lines 127-9.

11 Whiting (ed.), *Proverbs*, nos C193-231, particularly C194, C196 and C204. See too the opinion of Bartholomaeus Anglicus in the translation by John Trevisa: Seymour (ed.), *On the properties of things*, vol. 1, p. 300.

12 E.g. in the Master of the Transfiguration of the Virgin, *The Virgin and child with St Anne, c.*1480 (now in Cologne's Wallraf and Richartz museum) Christ plays happily with Mary's gown.

13 Klapisch-Zuber, *Women, family and ritual*, p. 315.

14 Herlihy, *Women, family and society*, p. 126.

15 Shirley (trans.), *A Parisian journal*, p. 369. Geremek, *The margins of society*, pp. 202–4.

16 Hsia, *The myth of ritual murder*, p. 3. Shahar, *Childhood*, p. 135. Cowgill, 'Chaucer's missing children'; Rubin, *Gentile tales*, pp. 156–7, 160, fig. 21.

17 *Angela of Foligno's memorial*, pp. 1–2; Huizinga, *The autumn of the Middle Ages*, p. 35.

18 See p. 30 above. Haas, 'Women and childbearing', p. 87; Beer, *Eltern und Kinder*, p. 207.

19 Klapisch-Zuber, *Women, family and ritual*, p. 318; Gibson, *The theater of devotion*, pp. 63–4, 105; Origo, *The merchant of Prato*, pp. 161–3; Cadden, *Meanings of sex difference*, p. 229 and ch. 5 in general; Bell, *How to do it*, p. 35.

20 Klapisch-Zuber, *Women, family and ritual*, pp. 317–19; Bell, *How to do it*, pp. 24–5; Cadden, *Meanings of sex difference*, p. 237; Ross, 'The middle-class child', p. 206. There was a very limited literature on how to produce a female: Rowland (ed.), *Medieval woman's guide to health*, pp. 168–9.

21 Extract from *Book of fortune's transformation* in Blumenfeld-Kosinski and Brownlee (eds), *The selected writings of Christine de Pizan*, p. 94.

22 Seymour (ed.), *On the properties of things*, pp. 295–7; Dunstan, 'The human embryo', p. 43.

23 Haas, *The Renaissance man and his children*, p. 34.

24 Christine de Pisan, *Treasure*, p. 154.

25 Stoertz, 'Suffering and survival', p. 111; Gibson, 'Scene and obscene', p. 9.

26 Larrington (ed.), *Women and writing*, p. 79; Finucane, *The rescue of innocents*, p. 30.

27 Haas, *The Renaissance man and his children*, pp. 28, 56–7.

28 Finucane, *The rescue of innocents*, p. 39; Shahar, *Childhood*, p. 87; Beer, *Eltern und Kinder*, p. 261.

29 Coulton, 'Infant perdition in the Middle Ages', pp. 19–23.

30 Haas, *The Renaissance man and his children*, p. 7.

31 Goodich, *Violence and miracle*, p. 91; Finucane, *The rescue of innocents*, p. 45; Arnold, *Kind und Gesellschaft*, p. 31; Beer, *Eltern und Kinder*, pp. 224–5.

32 Peacock (ed.), *Instructions for parish priests*, line 91; Taglia, 'The cultural construction of childhood', pp. 261–3.

33 Grubb, *Provincial families*, p. 41.

34 Alexandre-Bidon and Closson, *L'enfant à l'ombre*, p. 77, and see in general ch. 1, section 5.

35 Grubb, *Provincial families*, pp. 48–9; Le Roy Ladurie, *Montaillou*, pp. 126–7; Haas, 'Social connections', pp. 5, 20; Dinn, 'Baptism', pp. 97–8.

36 In fourteenth-century Cambridgeshire, before the baptism of Ivo Harleston, a neighbour ran to the house of the smith to heat an iron rod which was then used to heat the font's water: Kirby (ed.), *Calendar of inquisitions post mortem*, vol. 18: *1–6 Henry IV: 1399–1405*, no. 310.

37 *Ibid.*, no. 998; Delmaire, 'Le livre de famille', p. 310; Haas, 'Social connections', p. 18. Hanawalt, *Growing up*, pp. 46–7.

38 Grubb, *Provincial families*, pp. 42–7, 225–6.

39 Stargardt (trans.), *The life of Dorothea von Montau*, p. 5.

40 Brucker (ed.), *Two memoirs of Renaissance Florence*, pp. 115–17.

41 Freed, *Noble bondsmen*, table 3.1, p. 96.

42 Lorcin, *Vivre et mourir*, pp. 160–6; Delmaire, 'Le livre de famille', p. 310, table 8; Bennett, *Women in the medieval English countryside*, p. 69.

43 Ward, *English noblewomen*, p. 95; Harris, *English aristocratic women*, p. 29; Shahar, *Childhood*, pp. 59–64; Fildes, *Wet nursing*, p. 36.

44 Haas, *The Renaissance man and his children*, p. 114, table 1; Klapisch-Zuber, *Women, family and ritual*, p. 137.

45 Klapisch-Zuber, *Women, family and ritual*, p. 145; Ross, 'The middle-class child', p. 188.

46 Barbaro, 'On wifely duties', pp. 223–4; Arnold, *Kind und Gesellschaft*, p. 51.

47 Klapisch-Zuber, *Women, family and ritual*, p. 151.

48 Orme, *Medieval children*, p. 58.

49 Christine de Pisan, *Treasure*, p. 67; Haas, *The Renaissance man and his children*, p. 117.

50 Hanawalt, *Growing up*, p. 56; Le Roy Ladurie, *Montaillou*, pp. 207–8; Nicholas, *Domestic*, p. 120; Beer, *Eltern und Kinder*, pp. 248–50; Ozment, *Ancestors*, p. 67; Wunder, *He is the sun*, p. 19.

51 Shahar, *Childhood*, p. 113.

52 Barbaro, 'On wifely duties', p. 221; extract from Christine's *Vision* in Blumenfeld-Kosinski and Brownlee (eds), *The selected writings of Christine de Pizan*, p. 194.

53 Larrington (ed.), *Women and writing*, pp. 109–22.

54 Hanawalt, *The ties that bound*, p. 185; Orme, *Medieval children*, p. 60.

55 *Dante's Il convivio*, book IV, ch. 24, p. 221.

56 Hanawalt, *Growing up*, p. 94.

57 Alexandre-Bidon and Lett, *Children*, p. 61.

58 Gibson, *The theater of devotion*, pp. 57–8; Gibson, 'Scene and obscene', p. 17; Alexandre-Bidon and Lett, *Children*, p. 63; Grubb, *Provincial families*, p. 53.

59 Alberti, *I libri*, p. 45.

60 Hanawalt, *The ties that bound*, pp. 184–5.

61 Parsons, 'Que nos in infancia lactauit', pp. 298–9; cf. Beer, *Eltern und Kinder*, p. 269.

62 Haas, *The Renaissance man and his children*, p. 139.

63 Grubb, *Provincial families*, p. 57.

64 Ariès, *Centuries of childhood*, p. 37.

65 Arnold, *Kind und Gesellschaft*, pp. 31–2.

66 Haas, *The Renaissance man and his children*, p. 56; Dyboski (ed.), *Songs, carols and other miscellaneous poems*, pp. xiii–xiv. Humphrey Newton's manuscript is Bodleian Library, Oxford, MS Lat. Misc.c.66, fos 1–2.

67 Arnold, *Kind und Gesellschaft*, p. 37.

68 Webb, 'Friends of the family', pp. 183–95; Goodich, *Violence and miracle*, pp. 86–7.

69 Finucane, *The rescue of innocents*, p. 151; Krötzl, 'Christian parent–child relations', p. 31.

70 Brown (ed.), *Religious lyrics*, no.7, p. 13; Gibson, *The theater of devotion*, p. 99.

71 Johnston (trans. and ed.), *Galar Y Beirdd*, pp. 28, 74–5, 104–5. See too Patrick Sims-Williams's review in *Cambrian Medieval Celtic Studies*, 29 (1995), pp. 60–2; Trexler, *Public life*, p. 174; King, *The death of the child*, p. 143; Banker, 'Mourning a son', p. 354.

72 *Ibid.*, p. 353; Finucane, *The rescue of innocents*, p. 156.

73 *Ibid.*, pp. 96, 141, 160–3; Haas, *The Renaissance man and his children*, pp. 1–2; Grubb, *Provincial families*, p. 55.

74 Orme, *Medieval children*, p. 108.

75 Arnold, *Kind und Gesellschaft*, p. 60; Beer, *Eltern und Kinder*, pp. 268–70.

76 As Helen Kottanner did for the young King of Hungary: Williamson (trans.), *The memoirs of Helene Kottanner*, p. 47.

77 Klapisch-Zuber, *Women, family and ritual*, pp. 101–8. Hanawalt, *Growing up*, p. 58 suggests that boys received better care, but offers no evidence in support. Neither Shahar (*Childhood*, p. 81) nor Beer (*Eltern und Kinder*, p. 255) could find examples of sons favoured over daughters when it came to nursing. For Cerruti see Wunder, *He is the sun*, p. 22.

78 Dominici, *On the education of children*, p. 45; de La Ronciere, 'Tuscan notables', p. 224. For parents recognising children by their clothes see Gordon, 'Accidents among medieval children', p. 161; Finucane, *The rescue of innocents*, p. 181.

79 Weinstein and Bell, *Saints and society*, p. 30.

80 Dominici, *On the education of children*, p. 34; Haas, *The Renaissance man and his children*, pp. 142–3; Shahar, *Childhood*, p. 112; Ruggiero, *The boundaries of eros*, p. 152; King, *The death of the child*, ch. 1.

81 Eg. Finucane, *The rescue of innocents*, p. 114.

82 Gordon, 'Accidents among medieval children', p. 155; Alberti, *I libri*, pp. 83–4; Orme, 'Children and literature', pp. 219–20.

83 Arnold, *Kind und Gesellschaft*, p. 69; Bell, *How to do it*, pp. 160–1.

84 Bell, *Holy anorexia*, pp. 35–7.

85 Dominici, *On the education of children*, p. 45.

86 Alexandre-Bidon and Lett, *Children*, p. 97.

87 Finucane, *The rescue of innocents*, p. 112,

88 Alexandre-Bidon and Lett, *Children*, p. 98; Goodich, *Violence and miracle*, ch. 5; Hanawalt, 'Childrearing among the lower classes', pp. 1–22; Finucane, *The rescue of innocents*, p. 8.

89 Gordon, 'Accidents among medieval children', p. 157; Finucane, *The rescue of innocents*, p. 108; Webb, 'Friends of the family', p. 191; Krötzl, 'Christian parent-child relations', p. 35.

90 Hanawalt, *The ties that bound*, p. 176; Ozment, *Ancestors*, p. 62.

91 Useful discussion and illustrations can be found in Arnold, *Kind und Gesellschaft*, pp. 67–76 and Alexandre-Bidon and Closson, *L'enfant à l'ombre*, pp. 174–83.

92 An English translation is found in Rickert, *Chaucer's world*, pp. 96–8.

93 Orme, *Medieval children*, p. 182.

94 Haas, *The Renaissance man and his children*, p. 152.

95 Rickert, *Chaucer's world*, pp. 96–8. For examples of girls and boys playing

together see Ross, 'The middle-class child', p. 204.

96   Klapisch-Zuber, *Women, family and ritual*, p. 125; Trexler, *Public life*, pp. 163–7.

97   Boswell, *The kindness of strangers*, p. 400.

98   Shirley (trans.), *A Parisian journal*, p. 155.

99   Boswell, *The kindness of strangers*, p. 397; Shahar, *Childhood*, pp. 126, 297, fn. 25; Brodman, *Charity and welfare*, p. 110.

100 Tucker, 'The child as beginning and end', p. 244; Trexler, *Dependence in context*, p. 205; Brissaud, 'L'infanticide', pp. 232, 250; Shahar, *Childhood*, pp. 126–7.

101 Hanawalt, *Crime and conflict*, p. 154; Hanawalt, *Growing up*, p. 44; Helmholtz, 'Infanticide in the province of Canterbury', p. 384.

102 Hanawalt, *Growing up*, p. 44; Hanawalt, 'Medievalists and the study of childhood'.

103 Hsia, *The myth of ritual murder*, pp. 151–4.

104 Hanawalt, *Crime and conflict*, p. 155; Kellum, 'Infanticide', pp. 369–70.

105 Biller, 'Marriage patterns', pp. 75–82; Orme, *Medieval children*, p. 95. For general Christian attitudes see Arnold, *Kind und Gesellschaft*, pp. 43–5.

106 Shahar, *Childhood*, p. 129; Arnold, *Kind und Gesellschaft*, p. 52; Brucker (ed.), *The society of Renaissance Florence*, pp. 146–7.

107 Gauvard, 'Fear of crime', pp. 16–17.

108 Finucane, *The rescue of innocents*, p. 48.

109 Kellum, 'Infanticide', p. 374.

110 Attreed, 'From Pearl maiden to tower princes', pp. 131–43.

111 Hyatte (ed.), *Laughter for the devil*, p. 18.

112 *Ibid.*, pp. 54–62

113 Benedetti, *Gilles de Rais*, p. 118.

114 Hyatte (ed.), *Laughter for the devil*, p. 131.

115 Bataille (ed.), *The trial of Gilles de Rais*, pp. 109–10.

116 deMause (ed.), 'The History of childhood', p. 1.

117 Nicholas, *Domestic*, ch. 8; Nicholas, 'Childhood in medieval Europe', p. 38.

118 Finucane, *The rescue of innocents*, p. 25.

119 Orme, *Medieval children*, p. 91.

120 Smith, 'Fosterage, adoption and god-parenthood', p. 15; Haas, *The Renaissance man and his children*, pp. 24–5.

121 Orme, *Medieval children*, p. 57.

122 Otis, 'Municipal wetnurses ', pp. 83–7.

123 Haas, *The Renaissance man and his children*, p. 174; Hanawalt, *Growing up*, pp. 57, 89–92; Nicholas, *Domestic*, pp. 113, 140, 144.

124 Shahar, *Childhood*, p. 296, fn. 13; Clay, *The medieval hospitals*, p. 26; Rawcliffe, *Medicine and society*, p. 204; Orme, *Medieval children*, p. 88.

125 Herlihy, *Women, family and society*, pp. 233–4; Arnold, *Kind und Gesellschaft*, p. 46; Brodman, *Charity and welfare*, p. 112.

126 Cohn, *The Black Death transformed*, pp. 217–18.

127 Gavitt, *Charity and children*, p. 1.

128 Trexler, *Dependence in context*, pp. 225–58; Gavitt, *Charity and children*, pp. 188, 191–5, 204.

129 Brodman, *Charity and welfare*, pp. 114–15.

130 Epstein, *Genoa*, pp. 304–5; cf. Trexler, *Dependence in context*, pp. 232–3.
131 Gavitt, *Charity and children*, pp. 212, 218. In Santa Creu, Barcelona, between a half and two-thirds of infants died before the age of two: Brodman, *Charity and welfare*, p. 117.
132 While Trexler saw the deserter as signing the child's death warrant (*Dependence in context*, p. 251), Boswell doubts that the death rate was known (*The kindness of strangers*, p. 423).
133 Boswell, *The kindness of strangers*, p. 423.
134 Brodman, *Charity and welfare*, pp. 117–18.
135 Ozment, *Ancestors*, p. 63; Wunder, *He is the sun*, p. 20; and see p. 62 above.
136 Cohn, *The Black Death transformed*, p. 217; Herlihy, *Medieval households*, p. 117.

4

Boys and girls

CHILDREN do not stay babies for long. It appears from a number of medieval sources that a key turning point in the child's life occurred around the age of seven, although the timing depended on ability, gender and social status. In some 'ages of man' literature, the end of infancy was said to mark the beginning of a stage called, in Latin, *pueritia*, which extended to the ages of twelve to fifteen. The term itself was said to derive from 'pure' (*pura*), indicating that the child had not yet reached puberty and was still cloaked in the idea of innocence. Nevertheless, cracks in the image were beginning to appear. In the influential treatise *De regimine principum*, by Giles of Rome (d.1316), the stage between seven and fourteen was marked by the start of lustful thoughts. Some theologians saw sexual knowledge as common among boys, and there were moves in the fifteenth century to alter the canonical age of confession from fourteen down to ten or perhaps seven to take account of those feelings.[1]

Legislation further marked seven as an age of change: hospitals were no longer obliged to care for the children; legal innocence had ended in certain criminal actions; and canon law decreed that a child could be betrothed. The new responsibilities were linked to perceived physical and rational strengths. According to the Scottish poem *Ratis raving* the ages of seven to fifteen saw the setting of the roots (though not the fruition) of reason. The body was cooling down sufficiently for instruction to take place. Whereas care in infancy had focused on food and warmth, this next stage of childhood was the time when training for adulthood fully commenced and play was curtailed.[2] By around seven, decisions were being made about the child's future. For young daughters, the focus narrowed on the training for marriage and motherhood; a few among the elite could become betrothed. It may have been no coincidence therefore that seven was also the approximate age when many female saints first showed their spiritual leanings. Sts Bridget of Sweden (d.1373), Catherine of Siena (d.1380) and Dorothy von Montau (d.1394) initiated their spiritual careers around the ages of six or seven at a time when they were first becoming aware of their roles in society.[3] Conversely, sons had a larger range of options open to them, ones that focused on public careers. The Florentine friar Giovanni Dominici (1356–1419) stressed the necessity of choosing the profession for the boy, whether as farmer, merchant, banker or priest, which suited his aptitude and inclinations 'since nature aids art, and a skill chosen against nature will not be learned well'.[4] For both sexes and across social groups, education – literally meaning 'to lead out' – was directed at providing them with the skills required for adult life.

Upbringing

Medieval society took child rearing very seriously. A common English proverb ran, 'A child were better to be unborn than to be untaught and so be lorn [lost].'[5] Every child needed a degree of moral and technical education. Orphanages not only provided food and shelter, but the instruction necessary to give the child an adequate start in life. The ills of society were often traced back to poor upbringing, and a whole people might be condemned for its child-rearing customs. Irish and Welsh practices were frequent targets of English ecclesiastics and statute writers. Following the conquest of Wales, Archbishop Peckham advised Edward I that the best way to civilise the Welsh was to force them to send their children to England to acquire learning and good manners.[6]

Bearing the brunt of any criticism were parents, who remained the primary teachers of young children and whose duty it was to ensure good upbringing. Jean Gerson (1363–1429), Chancellor of the University of Paris, believed that parents who neglected to teach their children good morals 'will be held more accountable than if they let their offspring die of hunger'.[7] A popular story told of a young man whose criminal actions had led him to the gallows. On his way to the hanging he asked to kiss his father for the last time; but instead of giving him a kiss he bit his father on the nose and blamed him for his crimes because of inadequate education the young man had received in childhood.[8] For boys, as that tale implies, the move out of infancy corresponded with a greater male presence in their upbringing, as fathers (or surrogate fathers) took the primary role of educator and disciplinarian. For young girls, the mother and the domestic sphere continued to be major influences. Greater mobility and reasoning also brought the child into contact with a broader range of influences. Instruction and correction would be received from other household members, neighbours, the local priest, the schoolmaster or employers. All competed with advice offered by friends and peers.

Most of this advice and correction would be passed on orally, and it would be largely a private experience for each individual. Local customs as well as parental preference determined content and emphasis, nuances that are rarely recoverable from the texts that survive. What is more readily available is information on how certain sectors of society wanted children to be raised. As already mentioned, child rearing had far-reaching implications for society. While the Church and moralists focused on saving souls, civil authorities directed their attention to the need for social order. Florentine evidence in particular illustrates the belief that a society's future stability depended on the education of its youth.[9] There was no specific genre of children's instruction, but a number of didactic works included sections on child (mainly boy) rearing. Giles of Rome's *De regimine principum* and the pseudo-Aristotelian *Secretum secretorum* enjoyed widespread popularity among the nobility of Western Europe, and their chapters on childhood proved influential with other writers. Among the borrowers were Jean Gerson and Christine de Pizan, both of whom wrote works of advice for the young French dauphin, in addition to more general works on the upbringing of boys and girls. Wealthy families in other parts of Europe commissioned their own manuals: Giovanni Dominici produced his treatise on child rearing as the result of a private commission by a Florentine noblewoman.[10]

For a wider literary public, vernacular books of advice were increasingly produced during the fifteenth century, and were thought popular enough to be printed. They focused on training in the home and the correcting of personal habits. In 1476 William Caxton printed *Stans puer ad mensum*, a loose English translation by John Lydgate of a Latin poem on table manners. It rendered into verse advice against such habits as slouching, picking one's nose, scratching, gobbling down one's food, eating noisily, making faces, talking too much and playing with knives. Accompanying the text were simple religious poems and several proverbs, suggesting that children were Caxton's target audience. Children are likely to have been the intended readers of other short didactic works employing rhymes or mnemonics to aid learning. The *ABC of Aristotle*, a list of aphorisms on good behaviour, is one such example found in English miscellanies and household books. Ideas on upbringing were also promoted in sources as diverse as sermons, devotional handbooks, confessionals, saints' lives, histories, romances, morality plays and popular ballads.[11]

What, then, are the messages coming from medieval literature? Medieval society strongly believed that anything experienced during childhood would leave an indelible mark; it was the foundation of a person's life and personality.[12] Some likened the child to wax or soft clay: Dominici observed that 'this age is like soft wax that takes whatever imprint is put upon it'.[13] Others preferred the comparison of a clean slate – the *tabula rasa* – on to which the child's personality and abilities would be written. The alacrity with which the young could pick up information was widely commented upon. Christine de Pizan thought that what a girl 'absorbed in her early childhood she usually remembers all her life'. Gaston Phébus, Count of Foix and author of a famous hunting manual (written *c.*1387–89), argued that education should begin at seven, for 'what a man learns in his youth he will hold best in his old age'. Yet the process, as all these comments indicate, was one of the child passively accepting the input of the adult. It was imitation rather than thoughtful application that Konrad von Megenberg in his *Yconomica* (1352) saw as characterising the training of the child after seven.[14]

The malleable child was considered highly impressionable. Adults had a responsibility to make sure that the child was taught only good and right ways before the body hardened and became set in its ways. As a result, it was imperative that the behaviour of those around children should not lead the latter into irreversible bad habits. Both Dominici (on boys) and Christine de Pizan (on girls) believed that children should keep good company, with the emphasis on virtuous tutors guiding them away from perversity and frivolity. These desires were echoed in wider society in the supporters and founders of schools, who paid special attention to the character of the schoolmaster. The master of Ave Maria College, Paris, was not to be dishonest, a drunkard or wanton.[15] As this indicates, the focus of much of the literature on upbringing was directed towards moral and spiritual development. The main aim was to raise the person in good Christian values, teaching her or him how to worship and to stay away from the seven deadly sins. The strong belief that children, after infancy, were coming to know sin played an important factor. The Church thought that boys over the age of seven should not be allowed to sleep together, and it was not considered wise for them to remain in nunneries much beyond their infancy. In the English nunneries of Elstow and Bishop Stretton, boys had to leave at the ages of six and eight respectively.[16]

The outside world was full of temptation too. Christine de Pizan thought that the young girl should not be given books that contained 'vain things, follies or dissipation'. From his university in Montpellier about 1300, Bernard de Gordon warned that children under twelve should not read the bawdy twelfth-century comedy *Pamphilus* (a basic school text in many European schools), and he condemned indecent songs, evil music and dances as corrupting influences. As supervisor of several schools in Paris, Gerson was equally worried about corrupt images. In 1402, in his writings on youth, he urged secular and clerical powers to legislate against the public display of obscene pictures. This would help to prevent 'the filthy corruption of boys and adolescents by shameful and nude pictures offered for sale in the very temples and sacred places'. Parents were again targeted, and told not to pamper or indulge their children. Dominici, writing for a wealthy family, instructed parents to stamp out any predilection in their children for fine clothing. A boy should be strengthened by walking barefoot, sleeping on a couch or chest with the windows open, going on a fast and generally being treated 'somewhat as if he were the son of a peasant'.[17]

Related issues were routine and discipline, which were considered the best ways to keep a child from idleness. As the child grew older, harsher chastisement was encouraged as it was believed that the child learnt best when in fear of punishment. Often quoted were the lines from Proverbs 13:24, 'he who spares the rod hates his son'. Corporal punishment was normal for all age groups in medieval society and can be seen in both private and public contexts. It could be severe: in London in May 1324, a five-year-old caught stealing wool was hit so violently by an angry wool seller that he died. Yet views varied regarding the degree of severity required. The calls by fourteenth-century writers such as William Langland for greater parental discipline could suggest growing indulgence in the post-plague era; again parents were not doing their job properly. On the other hand, writers like Maffeo Vegio (writing in 1444) believed that severe beatings did more harm than good and advocated leniency, encouragement and reward.[18]

How far parents and guardians followed this advice is unknown. Most of the views considered above are those of religious and moral authorities who, it could be argued, are unlikely representatives of medieval society at large. Nevertheless, they were not writing in a vacuum, and most had some contact with the young, albeit mainly from the upper echelons of society. They appear to have produced the accepted wisdom on upbringing, which struck a chord with the nobility and merchants who owned copies of their texts. For parents and families in general, however, instilling good behaviour was only one element of a child's upbringing. Their energies were directed at socialising the child into a life suitable for her or his position and gender. Educating the young in the Middle Ages was not about broadening horizons or offering a comprehensive education; the emphasis was on vocational training. Whether children had any say in their future is doubtful, especially if they were the first born. In 1401 Jean Gerson wrote to his younger brother Nicholas complaining that as the eldest son he had been given little choice in his career.[19] The following sections consider the forms that vocational training took and the options available (or not, as the case may be) to the growing child in the years 1300–1500.

Nobility

For the aristocratic boy, later childhood saw him move out of the domestic sphere and the world of women, be that nursery or nunnery, and into the public arena for training among men. In England, Henry VI was nearly seven when in 1428 he passed from the care of Dame Alice Butler to that of the Earl of Warwick.[20] Of central importance was the inculcation of military skills and engendering an interest in war. It was a highly physical goal and required the toughening of the body with a regime of walking, racing, gymnastics, wrestling, hand-to-hand combat and fencing. A comparable toughening procedure for the mind was endured, and writers recommended dressing the child in plain clothes, giving him menial tasks and making him serve others.[21] The skills themselves included archery, horse-riding, hunting and jousting and were taught in a gradual fashion. Learning to be a good hunter, according to *The hunting book of Gaston Phébus*, began at seven with a series of lesser jobs, which were intended to improve discipline and strengthen the mind. The young boy would sleep in the same building as the hounds, and would learn their names and colours, clean their kennels every day, change the litters and put down fresh water.[22] Similarly, Christine de Pizan in her *Book of deeds of arms and of chivalry* stressed that training should increase in line with body strength; light staves should be used until the lad was strong enough to wield swords and axes.[23] Jousting too was practised first on foot before the boy progressed to riding a pommel horse with wheels. Nevertheless, children were given weapons at an early age, and a few were already learning to feel the weight of armour. The future Henry V of England owned a sword in 1397 at the age of nine; his son, Henry VI, had a suit of armour when he went to France in 1430 at the age of seven. While it was the case that serious training and the actual business of fighting would wait until adolescence, the learning process was already well under way. To all intents and purposes, Jean, Duke de Berry (d.1416), was fully equipped as a knight when he reached twelve.[24]

Noble training did not simply involve military skills. Education was required to develop the chivalric ethos and draw out the virtues of courageousness, generosity and honour, making the boy an accomplished defender and protector of the Church and society. To encourage bravery, young nobles were to hear about courageous words and deeds. To the young dauphin, Louis de Guyenne, Christine de Pizan recommended stories and songs about the ancients, while Gerson emphasised the more religious and moral matter of the saints' lives and the Ten Commandments.[25] A broad curriculum focused on the child's behaviour, with the general aim of making him less 'child-like'. The chronicler of the life of Don Pero Niño, Count of Buelna (writing c.1431–49), described how a ten-year-old Pero was entrusted to the education of 'a wise and learned man, who instructed him and taught him in all good habits and manners as befits a good and noble gentleman [*hidalgo*]'. The focus was on knowing God, eschewing the company of sinful men and women, and avoiding the sins of greed and a loose tongue.[26] Young noble boys would also have practical lessons in language, music, singing, dancing, playing chess and serving at the table. By the later Middle Ages, reading and to some extent writing were regular features of the curriculum. Noble children were unlikely to attend the schools that were developing in Europe's towns (see below), and instruction at the higher levels of society came from private tutors. Edward V of England was given a male governor at the age of three and a grammar master at six. Noble households doubled up as private schools. In 1471 an inventory of the castle of Angers (north-western France) included a large board filled with 'alphabets' in several languages.[27]

At all stages of instruction the emphasis was on boys being taught together and becoming accustomed to other people.[28] The group would not necessarily be from the same age cohort. In 1426–28 the young Henry VI, aged between five and seven, had as his companions the seventeen-year-old Duke of York and Earl of Oxford and the twenty-year-old Lord Roos. That young princes would mix with older children and particularly the household retainers caused some concern among their elders. In 1432 the Earl of Warwick complained to the Privy Council of England that certain people had been telling Henry VI inappropriate stories and diverting him from his studies. Princely and noble children also managed to escape the watchful eyes of adults and get themselves into trouble. Prince Arthur, son of Henry VII of England, played dice for money when he was ten, managing to lose 40s.[29]

For young aristocratic girls, upbringing remained within the domestic sphere. There was some limited physical training outside, such as learning to use the bow or ride a horse, but generally the emphasis was on household tasks. Parents, mistresses and servants focused on teaching those skills needed for later wifely duties. There was little need for a graduated education because ideas of physical strength and a developing reason did not impinge on a girl's upbringing. Didactic literature stressed the importance of obedience, submission and chastity, with prescriptions in conduct books focusing on secluding the young girls and keeping them from idleness. The three chapters devoted to educating girls in Giles of Rome's *De regimine principum* discuss the ways to keep young girls suitably occupied in spinning, weaving and reading so that they would not become, as John Trevisa's translation calls them, 'strumpettes and gygelottes'. An example of a conduct book written specifically for aristocratic girls was the *Livre du chevalier de la Tour Landry*, compiled in 1371–72 by a knight of Anjou for his three daughters. It enjoyed some success among the aristocracy of France, England and Germany, although its popularity lay in the fifteenth century with socially aspiring audiences. The book is a mix of the courtly and the clerical and is a compilation of viewpoints drawn from, among others, the Bible, sermons, female saints' lives and popular tales of fabliaux. The message reiterated a common view: the well-born girl was to learn her prayers and be courteous, gracious, meek and abstemious in food and fashion. Whether girls themselves read these conduct books is unknown, but literacy does appear to have been a feature of an aristocratic girl's upbringing. By 1400 most daughters of English nobles and gentry had learnt to read. Recommended texts were overwhelmingly religious, with tales of the Virgin or virgin martyrs considered particularly suitable.[30]

The education of Europe's elite did not always take place in the parental home. In German-speaking areas, Spain, France and England, noble youths were placed in other households for their upbringing. The Alphonsine law code, the *Siete partidas*, observed that in Spain it had 'always been customary for honourable men to send their sons to be brought up in the courts of kings so that they might learn to be courteous and educated, and free from villainy and all defects'.[31] England too had a long tradition of sending children into other noble or royal households, which exaggerated the change from the informal surroundings of the nursery to the formalities of regulated study. The move commonly occurred towards the end of childhood or in early adolescence, but there are a number of examples to show that the move came sooner for some, among both boys and girls. Katherine, daughter of John of Gaunt, was only seven in 1380 when she went to live with Lady Mohun at Dunster Castle in Somerset. All of the major houses in England potentially provided a home for aristocratic children. The largest was the royal household, whose departments provided employment and training for dozens of children who acted as pages or choristers and would serve and carve at dinner. Religious establishments offered a number of places for both boys and girls, with nunneries proving particularly popular as temporary 'crèches' or boarding schools for noble and gentry girls. In early fourteenth-century Cork (Ireland) the Anglo-Irish community petitioned for a local nunnery where 'the knights and other free men might have their daughters brought up and maintained'.[32]

The custom had many supporters within the English elite. In the fifteenth century Sir John Fortescue thought the household was the chief academy (the *gignasium supremum*) for athletics, good manners and moral integrity. For parents, placing a child in another household could further bonds with important families. For the child, it was felt that she or he would be better disciplined, learn the value of service, gain new experiences and secure social advancement. There were dissenters, however. A number of religious writers criticised the practice on moral grounds: the preacher John Bromyard believed that parents who placed their children at court were less concerned for their children's souls than they were for their potential as 'a marriage ticket to riches'. Around 1498 a Venetian visitor to England considered the sending out of children a callous custom. The practice evidently struck him as highly irregular; Venetian nobles did not send their children away to learn. Yet while his views as a stranger to England must be treated with caution, English children themselves could suffer from the move. Aged eleven, Sir Stephen Scrope was sold by his stepfather (*c.*1409) to be a ward and resident of William Gascoigne, the Chief Justice of the King's Bench. In later life Scrope's anger at his stepfather and mother had little abated. He thought it unnatural that a boy of such 'tender years' should be removed from his natural family. In the words of Jonathan Hughes, 'the introspective man's obsession with compensation for these injuries dominated his personality and he probably lost no opportunity in reminding his mother and stepfather of their cruelty'. It did not stop Scrope, however, placing his own children in other households.[33]

Labour

The duty of parents and guardians was to prepare the child to live and work independently. In England, around 1470, John Fortescue asked rhetorically what craftsman 'is so negligent of his child's profit that he does not instruct him in crafts when he is young, by which he may afterwards gain the comforts of life? Thus a carpenter teaches his son to cut with an axe, the smith his son to work with a hammer'.[34] As in the higher levels of society, most children of merchants, artisans or peasant communities learnt adult roles through practical experience and hands-on training. Children were expected to contribute to the economy of the household, which, in both rural and urban areas, formed the basic unit of production. By seven, children were already helping out their parents or guardians in simple tasks; as they grew older they were given jobs to perform on their own. In the countryside the range involved babysitting, chasing birds away from crops, feeding chickens, herding geese, gathering wild berries and fetching water from wells. If infancy kept children close to the home, the work of later childhood took them further afield. Boys in particular were used as messengers and could travel considerable distances. In the fourteenth-century *Meditations on the life of Christ*, based on apocryphal texts, a five-year-old Christ is described as acting as his mother's messenger, helping to sell her cloth and spinning to others. That this was conjecture on the part of the writer indicates the assumptions made about the life of young boys.[35] While both sexes worked in the fields and in the home, a gender division of labour was becoming more discernible, with girls preparing food, cooking and helping with the laundry, while boys took on more demanding physical tasks such as climbing trees for fruit and nuts, digging in the fields and caring for animals.[36] Nevertheless, even for boys, the introduction to the world of work appears to have been a gradual progression. The different degrees are related in a book written for King Charles V entitled *Le bon berger* ('The good shepherd'). At the age of eight a boy is employed to watch the geese before being allowed to mind the pigs. At around nine or ten he is leading horses at the plough. At eleven he watches the sheep, and by fourteen he is in charge of 200 ewes.[37]

Children in towns and cities across Europe were expected, at the very least, to work for the family business. In fifteenth-century Auvergne, children minded their father's cloth-cutting store in his absence and boys of eight to ten years acted as candle sellers. In London boys sold eels and other goods, while in Venice girls were employed as silk workers. Children of artisans in Ghent appear to have worked regularly too, earning a little money even when working for their own families. The small incomes did not permit independence, but they did make the children a little less reliant on family or guardians, and gave them early responsibility with money. Some independence was also gained by working away from home. In the Upper Swabia and Voralberg regions, children from the age of eight were hired out to farms from spring to autumn to help out at a time of intensive labour activity. Such work was seasonal, and most working children continued to live with their families. However, for some, particularly in southern Europe, a more permanent move away from home was experienced at an early stage in their lives. In fifteenth-century Venice, Florence and Barcelona, girls and some boys could become servants as young as eight or nine. Evidence from the memoir writers of Vicenza and Verona shows that nearly a quarter of female servants in their households and nearly ten per cent of male servants were under fourteen. In Castile and Catalonia, examples of very young servants and apprentices appear to have come from the disadvantaged children of society – foundlings, orphans or paupers – who would provide cheap sources of labour. In Castile in 1427, Mateu Esteve was only six months old when he was apprenticed as an apothecary.[38]

Families thought little of using their children as labour; for most there was no option. When his young son Raymond died, a distraught Guillaume Benet, a farmer in Montaillou, wept to a neighbour, 'I have lost all I had through the death of my son Raymond. I have no one left to work for me.' [39] Harvest time meant using all available hands, and employing children may have intensified in the labour shortage of the later fourteenth century. The sad accounts of missing children in the trial of Gilles de Rais in 1440 illustrate the normal, regular work and mobility of children between the ages of seven and twelve. Parents tell of sons who went out to carry milk, buy bread, gather apples, watch the flocks or work as haberdashers, and never came back. For a significant number of children, their daily task had been begging. Several likely victims of Rais came to his attention while queuing for alms at his castles in Machecoul and Champtocé; some had entered believing they were to be employed as household servants. Even while suspicion hung over Rais as child murderer, the possibility of food and shelter and the promise of social advancement were too tempting.[40]

Murder was not an occupational hazard for most, but children did suffer accidents while working. In the fourteenth century, a nine-year-old girl was washing clothes in the Sarthe river, near Le Mans (in the Loire, France), when she fell into the river and was carried under a mill dam. In fifteenth-century England a six-year-old housemaid was sent to draw water from a well, but lost her balance and fell in. In medieval Scandinavia children aged seven to twelve suffered accidents while fetching hay for animals and leading horses.[41] Some accidents were caused by children being allocated tasks that were unsuitable for their age. In the late fifteenth century an eight-year-old boy in Devon was goading the oxen pulling his stepfather's plough when one of them gored him to the point of death. The recorder of the incident noted that 'he was really too small' for the task.[42] Dangerous work too was given to the young miners found working in the narrow clay tunnels of fourteenth-century Montagne Noir (southern France).[43] Nevertheless, while it is possible to uncover individual cases of exploitation, medieval society as a whole recognised that children should not be given adult tasks and commented on the exceptions. To emphasise the reduction in the labour force following the Black Death, a monk at Malmesbury Abbey stated that children had to be used to operate ploughs and carts, 'which was unheard of'.[44] From around seven onwards, children were carrying out many of the tasks that would be a regular feature of their adult lives. Yet they were not recognised as adults, and the opinion of Bartholomaeus Anglicus appears to have been a common one: 'because of tenderness of body they are soon injured and cannot endure hard work'.[45]

Schooling

Since the nineteenth century, the fundamentals of a child's early education in Western Europe have been reading, writing and arithmetic. Schools are the main forums for this training, as well as providing common cultural and social experiences for five-to-fourteen-year-olds. In late medieval society, reading and writing were not synonymous with education and they were not considered skills necessary for all. Formal schooling was neither compulsory nor the choice for the majority of children. Most learnt through labour and experience rather than pen and paper, and literacy levels could vary considerably between social groups.

Nevertheless, the period 1300–1500 witnessed a growing number of voices expressing the value of literacy skills and formal education to individual, familial, spiritual and commercial development. The Church, with its sights on facilitating religious instruction, had already made the provision of schooling a canonical requirement. In the third and fourth Lateran councils (in 1179 and 1215 respectively), the Church had ruled that a master capable of teaching should be made available in each cathedral, and lessons should be free to both young clerics and students from poorer backgrounds. The legislation was successfully implemented and developed at a local level. By the end of the fourteenth century every diocese in the Spanish kingdoms had a school of some sort. At the same time in France, synodical statutes required that parish priests encourage parents either to send their children (at the age of six or seven) to the local schools or to place them with priests who could offer a basic religious teaching. National governments and urban authorities similarly moved to establish formal schooling, influenced by commercial needs and the hope that it would further good citizenship and promote civic values. The optimistic Estates of Scotland required all barons and freeholders to send their children to school at eight or nine; the council of Hamburg founded several schools in 1402; and tax exemptions and free accommodation were used to tempt teachers into Italian cities. Craft guilds too began to lay more emphasis on reading and writing skills. Several craft guilds in England, such as London's Goldsmiths' guild in 1478, refused to take apprentices who could neither read nor write. But the development of formal education also owed much to the individual efforts of passionate supporters of schooling, from the high-profile campaigners like Jean Gerson to the lesser-known founders of small chantry schools, and to the numerous parents who wished to further their child's and family's development. When one of Gille de Rais's men tried to persuade Peronne Loessart from La Roche-Bernard (Brittany) to part with her ten-year-old son, she replied that he was going to school and was learning well. She only yielded when she gained an assurance that the boy would be kept at school.[46]

Precisely how many schools were established in medieval Western Europe is impossible to know. Medieval authorities produced no surveys of schools, nor did contemporary writers give much attention to their number and purpose. Most of our evidence has come about accidentally, and remains patchy. It does appear, however, that opportunities for schooling depended in part on where one lived: schools were more numerous in northern Italy than in Flanders; more numerous in south Wales than in the north.[47] Lay education was most advanced in northern and central Italy, where the actions of parents and governments had resulted in a large educational network spreading across numerous towns and villages. Even during the fourteenth century, Venice could boast fifty-five teachers in a single year. Florence has received particular attention because the chronicler Giovanni Villani (c.1338) offers a rare contemporary estimation of school numbers: 'we find that 8,000 to 10,000 boys and girls are learning to read. There are 1,000 to 1,200 boys learning abbaco [a form of business mathematics] in six schools. And those who study grammar and logic in four large schools are 550 to 600'. This would mean roughly 9,550 to 11,800 boys and girls, or between thirty-seven and forty-five per cent of Florence's school-age population. This extraordinary number has not stood up to later scrutiny, and the figure has been reduced to a more conservative, yet still impressive, estimate that just over a quarter of boys aged six to fourteen attended formal schools in Florence.[48]

Estimates for northern Europe are lower, but schools can also be traced to most of the major towns and cities. For Paris in 1357, there is mention of around forty-one schoolmasters and twenty-one schoolmistresses of 'little' (elementary) schools, which may suggest at least sixty-two separate establishments. While little credence can be given to the Parisian journal writer's total of 12,500 schoolchildren in a Paris procession in 1449, it at least suggests that schoolchildren were perceived as a substantial subgroup of the city.[49] Elementary and grammar schools were a familiar sight in the larger and some smaller towns of England. It has been estimated that there were somewhere between 8,000 and 16,000 school-children in private, public and religious schooling in fifteenth-century England. This amounts to approximately one in twenty of England's boys aged seven to eighteen.[50] Some of these children would be based in rural areas, but schools were rarer in Europe's countryside. The inquisition records of Montaillou show only one schoolboy, and he was under the tuition of the local priest. Some areas did do better. Villages in the Ariège valley and the lowlands of southern France had a number of schools, mainly run by the church: thirty villages in one Champagne diocese (of 300 parishes) contained a school.[51]

Opportunities for schooling also depended on resources. There was no universal free education, and significant costs could be incurred by those who sent children to school. There were fees, ink and wax tablets, possibly books and perhaps accommodation to be paid for, as well as the prospect of lost earnings or the need to provide extra labour.[52] While these would exclude a substantial proportion of Europe's population, they did not necessarily mean that only the wealthy could attend schools in the Middle Ages. In northern Italy, schoolchildren came from across the social spectrum, although the numbers progressively diminished down the social scale. In 1498 a Genoese schoolmaster taught children whose parents included a banker, baker, barber, boat maker, spinner, tanner and wool worker. Even in rural France and England motivated peasant boys wanting to learn could generally do so, especially if they possessed a good singing voice. They did however have to be free: serfs in England could not be educated without their lord's permission, and he seldom gave it without attaching time limitations.[53] A significant development in the later

Middle Ages was the introduction of a limited free schooling. In fourteenth-century England wealthy benefactors began endowing schools, which paid the master a regular salary and offered free places. The school at Wotton-under-Edge (Gloucestershire), which was endowed by Lady Katherine Berkeley in 1384, offered free lessons to anyone who wished to attend.[54] Similarly in Paris, there were at least five colleges for poor schoolboys by 1342. The statutes of Ave Maria College, founded in 1339, declare it to be a hospice for schoolboys aged between seven and sixteen who were poor and of legitimate birth, lived by their own labour, were capable of being taught and were free from physical deformities.[55] Schoolboys additionally benefited from private charity, as testamentary evidence from Paris in 1200–1348 and England in 1340–1548 demonstrates.[56]

It will be noted that the emphasis here is on school*boys*. None of the scholars at Ave Maria College were to be girls, nor were female servants or householders' daughters over the age of ten allowed to remain in this male-only environment. Gender too prevented girls from attending cathedral schools. Opportunities were available elsewhere. An English statute of 1406 explicitly noted the right 'of every man or woman, of whatever estate or condition he be, to set their son or daughter to take learning at any manner of school that pleaseth them'. Nevertheless, the evidence of actual attendance is fragmentary. Northern Italy is the most promising, with female teachers noted in several Italian towns – Florence, Siena, Venice, Vicenza, Modena – teaching both boys and girls. This supports Villani's inclusion of girls in the numbers learning to read in Florence. French towns such as Paris and Reims had schoolmistresses who kept grammar schools, possibly single-sex schools, while in the county of Hainault (north-east France) Froissart's account of early schooldays assumes that boys and girls were taught together. Elsewhere there are only scattered references to suggest that girls attended schools in London, Ghent, Cologne and Armagh (Ireland): the last example is known because a marriage contract was made for a young girl and boy when they were still at school together.[57]

While it was not unusual, therefore, for girls to attend schools, they did not do so in large numbers. In urban families, the basic literary skills required of the prospective merchant's wife could be taught in the household. Mothers could play a key role, and the numerous surviving images of St Anne teaching the young Virgin Mary to read may well reflect this expectation. Richer families were able to pay a tutor for private tuition. In 1401 Francesco di Marco Datini of Prato recorded paying a gold florin to the lady who taught his nine-year-old daughter to read. It is noteworthy that those girls who received formal education did so only at an elementary level, with study largely in the vernacular. The reasons are not hard to find. Schooling for boys was justified in terms of its utility for later life and the public work undertaken in adulthood, whereas a girl could not go to university or become a lawyer, a member of the clergy or a civil servant. As Latin was the language of Church and law, there was no practical reason why girls should need to learn it. The attitude of Agnes, a widow of Barcelona, was a common one. When she took into care two eight-year-olds, she promised to have the boy taught to read, and the girl presented with a dowry of £20.[58]

Those women who took their education further were a very small minority, and learning was thus an individual experience. A case in point is that of Laura Cereta (1469–1499), from a wealthy family in Brescia. Because of her status, she was sent to a nunnery rather than a school, but it is useful to consider her experience of learning. At seven she was placed in a convent under the care of a female teacher 'highly esteemed both for her counsel and sanctity'. After a brief spell back with her family when she was nine, her father returned her to the convent to improve on her studies. He worried, Laura said, that she was getting 'bored with childish pursuits and he feared that at my age I might slip into indolent habits and grow dull from the free time I would have'. In common with most female monastic education, direction from the nuns was largely in practical skills such as embroidery, which Laura enjoyed and in which she excelled. It was rather during her own time that she turned her attention to the accumulation of knowledge, and she spent long periods 'blinking back my fatigue' studying into the night. Even when she returned home, aged eleven, and was expected to look after the household, she continued her studies. She attended lectures on mathematics in her free time, read Cicero and Seneca, and 'devoured' the Bible late into the night.[59] For girls, learning was always something that had to be fitted around domestic duties.

What then of the school experience? School had no fixed entrance or exit ages, and the number of years a child attended varied according to individual ability, the purpose of attending and finances. In 1312 Nicholas Picot, a London alderman, simply wanted his sons to attend school until they could write Latin poetry.[60] It meant that some children only attended school for a brief time. As with physical labour, lessons developed with the child's ability. Early instruction was in singing and reading, focusing on the basics of the alphabet. Latin was introduced gradually and by rote through basic religious texts such as the Pater Noster and Ave Maria. Chaucer's seven-year-old clergeon in the *Prioress's tale* offers a rare and sympathetic glimpse of the young boy at school who cannot understand what he hears and asks an older, though not much more enlightened, boy to explain the words. Lessons became more demanding as the boy's reasoning developed. At the grammar school of St Davids, Pembrokeshire, boys began learning choral music and were allowed to progress to 'scientia' or knowledge in grammar only when sufficient improvement had been noted. In Ave Maria College, Paris, Latin grammar was introduced for pupils between the ages of eight and twelve, but it was only after the age of twelve that pupils were introduced to the Roman poets like Cato, and were allowed to dispute and compose Latin grammar. Some topics remained inappropriate to those under fourteen, especially moral philosophy. An alternative to grammar school was a school of commerce, where practical skills such as book-keeping were taught. Niccolò Machiavelli (b.1469), for example, began school in Florence with a master of grammar at the age of seven, before moving on to an *abbaco* course at the age of ten and completing it at the age of twelve.[61]

The schooling experience was not confined to lessons, and memories of this life stage evoke the sights, smells and extra-curriculum activities of the school day. Gone was the freedom of infancy as life became tied to the rhythms of the school timetable. It was an early start, around five or six o'clock in the light June mornings, and earlier if chores needed to be carried out first. Schoolchildren were not exempt from family duties, and the long summer holidays, a feature of European schools, allowed pupils to help harvest the wheat or, like the schoolchildren in Soissons (France), contribute to the grape harvest. Depending on the type of school, lessons could take place in a church, a cathedral, a hospital, a private house or sometimes a specially designated building. At Agen (south-western France), the re-use of an old prison as a schoolroom may have drawn a few wry smiles from schoolchildren. As their names were called out, the children sat cross-legged on cobbled floors strewn with straw or on long, hard benches. Class sizes varied. In the 'little schools' of France only a few pupils were accepted at a time, perhaps six or seven in total, while the symbolic number of twelve (imitating the apostles) were taught at the cathedral school in Lyons. In contrast, in Florence, a typical communal master taught around thirty pupils. The evidence from England suggests that class sizes could be larger again. In 1369, for example, Richard Beckingham, a canon lawyer, bequeathed 2d each to sixty clerks at the grammar school of York in order for them to pray for his soul. That he specifically requested they not be 'bad' boys suggests there were more than sixty to choose from.[62]

Breaking up the school day were meal times. Schoolmasters sometimes used the child's love of rich and sweet food to aid instruction. Luxury dishes are mentioned in the school exercises used by Exeter High School around 1450; they include pheasants, partridges, cream cheese and sausages.[63] Such mouth-watering luxuries, however, contrasted significantly with the actual 'school dinners'. The school meals at the College de Trets in southern France in 1364–65 may have been common fare. On the positive side, they included about a pound of bread per student, accompanied by a little meat, fish, eggs, a few fresh fruits and just over half a litre of wine (which may have been believed, as in Ave Maria College, to sharpen the intellect). However, the main meal at Trets was vegetable soup, with a clear preference for cabbage. Cabbage appeared in soup on 302 days out of 365 days that year, which must have given a particular smell to the school and suggests that the place of school cabbage in a Western European's development has a long history.[64]

A dominant feature in descriptions of schooling was punishment. In woodcuts, illuminations and carvings, schoolmasters are commonly depicted with birch rods. Gerson allowed whipping in Paris schools in his care, although he believed it should be carried out only for serious offences and not administered in a harsh manner; schoolboys may have felt a different interpretation. Froissart remembered his schooldays as a time when he received a number of beatings for neglecting his lessons. Adult songs of school life express bitterness at the beatings and imagine suitable punishments to inflict on masters. We may suppose that there were some relieved and perhaps joyful schoolboys who heard of the death of John Newsham, an Oxford schoolmaster who was found dead in the river Cherwell in 1301. He had climbed up a willow tree to cut rods with which to beat his pupils, but had fallen and drowned.[65]

Poets recalling schooldays suggest that it was school's extra-curricular activities that interested them more than lessons. John Lydgate presents a stereotypical picture of a schoolboy who pays no attention to lessons, but wants to quarrel and joke with other boys. Froissart shows himself far more fascinated by his fellow pupils than in learning, especially the girls, whom he tried to win over with offers of jewellery and fruit. Play still defined the growing child. Boys at Ave Maria College played with spinning tops and marbles and enjoyed quiz games. Fighting was also commonplace, and Froissart described his scuffles both at school and on his walk home. This could lead to serious injury. In Ghent in 1377, Colard Van Den Gardine was forced to pay a hefty compensation because at school his son had stuck an object into a fellow schoolboy's eye and blinded him. Such boisterous activity led Bernard de Gordon to characterise the age group from seven to fourteen as the age of concussion.[66] Children of school age might still be classed as 'innocents', but schoolboys were more likely to be caricatured by their naughtiness, bad language and appalling manners. Sermon writers despaired of them, and railed against parents for failing to stop the bad habits. In the English morality play *Mundus and infans*, the schoolboy Wanton (representing the ages seven to fourteen) is characterised by his love of games and naughtiness. On his way to school Wanton jumps into a neighbour's garden, steals fruit and has an eye for a sparrow's nest. His boisterous speech is peppered with the exclamations 'Aha', 'Lo' and 'Yea' and the growing self-knowledge of the demands of 'I can' and 'I will'. Brimming with energy, he hits people with 'my scourge-stick', sticks out his tongue, fights with his siblings, and calls his angry mother a shrew.[67] What was liberating self-expression for the young provided grist to the mill of the moralising adult.

Public life

Children could be seen every day in public spaces, playing in the streets, on errands or going to school. With their growing physical strength and abilities, they made their presence felt in ways that could leave adults outraged. Boys (and, it appears, exclusively boys) were criticised for climbing trees to steal fruit or birds, or hanging around in the streets, throwing rocks and shooting arrows; in 1385 the stained glass windows of St Paul's Cathedral, London, suffered the boys' aim. Florentine officials condemned boys for their violence at Carnival and their habit of dismembering the bodies of executed criminals. One distasteful example occurred in 1381 when children of various ages chopped off the hands of an executed Ghibelline to use as footballs.[68] In the same city, in the early fifteenth century, Franco Sacchetti was so outraged at boys' general behaviour that he gave up a prayer for Herod's return to put an end to the:

> bothersome and vain songs of those who never go down the street quietly. Thus the cruel Herod could return, but [this time] to kill those from four to twelve years, once he hears them … Certainly if that were done he would not be so much scorned as praised by the celestial choirs. For they displease everyone alive.[69]

Being conspicuous in public did not render children a formal political or legal role, and they continued to occupy a marginal position in society, still primarily located in the private sphere. Nevertheless, in certain contexts and as a result of their particular qualities as children, they were given a prominent role in public events and became the voices of their communities.

One important role saw children as the 'memories' of their community, as society made use of a child's sharp, receptive mind and the possibility of several further decades of life. The settlement of a boundary dispute between the towns of Andújar and Jaén on the Castilian−Granadan border in 1470 used child's play as a means to establish a collective memory. A crowd dominated by children and youths of both towns was led around the agreed bounds. At each important landmark a 'happening' occurred that was intended to imprint the place on the minds of the young. At one stop the children were encouraged to indulge in a water fight, at another they played a game called 'mares in the field' and had a fistfight. In other words, in order that the children held these memories, the communities were encouraging them to do what they did best.[70]

Children were valuable contributors to major festivals and feasts. In 1430 boys from Maxstoke Priory, Warwickshire, acted in a Candlemas play at the local castle, while at Christmas 1479 five young girls sang during feasts organised for King René of Anjou.[71] In the wider public, children took part in Christmas dances, funeral processions and Easter and May Day events. In Frankfurt-am-Main, Germany, boys dressed in white and carrying white candles accompanied the Eucharist through the streets. On Palm Sunday they walked alongside the donkey symbolising Christ's entrance into Jerusalem.[72] Whether singing for a king or among the throng of urban processions, the child's role reflected her or his symbolic innocence. In late medieval Spanish communities, children's innocence and associated sacredness made them 'privileged communicators with the divine'. Young children were placed at the head of religious processions at Cubas, near Madrid, as a way to 'put the village's best foot forward'. At times, they became even more active. In 1427 boys and girls in Barcelona flagellated themselves in a penitential procession because of an earthquake. Between 1455 and 1459 young children from Switzerland, Germany and Belgium went on pilgrimages to Mont-Saint-Michel to pray for aid against the Turks.[73] The common trend appears to have been that when ordinary prayer was deemed to have failed, communities organised special processions of their children to ask for God's forgiveness.[74]

Certain festivals were closely associated with children, who helped to lead the liturgy. The feast of St Nicholas (6 December), the patron saint of schoolboys, was an important day when children received gifts of clothes, coins and pastries. Three weeks later, the festival of the Holy Innocents (28 December), known in England as 'Childermas', drew large crowds of boys. A good example comes from Paris in 1449, when a procession of schoolchildren, carrying candles, followed behind relics of the Holy Innocents towards Notre Dame de Paris.[75] A development from this event was a celebration which drew on a child's more unruly side. This was the festival of the boy bishop, which enjoyed European-wide popularity and sprang from medieval Europe's sense of carnival and authorised role-reversal: a pupil from a reading or song school was chosen to act as bishop for a day and would deliver a sermon, bless the gathered throng, receive donations and have other young children assist him as prebends and priests. It was a boisterous, colourful event, and presumably a welcome break from school. While the action confirmed the everyday subordinate status of the young, it also allowed children an important place in the religious and social calendar.[76]

Not all roles were intended to diffuse tension. The Florentine reformer Girolamo Savonarola (d.1498) used young boys to police his moral reforms, giving them broad scope to act vigorously against gambling tables and the immodest dress of women. David Nirenberg's analysis of violence against minorities in fourteenth-century France, Aragon, Catalonia and Valencia has shown these 'festivities' to have been typically a 'children's game'. Children and adolescents took the main role in the crowds who hurled stones and insults at the Jews during Holy Week. In Valencia in 1391 around fifty children marched around the Jewish quarter, which sparked off violence, killings and conversions. Children's violence was sanctioned and protected by the Christian community. A letter written by James II to the university at Lleida in Cataluna, Spain, forbade adults to dress as Muslims and Jews as part of the festivities of St Nicholas and St Catherine, but gave permission for children under the age of fourteen to do so.[77] Children therefore had a dual function: they acted as symbols of the Christian faith, while taking on the roles that 'wise' adults were prohibited from expressing.

In all cases, children were acting as both the conscience of the community and its raucous voice. The dangerous combination of innocence and violence, particularly among young boys, gave children a central role in important ceremonies that bound medieval communities together.

Conclusion

In later childhood, somewhere between the ages of five and eight, the child's world began to change. No longer was there the same degree of free time and unlimited play. The experience is glimpsed in a fifteenth-century school exercise, probably written at Magdalen College, Oxford. While composed by an adult, it tries to evoke the life of a ten-year-old schoolboy and describes a situation where 'nowe the worlde rennyth upon another whele'. The protagonist reminisces about a time, in his infancy, when he could get up when he wished and had breakfast brought to him in bed. On beginning school, he is forced to get up before sunrise and is more likely to be awakened by his master's punishment than by a candle and breakfast.[78] Life would have become similarly regimented for the ten-year-old in the world of work. By that age, children of peasant, artisan or merchant stock would be helping the family's economy and paying their own way, although not earning sufficient sums to maintain themselves. Children between seven and fourteen were considered old enough to begin vocational training and take on certain responsibilities. Yet they never escaped their dependent status in social and political terms: they continued to be characterised by vulnerability, and few would have left home unless it was a home already broken. Parents, householders and teachers were duty-bound to guide the young; in turn children were expected to serve and honour their elders. The message was to obey rather than choose one's life path.

There is an irony for modern researchers trying to uncover the experience of growing up in the later Middle Ages. Medieval society clearly devoted time and attention to the upbringing of the young. Through a range of informal and formal activities children were socialised, instructed in Christian belief and patterns of behaviour and trained for their future social roles. Failures in later life were traced back to poor instruction during childhood. Gilles de Rais was only one of a number ending up on the scaffold who blamed poor upbringing for later crimes.[79] It is also the case that a few Italian writers commented favourably on their early years: Francesco Petrarch believed that his boyhood years were some of the happiest of his life, and several of his letters are nostalgic for those days.[80] However, these comments are rare finds, particularly in northern Europe. Few medieval chronicles, biographies and autobiographies draw attention to specific childhoods. Those who benefited from formal education rarely saw any reason to comment on their schooldays. It is appropriate that one of the few apparent pieces of children's handwriting surviving in England comes from a manuscript where a child has copied out the forms and structure of an adult's letters.[81] Education in childhood was about imitating adults and becoming less child-like, and this may explain why few adults mention their formative years. Childhood was a brief prelude to the more active and public phases of life. Philippe de Commynes (b.1447) began his memoirs with the words, 'When I left my childhood behind me and at an age when I could ride, I was taken to Lille to Charles, duke of Burgundy ...'.[82] For him it was the more active stages of youth and adulthood that were worthy subjects of discussion.

Notes

1 Fowler, Briggs and Remley (eds), *The governance of kings and princes*, ch. 16, p. 239; Brown, *Pastor and laity*, p. 242.

2 Shahar, *Childhood*, p. 178; Lumby (ed.), *Ratis raving*, lines 1152–3.

3 Weinstein and Bell, *Saints and society*, pp. 25, 30–4, 38 and 42; Voaden and Volf, 'Visions of my youth; Stargardt (trans.), *The Life of Dorothy von Montau*.

4 Dominici, *On the education of children*, p. 46.

5 Quoted in Hanawalt, *Growing up*, p. 70.

6 Martin (ed.), *Registrum epistolarum Fratris Johannis Peckham*, p. 777.

7 Brown, *Pastor and laity*, p. 238.

8 Shahar, *Childhood*, p. 172. For criminal tendencies linked to poor upbringing see Dean, *Crime in medieval Europe*, p. 21.

9 Owst, *Literature and pulpit*, pp. 462–70; Gavitt, *Charity and children*, pp. 22–3.

10 Dominici, *On the education of children*; Christine de Pizan, *The book of the body politic*; Brown, *Pastor and laity*.

11 Lydgate, *Table manners for children*. See the selections of writings in Kline (ed.), *Medieval literature for children*.

12 Folts, 'Senescence and renascence', p. 230.

13 Dominici, *On the education of children*, p. 37.

14 Christine de Pisan, *Treasure*, p. 68; Christine de Pizan, *The book of the body politic*, p. 5; Phébus, *The hunting book*, ch. 22; Goodich, *From birth to old age*, p. 94.

15 Gabriel, *Student life*, p. 99; Dominici, *On the education of children*, pp. 40–1; Brown, *Pastor and laity*, p. 245.

16 Peacock (ed.), *Instructions for parish priests*, pp. 216–21; Power, *Medieval English nunneries*, pp. 263–72.

17 Christine de Pisan, *Treasure*, p. 68; Demaitre, *Doctor Bernard de Gordon*, pp. 16, 23 and 121; Brown, *Pastor and laity*, pp. 240, 245; Dominici, *On the education of children*, p. 67.

18 Sharpe (ed.), *Calendar of coroners rolls of the city of London*, p. 83; Shahar, *Childhood*, pp. 177–8; Cohn, *The Black Death transformed*, pp. 216–17; Christine de Pizan, *The book of the body politic*, p. 6; Bell, *How to do it*, pp. 156–7.

19 McGuire (trans.), *Jean Gerson. Early works*, p. 198.

20 Christine de Pizan, *The book of the body politic*, p. 8; Orme, *From childhood to chivalry*, p. 17.

21 Christine de Pizan, *The book of the body politic*, p. 59.

22 Phébus, *The hunting book*, ch. 22, pp. 36–7.

23 Christine de Pizan, *The book of deeds of arms and of chivalry*, pp. 30–1.

24 Orme, *Medieval children*, p. 182; Alexandre-Bidon and Lett, *Children*, p. 108.

25 Christine de Pizan, *The book of the body politic*, p. 9; Brown, *Pastor and laity*, p. 248.

26 Evans (trans. and ed.), *The unconquered hero*, p. 17.

27 Orme, *From childhood to chivalry*, p. 15; Alexandre-Bidon and Lett, *Children*, p. 119.

28 Christine de Pizan, *The book of the body politic*, p. 6.

29 Orme, *From childhood to chivalry*, pp. 29, 31; Orme, *Medieval children*, p. 178.

30 Harris, *English aristocratic women*, pp. 32–3; Fowler, Briggs and Remley (eds), *The governance of kings and princes*, p. 246; Phillips, *Medieval maidens*, ch. 2; Orme, *From childhood to chivalry*, pp. 156–63.

31 Boase, *The troubadour revival*, pp. 60–1; Wunder, *He is the sun*, p. 23.

32 Orme, *From childhood to chivalry*, pp. 45, 49; Hall, *Women and the Church*, p. 175.

33 Sneyd (ed.), *A relation*, pp. 24–6; Owst, *Literature and pulpit*, p. 466; Hughes, 'Stephen Scrope', pp. 122–4.

34 Bennett, 'Education and advancement', p. 82.

35 Ragusa and Green (trans.), *Meditations on the life of Christ*, p. 69.

36 Hanawalt, 'Childrearing among the lower classes', p. 19; Shahar, *Childhood*, pp. 244–6; Orme, *Medieval children*, p. 307.

37 Alexandre-Bidon and Lett, *Children*, p. 79.

38 *Ibid.*, p. 82; Nicholas, *Domestic*, p. 134; Ruggiero, *The boundaries of eros*, pp. 150–1; Klapisch-Zuber, *Women, family and ritual*, p. 173; Grubb, *Provincial families*, table 4.3; Romano, *Housecraft*, pp. 152–3; Shahar, *Childhood*, p. 247; Brodman, *Charity and welfare*, p. 121.

39 Le Roy Ladurie, *Montaillou*, p. 210.

40 Hyatte (ed.), *Laughter for the devil*, *passim*.

41 Alexandre-Bidon and Lett, *Children*, p. 82; Finucane, *Rescue of the innocents*, p. 103; Goodich, *Violence and miracle*, p. 98; Krötzl, 'Christian parent–child relations', p. 27.

42 Orme, *Medieval children*, p. 308.

43 Alexandre-Bidon and Lett, *Children*, p. 77.

44 Horrox (ed.), *The Black Death*, p. 64.

45 Seymour (ed.), *On the properties of things*, p. 300.

46 Gerli (ed.), *Medieval Iberia*, p. 294; Alexandre-Bidon and Lett, *Children*, p. 122; Orme, *English schools*, p. 117; Nicholas, *The later medieval city*, p. 291; Denley, 'Governments and schools', pp. 95, 97–9; Hyatte (ed.), *Laughter for the devil*, p. 129.

47 Nicholas, *The later medieval city*, p. 291; Knight, 'Welsh cathedral schools'; Knight, 'Welsh schools', pp. 3–5.

48 Grendler, *Schooling*, pp. 30, 77.

49 Shirley (trans.), *A Parisian journal*, p. 371.

50 Orme, 'Schools and school-books', pp. 450–1.

51 Le Roy Ladurie, *Montaillou*, p. 214; Alexandre-Bidon and Lett, *Children*, p. 126.

52 Orme, *English schools*, p. 118.

53 Alexandre-Bidon and Lett, *Children*, p. 124; Orme, *English schools*, p. 52; Bennett, 'Education and advancement', p. 81.

54 Orme, *Medieval children*, p. 241.

55 Farmer, *Surviving poverty*, pp. 82–6.

56 *Ibid.*; Moran, *The growth of English schooling*, pp. 160–4.

57 Nicholas, *Domestic*, p. 128; Nicholas, *The later medieval city*, p. 289; Barron, 'The education and training of girls', pp. 139–53; Cosgrove, 'Marriage in medieval Ireland', p. 44.

58 Origo, *The Merchant of Prato*, p. 199; Grendler, *Schooling*, pp. 90–120; Brodman, *Charity and welfare*, p. 200, fn. 78.

59 Robin (trans. and ed.), *Laura Cereta*, pp. 25–7.

60 Hanawalt, *Growing up*, p. 83.

61 Grendler, *Schooling*, p. 76.

62 Alexandre-Bidon and Lett, *Children*, p. 134; Grendler, *Schooling*, p. 17; Orme, *English schools*, pp. 121–2.

63 Orme, *Medieval children*, p. 73.

64 Alexandre-Bidon and Lett, *Children*, p. 130; Gabriel, *Student life*, p. 224.

65 Brown, *Pastor and laity*, p. 247; Orme, *English schools*, p. 128.

66 Rickert, *Chaucer's world*, p. 98; Gabriel, *Student life*, pp. 213–15; Orme, *English schools*, p. 132; Nicholas, *Domestic*, p. 127; Shahar, *Childhood*, p. 26.

67 *Mundus and infans*, lines 76–114, in Lester (ed.), *Three late medieval moralities*, p. 115.

68 Rickert, *Chaucer's world*, p. 48; Trexler, *Public life*, p. 367; de La Ronciere, 'Tuscan notables', p. 243; Scott, *A visual history of costume*, plate 9, p. 26.

69 Trexler, *Public life*, p. 368.

70 MacKay, 'Religion, culture, and ideology', pp. 235–6.

71 Orme, *Medieval children*, p. 191; Alexandre-Bidon and Lett, *Children*, p. 105.

72 Ozment, *Ancestors*, p. 72.

73 Christian, *Apparitions*, pp. 217, 219.

74 Weinstein and Bell, *Saints and society*, p. 28.

75 Shirley (trans.), *A Parisian journal*, p. 371.

76 Orme, *English schools*, pp. 131–2; Shahar, 'The boy bishop's feast', pp. 243–60; Owst, *Preaching in medieval England*, p. 220.

77 For an account of Savonarola's boys see Landucci, *A Florentine diary*, pp. 101–5; Nirenberg, *Communities of violence*, pp. 223–4, 248.

78 Orme, *English schools*, pp. 138–9.

79 Dean, *Crime in medieval Europe*, p. 21.

80 Folts, 'Senescence and renascence', p. 230; Herlihy, *Women, family and society*, p. 242.

81 Hardman (ed.), *The Heege manuscript*, pp. 22–8, 40–3; Orme, *From childhood to chivalry*, pp. 218–19.

82 Kinser (ed.), *The memoirs of Philippe de Commynes*, p. 1.

5

Adolescence and youth

B Y the age of twelve to fourteen, childhood was coming physically to an end. The onset of puberty brought not only significant biological change, but also new social expectations and concerns. Canon law, certain criminal laws and social customs gave a fourteen-year-old male a new legal standing, with some of the rights and responsibilities of his elders. The transition to maturity, what modern society terms adulthood, would appear well under way. It was not, however, completed instantaneously: it was a process the length of which differed according to gender, status and employment as well as individual circumstances. In this time of transition the young person was neither a child nor an adult, but would exhibit qualities attributable to both life stages.

Medieval society recognised this transition period as a distinctive phase of the life cycle. Some of the most popular 'ages of man' literature describes a stage between childhood and maturity that shared a distinct set of characteristics and was called in Latin *adolescentia* (meaning 'growing up'). During the fourteenth and fifteenth centuries the term also began to appear in the vernacular, with a limited usage in Spanish, Italian, French and English literature. The ménagier of Paris, for example, described his fifteen-year-old wife as an adolescent ('vostre adolescence feminine').[1] While the term did not have the connotations of the modern word – such as teenage angst and alienation – it was used to describe a life stage prior to adulthood. Philosophical discussions attempted to fix chronological limits to this life-cycle stage. Isidore of Seville in his *Etymologiarum* located adolescence between fourteen and twenty-eight. Others, like Bartholomaeus Anglicus, hedged their bets and suggested it could end at twenty-one, twenty-eight, thirty or thirty-five. The variations were a recognition that the onset of maturity differed according to the individual.[2]

Beyond theory, medieval society at large acknowledged the existence of young people who were going through a period of formation and transformation before full adulthood. This might be because they were still pursuing education and employment training, had not yet received their inheritance, or had not yet married and taken responsibility for their own lives and those of others.[3] For women, this stage of life was commonly defined by their unmarried state, indicated by the descriptive terms 'maiden' (English), *Maget* (German) or *bun* (Welsh). Records in a broad range of European vernaculars also show the widespread use of the descriptive terms 'young' and 'youths'. There is little to be gained from trying to pin these terms down precisely. As today, they were flexible enough to cover a range of ages from nought to thirty-five.[4] However, this ambiguity should not be taken to mean, as some have argued, that medieval society did not distinguish between younger and older youths.[5] There is evidence of some sensitivity to the development of the young. Fifteenth-century Florentine confraternities separated their youth into two groups: those aged nineteen and under were in one hall, and those aged nineteen to twenty-four were in another. The latter group was defined as 'too old to be among boys, too young to be among mature men'. Elsewhere the age of eighteen was not uncommonly used as a dividing age: under-eighteens were banned from entering taverns in Florence and brothels in Burgundy. Similarly, Georges Duby has suggested the following age division among Europe's aristocracy: boys aged fifteen to nineteen were considered adolescents during their training to become knights, but became youths (*juvenes*) when their training finished; they continued in this stage until full adulthood was attained through marriage or the acquisition of a fief.[6]

This chapter will consider those in their teens and twenties whom society recognised as physically young and still in a developmental stage. The focus will be on the image of and attitudes towards youths and the opportunities open to them. At the same time, the aim will be to highlight the type of training and life experiences gained by adolescents as they gradually assumed their adult roles.

Bodies

During the teenage years the body continued its growth stage; it had not yet fully 'grown up' and reached a sense of completion. Nevertheless, the body had largely shaken off its childish incapacity and was becoming more adult-looking and gender-defined. Both male and female bodies were becoming physically stronger and capable of reproduction: medieval society generally assumed that menstruation would begin in girls between twelve and fifteen.[7] In reality, not all youths showed their bodies off to the best advantage: Francesco Petrarch cast an exasperated eye at sullen youth who dropped their faces and stooped their shoulders.[8] In image, however, and in contrast to childhood, the youth stage of life was characterised by physical beauty. The male youth was portrayed in the spring of life, possessing an agile, well-ordered body. According to *Ratis raving*, the stage between fifteen and thirty was when the body 'growis bewtee & bountee / And strenth of body and qualitee'.[9] From the twelfth century, the vernacular literature of France had shown a growing preference for young protagonists and their adventures. Courtly romances reflected the lives of young knights, with figures like Gawain and Tristan providing role models of valiant youth.[10] For young females, Kim Phillips has argued that youthfulness was 'a key attribute of feminine perfection': rosy cheeks, sparkling blue or grey eyes, slender body, small breasts and protruding belly are the ideal characteristics of the girl just past puberty. It is significant that the Virgin Mary, virgin martyrs and female souls in paradise are all presented as perpetual maidens, with slight attention to the passage of time.[11] For religious writers a cult of youth was predicated on the idea that outward beauty reflected inner goodness; only the evil young would have facial and bodily deformities. Nevertheless, society at large was more likely to see beauty as skin deep. Prostitution was considered a young woman's game, and it was rare for a prostitute to stay in a brothel past thirty: in Avignon, applicants to the repentant Magdelenes (a reforming house) had to be under twenty-five and 'beautiful'.[12]

These newly developed bodies were put on display. The fourteenth- and fifteenth-century fascination with luxury clothing saw fashion, at least among the elite, become part of the process of accentuating the beauty of youth. Royal account books reveal that in late medieval France, it was young men who spent the most money on clothing and were the first to adopt the latest fashions.[13] The difference between male youth and maturity could lie in a short garment instead of a long one, tight clothes instead of loose, colourful rather than sombre, decorated rather than plain. In Chaucer's prologue to the *Canterbury tales* a contrast is drawn between the mature knight's dark, fustian garments and the clothes of his twenty-year-old son, dressed in a short gown with fashionably wide, long sleeves and embroidered like 'a meede [meadow] al ful of fresshe floures'.[14] In romance literature youth's colour was usually green, the colour of spring, but they could be dressed in patterns, checks and stripes. Illustrations of the ages of man show the male youth standing in a cocky stance, full of pent-up energy, and dressed in tight hose, a short jerkin, a feathered hat and a knife slung in a belt and prominently displayed. Likewise in the vibrant colours of fifteenth-century Venetian paintings discussed by Stella Newton, male youth's 'innocent arrogance' and 'casual assurance' are displayed through their fashionable attire.[15]

Youthful desire for clothing could cause intergenerational tensions. The young Count von Zimmern recounted his struggles with his parents in the late fifteenth century as they had no sense of fashion and had dressed their adolescent son in a long robe at a time when the fashion was for short robes.[16] Moral commentators expressed dismay at youthful fashions. In the fifteenth century Bernadino of Siena launched an attack on young men for wearing tight hose with their legs exposed. Geoffroi of Charny (d.1356) had some understanding for youth's need to dress well, but they should be 'dressed decently, neatly, elegantly, with due restraint and with attractive things of low cost and often replaced'.[17] Governing authorities also voiced their disapproval over young males' dress. Apprentices were criticised for their fashionable tastes, with guilds laying down dress codes for those apprentices serving abroad. In southern France, Italy and parts of Spain, university regulations prohibited certain clothing: law students were ordered not to adopt an 'aristocratic lifestyle'. There is an element here of the youths attempting to emulate adult styles. In 1432, Oxford legislated to prevent undergraduates from wearing the linings and furs appropriate to their masters and noblemen.[18] From the fourteenth century onwards city regulations began to take note of the style of young men's clothing. In Venice, growing restrictions in the fourteenth and fifteenth centuries culminated in 1506 when the Great Council passed legislation on the design of young men's clothing. Condemned were shirts cut too low, gold-trimmed collars, elaborate embroidery and hose trimmed with cords or fringes.[19] Medieval sartorial prohibitions grew out of a desire to prevent individuals dressing above their status, which generally meant 'social' status but could, as shown here, apply to 'age' status.

Women generally drew greater criticism for expensive and provocative attire.[20] However, these comments were not specifically directed at the young, and some latitude may have been given to the young woman in search of a husband. Geoffroi of Charny clearly believed that 'young damsels sometimes achieve better marriages when they are seen in rich apparel which suits them'.[21] Having the opportunity to wear such clothing came at a price: the young girl at the upper levels of society would need to get used to tighter clothing than she had enjoyed during childhood, which restricted her movements. Artwork helps to show the clear difference in dress between the young (unmarried) and the adult (married) woman. In Frederich Walther's painting of Barbara Vetzer of Nördlingen, south Germany, and her daughter (1467) the mother's pleated, modest gown is almost covered with a fur-lined cloak, whereas the young girl has more on show with a gown of tight sleeves, laced collar and waistline immediately below the bust.[22]

A final badge of youth was hair. Symbolically for male youth it was often, in Michel Pastoureau's words, a 'minus attribute', as youths in medieval images are shown clean-shaven.[23] Nevertheless, for both men and women long hair was a sign of youth. In Chaucer's *Cook's tale* the apprentice Perkyn is characterised by his black locks that were 'ykembd [combed] ful fetisly [elegantly]'. While preachers habitually condemned male youths who wore their hair long as immoral and effeminate, this appears to have had little effect.[24] In his old age Francesco Petrarch reminisced entertainingly on his youthful nights out with his brother when the two of them spent hours getting ready. They would curl their hair with hot irons, and worry that the wind would blow it out of place.[25] For women, long hair signified both virginity and availability, with blonde hair a particular sign of youth. With prostitutes generally displaying their services with long flowing locks, respectable young girls would restrain their hair, by covering or plaiting, as a sign of modesty. Head-dresses too signalled age. In the brass of the Englishman Robert Ingylton of Thornton, Buckinghamshire, and family (c.1472), Robert's wives have old-fashioned short veils over small horns drawn together, while his daughters wear fashionable, large pill-box caps on the backs of their heads and butterfly veils underneath.[26]

Reason and emotions

The growing strength of the youth's body was matched by an increasing sharpness in the mind. Reaching the age of twelve or fourteen was entering an age of reason and understanding, and to some extent those in their teens were considered capable of making rational choices. At this point a person could receive the Eucharist, go to confession, do penance, give evidence in civil courts, be tried for criminal offences and marry.[27] Those who had been betrothed at earlier ages had a chance at twelve or fourteen to change the decision. A similar opportunity was available to those promised to nunneries: in 1505 Lady Beatrix Constable put her eight-year-old daughter into Watton Priory, Yorkshire, leaving orders that she would be able to choose her future at twelve.[28] Nevertheless, the strength of the mind lagged behind the strength of the body. For many religious commentators and moral philosophers youth was a 'contested territory', poised between vice and virtue, the individual only gradually developing the ability to divide and decide between good and evil. For example, the Florentine humanist Matteo Palmieri described youth as a fork in the road of life, where the person required guidance to choose the correct path.[29]

Particular prominence was given to sexual emotion, and adolescence was characterised as a period of lust. In the English morality play *Mundus and infans* the protagonist's name changes to 'Lust and Liking' when he reaches fourteen; his major characteristic remains as a lover until he reaches the age of twenty-one. The reason was explained by medical literature, which stressed that the heated humours in the male youth's body (necessary for growth) were in constant flux. While having the positive effect of making the young man generous and hopeful, the hot, moist humours also served to destabilise him, turning him into a victim of passion who was driven to extremes. In medieval romances, ballads and madrigals, love is the natural and laudable pursuit of young heroes and heroines. Nothing is finer than youth's pursuit of a maid's love in the fourteenth-century Welsh poetry of Dafydd ap Gwilym, while Chaucer's twenty-year-old squire, 'a lovyere and a lusty bachelor', is only one of many literary youths governed by Venus and Mars.[30] By contrast, in religious and moral writings, St Augustine's comments on the 'impure lustfulness' of youth are dominant.[31] In 1425 Bernadino of Siena wrote that men between fourteen and twenty-five are ruled by sexual licence, which leads to a loss of reason. Ave Maria College, Paris, thought in similar terms: boys were made to leave at the age of sixteen in case their 'evil' inclinations corrupted the younger 'innocent' boys.[32]

As victims of passion, youths were considered vulnerable and likely to succumb to bad influences. These were not just the wild company of friends. Friars were accused of preying on the weakness of adolescents for recruitment purposes. In 1358 the University of Oxford passed a statute forbidding the admission of boys under the age of eighteen into any religious orders. The statute's preamble refers to the fears parents had of their sending their sons to university 'in tender years' lest the friars get 'such children'. Parliament disagreed and, in 1366, ordered a lowering of the age to fourteen, but it was not a popular move. In 1402 Parliament was petitioned in an attempt to raise the age to twenty-one.[33]

An inability to control the body was also considered the reason why some boys engaged in same-sex activity. According to the chronicler

Fernando del Pulgar, the young Enrique IV of Castile 'gave himself some delights which youth demands to be satisfied and honesty calls to be denied. They became a habit because ... weak youth [did not] know how to refrain'.[34] The association between youth and homosexuality is fully explored in Michael Rocke's work on sodomy cases in Florence, where he argues that homosexual behaviour was 'organised around age difference'. The focus of male desire was on adolescents, with same-sex sodomy usually involving a youth over the age of eighteen who took the 'active' role and a 'passive' adolescent usually between the ages of twelve and eighteen. In 1478–1502, ninety per cent of those taking a passive role were eighteen or under.[35] As a youthful transgressor, the passive adolescent was treated with a degree of leniency. Whereas the age of majority in most Florentine criminal laws was sixteen, those boys engaging in homosexual activity were treated as minors until eighteen. Similarly, in Venice, adolescents engaging in same-sex activity were absolved of the most serious penalties, which suggests that some sexual experimentation was permitted. Nevertheless, the growing numbers accused of sodomy did eventually lead to a harshening of the law.[36] Lenience did not mean acceptance, and in being unable to control the flesh adolescent boys were deemed to have the bodies and weaknesses of women. While northern Europeans were less fixated with the issue of sodomy, they too made the link between adolescent boys and women. Writing in Paris, Jean Gerson believed that 'the ardour of adolescents and women is too great, too eager, unstable, unbridled and therefore suspect'.[37]

The wording of this comment is instructive. For the male, this emotional stage was a temporary life-cycle phase, and, all being well, the adult male's innate rationalism would ultimately triumph. This was not the case with women, who were considered for ever trapped by their lustful bodies and therefore a danger to mankind.[38] As a girl entered her teenage years, her body cooled rapidly, and it took on the distinctive characteristics of the adult female, with a body much colder and wetter than the male's. For medical writers, this made women irrational, fickle and indecisive, but did not dampen their sexual ardour. This was especially so while they remained unmarried. Pubescent single women were seen as a danger to society's morals, and urban authorities across Europe seem to have been particularly concerned with the migrant population of single females, especially servants, far away from the watchful eyes of their families. English laws treated single women harshly, sometimes fining them or banning them from town. In German cities the boundary between unmarried women and prostitutes was often obscured.[39] This turning point in female identity from childhood to adolescence is witnessed in the prosecution of rape cases in fifteenth-century Venice.[40] Whereas the city meted out its most serious penalties to those who had raped children under the age of twelve (later thirteen), whom it saw as helpless and innocence, it was lenient on rapists of single pubescent women. These rapists were less likely to be charged, and were usually offered the choice of paying a penalty or marrying the victim. Only when she married did a woman's value increase again and her ability to prove a rape charge improve. Such attitudes meant that the onset of puberty significantly took away a girl's freedom. The life of St Catherine of Siena (d.1380) is just one example that shows the restrictions placed on a young girl of marriageable age: while Catherine could play freely in the streets as a child, from puberty onwards she was increasingly pressurised to take a groom.[41]

Medieval society therefore viewed youth as a stage full of contradictions. On the one hand it was a time of beauty, agility, sharpening minds and opportunities, an age of promise, and one where women reached their physical ideal. On the other it was a period of lost innocence, uncontrollable passions and vulnerability, and the point where women took on the mantle of temptress.

Misbehaviour

Youth has long had an association with social disorder, and the young in late medieval society were no exception. Some groups, characterised by their youth, acquired poor reputations. Students were accused of brawling, whoring, gambling, carrying weapons and drunken misbehaviour. In Paris in 1395, there were clashes between students and the butchers of Sainte-Geneviève. To Bronislow Geremek the students of Paris irritated the townspeople with 'their youth, the casualness with which they spent their spare time, their sense of being special, their independence … and their active, daily participation in the world of pleasure and laughter'.[42] Apprentices and servants had similar reputations: suspicions abounded that they wasted earnings on gaming and would steal their masters' possessions to feed their betting. In 1492 Coventry's tavern keepers were warned not to receive apprentices or servants without the permission of their masters.[43] The rowdy characteristics of these groups formed the stereotypes of late medieval literature. In Sebastian Brant's *Ship of fools* students go 'carousing, roistering, drinking', spending all their money and having to return home in disgrace with little learning.[44]

While some groups attracted opprobrium, most fourteenth- and fifteenth-century complaints were directed at youth in its broadest sense. The problem of youthful misbehaviour raised its head in fifteenth-century Ghent, where city leaders deemed adolescents 'problematic and threatening' and regulated youth gangs during festivals.[45] David Nicholas's work on Ghent suggests that the city leaders may have had a point, for young people were frequently caught up in violence, with at least a quarter of all homicides involving youths.[46] In fifteenth-century England, church courts and urban courts began to clamp down on a range of misbehaviour such as sexual misconduct, disorder in alehouses and illegal games. As part of this drive the actions of young people were scrutinised by jurors. The reason appears to have stemmed from a fear of what youngsters did in their free time, what habits they were forming and what they were spending their money on.[47]

England at least appears to have been free from the criminal youth gangs that plagued certain continental towns.[48] Jacques Rossiaud's research on gang rapes in fifteenth-century Dijon reveals that eighty-five per cent of rapists were young townsmen and unmarried journeymen, with half of all rapes in the city committed by youths aged between eighteen and twenty-four. They made no attempt to hide themselves, did not always seek secluded spots, and did not appear concerned at the presence of witnesses. For Rossiaud, this suggested that young men used rape as 'a rite of passage of manhood and admission to neighbourhood gangs'.[49] The situation in Venice appears to have been comparable. Gangs of young men from the same age cohort committed gang rapes, though usually at night, and considered violence against policing bodies a sign of their virility and part of their code of honour. In response, fifteenth-century Venice took a number of repressive measures against social disorder and criminal activity, coming to portray youth as threatening and unrestrained.[50]

Drawing on her research into Venetian youth, Elisabeth Crouzet-Pavan argued that 'the dark and dangerous dynamic image of young men took shape during the late Middle Ages'.[51] Others have similarly argued that during the fourteenth- and fifteenth-centuries communities increasingly saw youth as a social problem and grew alarmed at the rate of juvenile crime. This problematisation of the young has been linked to changing social and economic conditions: the onslaught of war and plague, plummeting population levels, new economic opportunities and changes in marriage patterns. While David Herlihy sees a real rise in youth violence, others like Barbara Hanawalt and Crouzet-Pavan focus on society's growing anxiety about the young, whether that be debating the values to be inculcated in their offspring (in England) or worrying about dangers like sodomy (in Florence).[52] However, no quantitative or qualitative evidence has been produced to demonstrate conclusively that youth crime rose in later medieval Europe. Modern perceptions that it did may be the result of the better survival of documentation, thanks partly to the formulation of new laws by city and central governments directed at misbehaviour in general. It is also the case that the crimes that came under increasing scrutiny in the later Middle Ages – gambling, gaming, prostitution, sexual deviancy – were areas where young men were often blamed. Finally, while fear of crime increased in the later Middle Ages, there was little new about the moral panic over wayward youth: Duby's twelfth-century bachelor knights and the marauding young lads (the *Gweison bychain*) of thirteenth-century Wales are cases in point.[53]

Contemporary writers preferred to link misbehaviour to qualities seen as innate in youth – like laziness and hot-headedness – rather than changing social conditions. François Villon (b.1431) did not blame his misspent youth on his circumstances, simply on youth itself. The English writer Thomas Hoccleve (*c*.1368–1454) concurred, writing in his quasi-autobiographical poem *La male regle* that 'As for the more paart, youthe is rebel'.[54] Being hot-headed, youths were considered prone to frustration, particularly sexual frustration, and single men were viewed as more likely to get drunk and commit violence than married men. This caused particular worry in Tuscan cities: nearly three-quarters of men aged between eighteen and thirty-two were single in fifteenth-century Florence.[55] The establishment and regulation of public brothels in continental Europe reflected an official fear of unchannelled male sexuality. The brothel at Castelnaudary (Languedoc) was founded in the hope that young unmarried men could fulfil their sexual needs without recourse to rape, sodomy and propositioning 'decent' women.[56]

Frustration could also occur among those denied full participation in adult activities such as holding positions of public authority or entering into an inheritance; both would have curtailed economic autonomy. Venice provides examples of young nobles in lowly and poorly paid posts showing their disapproval by disrupting council chambers with what Stanley Chojnacki calls 'youthful shenanigans'.[57] The issue of inheritance could also spark intergenerational conflict between father and son. The extent is difficult to gauge from the literature: it was not a common theme in medieval prose, barely registering in German and Castilian narrative texts, but it does appear in French poetry. In the *Quinze joies de mariage*, the ninth 'joy' describes the impatience of the eldest son as his impotent father remains alive and in charge of the family business.[58] Individuals did voice concerns over sons' frustrations and the fear of betrayal by fathers. As Francesco Sassetti commented in fifteenth-century Florence: 'A man wants to have sons. But five times out of six they become his enemies, desiring their father's death so that they can be free'.[59] In this analysis, young men used their gangs as an alternative source of power.

If social conditioning was blamed for the problems of youth, then fault was laid at the door of parents for failures in early upbringing.[60] The family was considered a stabilising force for the young. Its absence, particularly the lack of paternal influence, was considered dangerous. For Leon Battista Alberti, the job of the male head of the family was 'to restrain and curb the excessive license of youth'. Writers like Boccaccio warned that if a father died too soon, the son would fall into bad ways and dissipate his patrimony.[61] Using this evidence, Herlihy argues that an absent father, or a 'diminished masculine influence', contributed to the violence in Italian city states. Similarly, for Dijon, Rossiaud believes that many youths involved in rape cases 'lacked the presence in the home of a father capable of providing an adult role model'.[62] An absent or incapacitated father inevitably raises the issue of the present mother. Later medieval society held that an education dominated by women, naturally indulgent, was not a healthy influence on boys. Hence, while seemingly blaming absent fathers, medieval society, and indeed modern historians, laid the fault for society's ills at the hands of the single mother.

Discussions of youthful rebellion and violence tend to focus wholly on young men. There is some justification for this in terms of numbers, gang membership and medieval perceptions of criminal activity. Nevertheless, young women were not merely passive victims or angelic ladies. Puberty could lead to an identity crisis among girls, caught, as Kim Phillips has described it, between the asexuality of childhood and the call of sexual adulthood. Marriage, as the next chapter will show, was most parents' goal for their daughters; but for some young girls, marriage and the loss of maidenhood were unwelcome prospects. Far from desiring to embark on the next stage of their life cycle, these young women fought for continuity: they wanted to retain the innocence of childhood. This desire to take control of their lives and fashion their own identities inevitably brought the women into open rebellion with their parents. The stories of virgin martyrs are dominated by young women in their maidenhood. Rebellion did not, as with boys, lead to external violence inflicted on others, but took the form of internal acts focused on disfiguring the physical appearance by fasting or self-inflicted wounding – her body being the one thing a girl had some control over. Catherine of Siena for instance was fifteen when she protested against her marriage by cutting off her hair and scalding herself.[63]

Training and employment

During adolescence, men and women progressively took on their adult roles. Education and employment had begun earlier in life and, for some, adolescence saw a continuation of familiar work. For others, this period was one of new and intensive training in different locations. Those children who would not be following in their parents' footsteps experienced a more significant change. In all cases, the youth's potential to misbehave influenced modes of education.

For the aristocratic male, acculturation into military matters continued during adolescence. Once he reached the age of 12–14, a more rigorous teaching regime began, and skills were introduced that had been deemed unsuitable for younger boys. Writers like Giles of Rome, John Hardyng and Christine de Pizan thought that the physical activities of wrestling, riding and hunting should begin around fourteen. The standard manuals of the period laid emphasis on physical achievements to meet the growing strength of the young man's body. Much of this advice was influenced by the standard medieval textbook on warfare, the *Epitoma rei militaris*, written by the late Roman writer Flavius Vegetius Renatus, which detailed a programme that included fighting practice, wearing armour and carrying weapons. Youths would still hear about deeds of arms, but experience and observation were now more important. According to Ramond Lull (d.1316) in *The book of the order of chivalry*, apprentice knights should go with their masters to tournaments; in Montpellier, Bernard de Gordon thought boys from the age of twelve should become used to seeing dead bodies in an attempt to toughen the mind. Violence – inflicting it, feeling it, seeing it – was part of the maturation process of the young noble. It is little wonder that the death rate among noble boys was so high.[64]

The apprenticeship was brief, and many would have completed their military training in their early teens. Some would immediately become knights, while others became so between seventeen and twenty-one.[65] Contemporary writers appear to have believed that later was better. Giles of Rome thought that the best age to begin a military career was eighteen, while the poet Eustace Deschamps complained that knighthood was becoming little more than a rite of passage that marked the transition to adolescence: it was being bestowed on boys far too young, sometimes around ten to twelve.[66] This example indicates that in the 'real' world the onus was on the young man to prove himself as soon as possible. Edward III of England, for instance, led his first expedition into Scotland aged fourteen. Jean II de Maingre, better known as Boucicaut (b.1366), was twelve when he went on campaign with the Duke of Bourban, and was knighted at sixteen.[67] Skill rather than age was what mattered on the battlefield. Nevertheless, the young could still be seen as a particular age group, and as knights bachelor (young knights attached to a lord's household) these youths formed a company characterised by their mobility and sense of adventure. The footloose soldier is a favourite of medieval romance literature in which young heroes set off with youthful companions in pursuit of arms and lovers.[68]

Not all male youths at the upper levels of society, however, were destined for an active life on the battlefield. In Venice, patrician fathers helped their sons begin political apprenticeships in the Great Council, while across Europe the privilege of receiving an ecclesiastical benefice was bestowed on adolescents. Others were not so active. Among the noble families of Tuscany and the Veneto, young sons could pass through their adolescence without much responsibility or autonomy, living at home with few opportunities for employment.[69] They had various outlets to display their masculinity – including, of course, sexual activity – but in other ways they shared the life of the young, unmarried noblewoman. A girl's training for adulthood continued themes introduced in childhood, but her movements and behaviour were subject to greater scrutiny as grooming for marriage increased. Christine de Pizan's *Treasure of the city of ladies* recommended dressing modestly, having a chaperon, and avoiding dancing and laughing in public.[70] The 'training' period before marriage could be brief, as some girls were married shortly after puberty (as will be illustrated in Chapter 6). On the other hand, a longer adolescence, for both girls and boys, occurred in those cases where training involved a period of household service outside the family home. Movement into service became more common at twelve to thirteen, and could involve travelling a significant distance. In 1397, Christine de Pizan sent her thirteen-year-old son across the Channel to England to become the page of the Earl of Salisbury.[71] For others, the households were not necessarily unknown, and family networks were commonly activated. In the 1460s, for example, the Countess of Oxford took in one of the daughters of her cousin, John Howard, and arranged for a second daughter to lodge with the countess's own daughter.[72]

In the countryside and towns of Western Europe the teenager was making a more significant contribution to the economy. For males, reaching their teens in the countryside and destined to spend their lives working the land, there were new responsibilities. In Montaillou, becoming twelve brought the task of keeping a father's or employer's sheep.[73] In agricultural regions, growing physical strength allowed boys to progress to challenging responsibilities like ploughing. Politically too they gradually took on adult roles; at fourteen they became part of a tithing group. Nevertheless, the transition to full adulthood had yet to be accomplished. Judith Bennett identifies the adolescents on the manor of Brigstock in fourteenth-century England as those who had mixed dependence and independence. While the young male had become part of a tithing group, he was still barred from becoming a village or manorial officer, positions given only to married men. Ties remained strong with the parental household and many would still be living there. About one-quarter of all conveyances of land in Brigstock were carried out by those identified as 'son of' or 'daughter of' other villagers. In one sense, therefore, they remained defined by their parents; yet these unmarried men and women had acquired sufficient resources, generally though wages, to buy land and gain some economic independence.[74] This last example also shows that young peasant women could achieve a modicum of independence during their adolescent years.

As with the nobility, one way to earn that money was to enter service. In northern Europe servants of both sexes and from a variety of social backgrounds formed a significant part of the population of large and small towns, such as York, Ypres, Rheims and Nuremberg. They were overwhelmingly young and unmarried, usually entering service between twelve and fourteen and leaving in their mid- to late twenties. The timing and temporary nature of employment has led them to be termed life-cycle servants. They were attractive to employ as cheap labour and were generally put on short-term contracts, often lasting a year, during which time they were resident in their employer's household. Becoming a servant therefore meant moving out of the parental home, sometimes the locality. The greater opportunities were in the towns with migration occurring from the rural hinterland, boosting the number of their young.[75] Such possibilities to enter service were rarer in southern Europe. In Tuscany, it was usual for young women to remain within the natal household until they were married; only economic necessity or a broken family drove parents to place their offspring in service. At the same time it was maturity that mattered in hiring male servants, with men in the Veneto making service a career rather than a temporary posting. Nevertheless, to a lesser extent, life-cycle servants were present in southern Europe. In Venice,

Verona and Florence, young female servants began working around the age of eight and spent their later childhood and early adolescence learning domestic tasks and accumulating money for their dowries; they would leave around the age of seventeen to eighteen.[76] The stage of transition was earlier than in northern Europe, but the idea of preparation and training is comparable.

Moving away from home and receiving a small wage gave the young servant a sense of responsibility. Some modern commentators have seen it as a rare opportunity for women to gain freedom from their families. P.J.P. Goldberg has argued that servants in late medieval York had the opportunity to save money; some may even have delayed their marriages to retain the benefits that a single working life brought. Many servants were clearly valued by their employers and could benefit from bequests. In Barcelona, Venice, the Veneto, Siena, Lyons and several English towns, examples can be found of employers leaving gifts, such as tools for male servants and monetary contributions towards the dowries of female servants. Service too provided a degree of security for the young. The employer provided bed and board, clothing and potentially a degree of moral instruction.[77] Yet the picture was not all rosy. A servant's labour could be exploited with low wages and poor working conditions, and young women were vulnerable to sexual abuse. It is noteworthy that sixty per cent of foundlings at the Innocenti hospital, Florence, were born to servants or slaves, and servants regularly appear as victims in records of Venetian rape cases. It is little wonder that conduct books, didactic verse and popular vernacular songs considering the young single woman gave clear warnings on the deadly combination of late nights, alcohol and men.[78]

For those with some status and wealth, an alternative was apprenticeship. This provided the opportunity to train in a specific craft under the direct supervision of an employer, to whom the apprentice was bound by contract. The potential for social mobility encouraged some peasant and husbandman families to direct their children to apprenticeships rather than the plough, but the majority of apprentices were from the 'middling sort' of society – merchants, artisans, yeomen – and generally from the same social background as the masters to whom they were contracted.[79] Apprenticeship was also largely an opportunity for boys. The search for female apprentices has yielded a few results, but show that women had much more limited employment opportunities. In Montpellier in 1293–1348, only fourteen per cent of apprenticeship contracts related to young women; in Orleans in 1380–1440, the figure was just over ten per cent.[80] The main concentration was in textiles and food, which drew on traditional feminine skills or on female specific crafts such as midwifery. For prestigious occupations, such as the merchant tailors of London, there is little evidence for female apprentices.[81] This is not surprising as women would not have been able to work in the most esteemed industries, would rarely have become masters, and would not generally have been expected to be the major breadwinner in a family. Opportunities did improve in some areas following the fourteenth-century population collapse and labour shortages. In Wells, Somerset, women were given the chance to take up apprenticeships, though again in the cloth industry, and there are early fifteenth-century examples of men achieving the freedom of the city by virtue of their wives. However, economic recession in the later fifteenth century saw these options dry up, and no female apprentices are recorded for Wells in the 1490s. In Orleans too, the number of female apprenticeship contracts fell to under four per cent during the period 1440–90.[82]

The age at which apprenticeship began and the duration of the contracts varied considerably. In southern Europe, apprentices could begin at a very young age and were treated as little more than servants. For those intending to learn a craft, who were the majority in northern Europe, the starting age was in early adolescence. While statute and guild laws did provide some guidance, the age depended on several factors. The choice of work mattered: apprentice paviors in London had to be at least eighteen because of the physical strength required. Gender was an issue: in Montpellier, contracts were generally given to girls at twelve and boys at fourteen, the ages of puberty.[83] Prior education was another consideration: the Florentine chronicler Gregorio Dati began his apprenticeship in 1375 in a silk maker's shop 'when I had learned enough arithmetic'.[84] The length of the contract was also subject to several variables, not least the age at which the apprentice had started and the amount of money paid to the master as his fee. While in some Tuscan towns an apprenticeship could last only three years, elsewhere it was a potentially lengthy preparation for adulthood.[85] A period of between six to eight years was common: this was the case for weavers in Ghent, locksmiths in Paris, blanket makers in Girona (Catalonia), spice dealers in Genoa and the merchant tailors of London.[86] More demanding crafts stipulated a longer period; for example, training to be a silversmith in Marseilles could take ten years.[87] There is also evidence to suggest that during the fifteenth century the entrance age and length of term gradually rose. The reasons appear to have been a combination of growing demands for prior literacy, problems in recruitment and a desire to keep hold of apprenticed labour. It meant that the young of the late fifteenth century were potentially experiencing a longer adolescence than those of the fourteenth century: in Montpellier, there was a ten-year increase in the apprenticeship term over that period.[88]

In Florence and Genoa a male apprentice would generally learn his trade from his father at home, destined to follow the family business.[89] However, this was not the case in other parts of Europe. Sylvia Thrupp argued that the overwhelming trend among the aldermen's sons in London was to pursue an occupation other than the one their fathers were engaged in. Part of the reason appears to have been the growing opportunities in the Church and in law. One London merchant who died in 1361 made his younger son's inheritance conditional on him becoming a chaplain by the age of twenty-one.[90] In Marseilles, families blessed with a number of children, especially sons, sometimes chose to diversify the talents of the household.[91] Other families may not have had the resources to provide suitable training, may have felt it was better for strangers to teach and discipline their children, or were simply not there to give advice. In Orleans a substantial proportion of apprentices aged thirteen to fifteen were orphans.[92] But the trend could also indicate the growing voice of the adolescent and his wish to choose his own career path. In Nuremberg, Albrecht Dürer (1471–1528) began a goldsmith's apprenticeship with his father before he realised that his ambitions lay with painting. After a struggle with his father, who was aggrieved at the time lost in training his son, Dürer won his right to become an apprentice in a painter's workshop at the age of fifteen.[93]

Taking up an apprenticeship could, like becoming a servant, signal a point of departure from childhood and the parental home. For some, the break was underlined by a move of some distance. In Montpellier, apprentices were often drawn from more than fifty kilometres away.[94] In the British Isles, London acted like a magnet for provincial craftsmen. London's Tailors' guild drew fewer than a fifth of its apprentices from London itself, with well over a third coming from northern counties, particularly Yorkshire. For the young in north Wales, Shrewsbury was a favoured destination, whereas those living in south Wales and the Severn basin were drawn to Bristol.[95] Contemporary literature can reveal fears that family ties would be broken. The fourteenth-century English poem *Wynnere and Wastoure* (written and set in the midlands) warns fathers not to send their sons 'southewarde' (implying London) lest they never see them again. Yet these parental fears were not always well founded. Sons and daughters did return home after, sometimes before, their contracts ended (see below), and families stayed in contact with their children regularly enough to bring cases of maltreatment against employers.[96]

Leaving home may have offered a sense of freedom to the young, but becoming an apprentice meant attaining a new kind of dependency. The master took the position of a surrogate parent and the apprentice was a kept person, being fed and clothed as well as trained. Parents expected masters to look after the wellbeing of their offspring, and the contract contained moral comments on upbringing and the inculcation of class values. In London in 1451, when John Harrington was apprenticed to the merchant tailor Robert Lucy, he was expressly asked not to frequent taverns or to play dice, tables or checkers. John was also prevented from getting married or becoming betrothed without his master's permission. Control over sexuality and a prohibition on marriage appears to have been a standard feature of English and Genoese contracts.[97] At the same time, apprentices could suffer exploitation by being inadequately trained, or having their skilled labour used for little to no financial reward. Wages were not commonly given, and small allowances were usually offered only to older apprentices. Poor treatment may well have contributed to the significant drop-out rate among apprentices. Only forty per cent of apprentices who enrolled in the London's Tailors' guild during the years 1425–45 and 1453–58 completed their terms and became freemen. It may be that after working for three to five years they felt they had absorbed the basics of the craft, and could leave before they became too heavily exploited by the master.[98] Adults tended to blame the drop-out rates on youthful fickleness. Yet the semi-dependent state of the apprentices could serve to alienate youth and underline the point that apprentices were not yet full adults.

One reason for the delay in beginning an apprenticeship was the increasing value placed on prior education. For a small number of youths, training meant further schooling and entering university. In 1300 the students were generally tonsured clerics destined for the Church, but the next two centuries witnessed a growing number hoping it would advance their secular careers.[99] Study would have become more challenging, with the bachelor's degree traditionally covering the seven liberal arts: the *trivium* of grammar, dialectic and rhetoric, and the *quadrivium* of music, arithmetic, geometry and astronomy. Education in adolescence was also exclusively male. Females were barred from universities, and visits from female family members were discouraged or heavily supervised. The social background of the intake remained relatively similar across the later Middle Ages: few at the lower end of society, few from the social elite. In England undergraduates included sons of lesser gentry, merchants, artisans, lawyers and village officials. Nobles do appear in greater numbers in

Spanish, Italian, French and German universities, but only those students from the Holy Roman Empire included high numbers of the aristocracy. There was no set age of entry, but fourteen had become the minimum statutory age for the arts students of the universities of Oxford, Cambridge and Paris, while those studying law, medicine or theology in southern European universities tended to be older by about four to five years.[100] Overall the main body of students were in the age group fourteen to thirty, one generally broader than the twenty-first-century student body, but nevertheless distinctly youthful.

Going to university was a rite of passage for the students, underlined by the rituals associated with greeting the 'fresher'. In universities of Germany and southern France, the new boy, sometimes called *beanus* or *bejaunus* (possibly from *bec-jaune*: yellow-bill) was welcomed by rituals of hoaxes, bullying and feasting. The fresher was often humiliated by being presented as a wild beast in need of civilising or a criminal needing to be tried. Once the student had been welcomed and incorporated into the new society a feast was held at his own expense, which could help to impoverish him even before studies began.[101] For most students these rituals would have been experienced far away from the family home. Despite an expansion in the number of universities in the later Middle Ages, students needed to travel, sometimes across country or seas, for their education. Moving away was part of the training for adulthood. University bodies – unlike the apprentice's master – did not see their roles as surrogate parents. Students had to find their own lodgings and were left to fend for themselves, perhaps by getting a part-time job, securing a generous patron or, as was the case in Catalonia, receiving aid from almshouses. It is telling that model letters used in the education of students, which tried to reflect their learning experience, focused heavily on financial concerns.[102] Intellectually too, the universities believed the students were responsible for their own learning and achievements. Many of those attending university did not intend to obtain a degree, but were there in the hope that the process of studying in itself would lead to social and career advancements. It has been estimated that over half of the undergraduates in late medieval Oxford and Cambridge did not collect a degree.[103]

Nevertheless, the students had to abide by university rules, and statutes and treatises acknowledged the youth of their intake by focusing on their moral life. These regulations significantly increased during the fourteenth and fifteenth centuries to cover a wide range of issues. In 1442, additions to the statues at the University of Heidelberg ordered students not to engage in gaming, visit brothels, join dances during Lent or enter jousts. In English colleges, unexplained absences from hall, the carrying of weapons and creating discord were among the punishable offences. Parents too do not appear to have considered student life the equivalent of full adulthood and independence. Writing in 1457, Agnes Paston advised the tutor of her fifteen-year-old son, studying at Cambridge University, to 'truly belash him' should he do badly. One explanation for the successful recruitment to the friaries in university towns like Cambridge is that they provided not just education, but accommodation and a sense of security.[104]

It can be seen therefore that experiences of youth differed in the Middle Ages according to the type of training the young person received. Nevertheless, three common factors are discernible. First, adolescence was a period of semi-dependence. While young knights, servants, apprentices and students were being integrated into adulthood, they were still considered in need of instruction and could be treated as children. Second, the nature of the training demonstrates the concerns society had about the moral upbringing of youth. Apprenticeship contracts and university regulations dictated behaviour and the rhythms of the day, and were aimed at neutralising the threat of outside temptation, especially because these young people were living away from home. Several conduct books that survive from the later Middle Ages appear aimed at those who were not directly experiencing the mother's or father's guiding hand. In 1315, Peter Fagarola, a doctor from Valencia, tried to make up for his physical absence by sending a regimen to his sons, who were studying at Toulouse. The advice included what to eat, how much to sleep, the proper clothing and a recommendation for controlling the passions. Personal daily plans, emphasising routine and regime, were compiled for young English nobles, while more general texts were available in Middle English for apprentices and servants. Instruction could be found for the middle-class urban boy in *The childe of Bristowe* and *The merchant and his son*, while *How the good wife taught her daughter* may well have been written with itinerant female servants in mind; all were designed to instil moral precepts in the young. Images too proved popular: bust-length sculptures of angelic-looking boys, such as that of Antonio Rosselino's *Young St John the Baptist* of about 1470, showed the youth stripped of the sins of social life and as a model of chastity.[105]

A third common factor was mobility. Not everyone would spend their youth away from their family homes, but a significant number of knights, students, clergy, servants and apprentices did move away in order to receive training and gain experience, even if they later returned to their home villages and towns to settle. Travel involved the young most of all, as they had few family ties and could move around, picking up skills and finding better working conditions. It was also an opportunity to see the world and prove themselves in it. Fifteenth-century French criminal records reveal travel to have been common among young artisans. Guillemin Le Clerc, a hose maker, described how he had left Paris aged twelve and 'went off with other children and comrades to see the world'. He returned to the city twelve years later after living in several towns in southern Europe. Similarly, on completing his apprenticeship at seventeen, a tailor from Burgundy decided 'to see the world, like many other young children' and worked for eight months in a tailor's workshop to earn enough money for his travels.[106] For youths themselves, education for life was not seen solely in terms of service, labour and Latin grammar.

Youth groups

As well as expressing a general distrust of youth when left to their own devices, medieval writers often commented on the propensity of the young to band together. In late medieval society both these views found expression in youth associations attached to military, craft and religious guilds, which aimed at directing the actions of the young and integrating them into adult society. The crossbowmen of Ghent established a junior association in 1438 where the young were instructed in both military prowess and civic power. Its partial use as a recruiting ground and its close supervision by adults helped to ensure that the youth club was respected by the elders, although some intergeneration conflict was experienced, with arguments arising over deference and precedence.[107] English urban craft guilds, like the skinners of London and the merchants of Lynn, Norfolk, had youth fraternities which offered ideal opportunities for young men to establish a position in urban society and for single women to make respectable friendships.[108]

Further opportunities were provided by religious guilds, with young men's guilds and maidens' guilds documented for towns and villages across southern England. In fifteenth-century Bodmin (Cornwall) and Croscombe (Somerset), village youths belonged to guilds called the Younglyngs (for males) and the Maidens' Guild (for females). Ashburton (Devon) had separate altars for 'the maidens' and 'the bachelors', and young men's groups are recorded for Bassingbourn (Cambridgeshire). The guilds provided the opportunity for controlled pleasure as well as religious worship; this was particularly the case with sexual flirtation. At Hocktide (the second Monday and Tuesday after Easter) the Croscombe maidens' guild would block the main routes of the village and charge the young men for access, or sometimes they would capture them and demand a ransom; the following day the action would occur in reverse. In this way the young contributed substantially to the parish's income. The pride in their separate group identity is seen in Garboldisham church, Norfolk, where the young men's guild paid for the church's roof and its painting. An inscription on the boards reads that 'the yongling han payd for this cost'.[109]

The mix of adult supervision, religious worship and youthful pride is similarly seen in the youth confraternities of northern Italy, which were established from the end of the fourteenth century. Most appear to have been composed of young single men of the same age cohort; in Florence they were usually between the ages of thirteen and twenty-four. This was an age group felt most in need of controlling, partly to prevent disorder, but also because they were considered the best hope for producing a good Christian society. In the early fifteenth century, the youthful Compagnia di San Girolamo (Bologna) embarked on a recruitment campaign to draw the young away from the gaming tables and taverns and towards instruction in Christian life. From the outset the confraternities were modelled on adult societies and under the control of adult guardians who monitored their finances, development and decision-making processes. Adults provided education, and arranged games and other entertainments to keep the young occupied. Nevertheless, youths were not passive members: some clubs were established by the young, while boys held decision-making powers in most Florentine associations. Those of San Giovanni Vangelista, for instance, elected their own governor and had some say in the choice and dismissal of confessors. In addition, confraternity members gained prominent roles in Italian city life. In Florence, youths took part in a range of public processions and undertook embassies to foreign lands. In Venice, young men's societies had an important role in meeting and organising festivities for foreign dignitaries. In this way youths were drawn into public rituals while being socialised in adult values.[110]

Based on a similar desire to draw and neutralise youthful aggression, while preparing them for adult roles, were the youth 'abbeys' popular in France (although they appeared too in rural Germany and Flanders). The abbeys were controlled by urban collectives or village communities, who elected the 'abbot' from one of the leading local families. The abbeys celebrated at festivals, met together to play ball games, and formed a vociferous element in the raucous *charivaris* instigated on a local couple's wedding night. As *charivaris* were especially popular when a young girl was marrying a much older man, Natalie Zemon Davies suggests that the actions were partly a venting of youthful frustrations in the face of another young woman snatched away from the marriage pool. Abbeys also acted as the voice for the community, sometimes by setting up 'courts' to mock others; Lyons had a Judge of Misrule and a Bench of Bad Advice. They particularly patrolled the reputation of women. Youths would plant a sweet-smelling bush under the window of a marriageable girl – marking her out for the next stage in her life – or a foul-smelling bush if the girl's morals were questionable. In this way the young could undertake actions that the adults, now sad and wise, could not. Rather than rebelling against the body politic, the young were becoming integrated into its values.[111]

Outside these formal groupings, it is more difficult to uncover the occasions when groups of young people were by themselves.[112] By their nature, these social occasions tended to be informal, temporary, short-lived affairs. They may have involved a few communal drinks. In Denmark in 1425, the journeyman smiths of Fleisborg required any new journeyman to the town to join the group for a drink. Festivals and feast days were an obvious draw. It was common in French towns and villages for groups of unmarried young people to spend feast days together in search of amusement. In the village of Prades d'Aillon, young people of fifteen years and above formed a specific age group with their own dances, games and festivals.[113] Paintings and manuscript marginalia can give form to these details, as youth is depicted in a mass of colour, with musical instruments and boisterous exaggerated gestures. Examples include the maidens dancing and singing to the music of tambourines featuring in the frescos painted by Lorenzetti on the walls of the Palazzo Publico in Siena (1338–41), and the lively young group illustrating the *Roman d'Alexandre* manuscript made in Bruges in 1339–40.[114] Youth enjoyed playing sports, including football, tennis, wrestling, archery and shooting at cocks. These were not exclusively youth games, but it was apparently the young who were the primary participants, or at least the major concern for those legislating against the activity. In 1479 a London proclamation forbade football, tennis and dicing specifically among labourers, servants and apprentices.[115] Many similar prohibitions were voiced in governments' attempts to improve their city's or nation's fighting skills by ordering young men to eschew gaming for regular practice with bows and arrows.[116] In less violent ways, young females too might gather together while undertaking a particular task. As a twelve-year-old, St Bridget of Sweden (1307–73) practised her needlework with other girls of her own age.[117] Yet the sexes were not always apart. In Boccaccio's *Decameron*, ten young noble men and women aged between eighteen and twenty-eight escape plague-ridden Florence and entertain each other by exchanging tales. The ladies are suitably cautious about their reputations, but it remains a young people's trip, away from prying adults. A less restrained instance of youthful enjoyment is revealed in popular poetry. The fifteenth-century Middle English poem 'The serving maid's holiday', expresses the sense of release in the 'joy that it is a holiday' and the sexual activity that the young maid and her paramour hope to pursue.[118]

To what extent the available evidence suggests that a youth sub-culture existed in the Middle Ages is debatable. There has been strong opposition from some historians who point to the absence of juvenile law; a lack of exclusively youthful events, institutions and written material; the lack of personal wealth; and the control of leisure time by householder or employer. It should be noted too that students and apprentices were not isolated from other groups in society, nor did they congregate in particular spaces. In France, students circulated in an ill-defined group of wandering priests, itinerant story-tellers and singers, among the poor and criminal bands. They were distinguished only by the temporary nature of their association.[119] There appears to have been no ideological thrust to the rebellious behaviour of either university students or apprentices, and it would be difficult to argue for a common youth identity that cut across gender, class and geography. Nevertheless, we must be careful not to look for a 'modern' youth culture in the later Middle Ages. Paul Griffiths has suggested a more 'supple' definition of youth culture in his investigation of early modern English youth, one whose essential attributes are 'a different sense of place and time, and an alleged preference for play and leisure'. Here he focuses on the time engaged in playing games and sport.[120] While this in itself is not sufficient to claim a common youth culture in pre-industrial Europe, it is an important recognition that the young in past societies could share common experiences because of the stage of life they had entered.

Conclusion

This chapter has focused on young people who experienced a period of transition between childhood and adulthood. While the stage was distinguished from pre-pubescent childhood and from full adulthood, it was not a fixed life stage with defined age limits; rather it was characterised by movement, development and liminality. Thus, in different contexts, medieval society could see an eighteen-year-old male as a child, at other times as an adult.[121] He was vulnerable, in need of guidance, and the hope for the future; but he was also strong enough to be a menace – much more so than in childhood – and keen to demonstrate his manhood. In addition, variables like gender, social status and employment determined whether the transition was a brief stop or a long, drawn-out affair. Girls who were married and pregnant soon after puberty, or males who came into their inheritance at fourteen, entered adulthood before the apprentice and servant. The next chapter will provide more detail on the timing of these entrance points to full adulthood.

In holding this liminal position, adolescents had yet to achieve key political or administrative positions. A period of training generally kept them single and free from dependents. For some (largely male) adolescents this freedom was an opportunity to travel and gain experiences before settling down. Young knights and practising craftsmen travelled across Europe seeking their fortunes while contributing to society's wars and economies. While parents and guardians actively supported this movement, they were equally worried about young men and women living outside family influence. Society at large held several contradictory positions on the young, stemming from the view that adolescence marked a crossroads in life; danger and opportunity were bedfellows.

To some extent, experimentation was allowed and bad behaviour among male youths considered only natural. Records from Paris University's administration, Florence's youth confraternities and fifteenth-century Venetian criminal trials contain cases of disorder explained away on the grounds of 'youthful behaviour'. That three-quarters of criminals who received royal pardons from the French king in 1419 were aged between eighteen and thirty may show that the young featured prominently in criminal activity, but it may equally indicate that youths were the ones mainly pardoned. [122] Such allowances were rarely extended to women, however. While their youth was acknowledged, the perceived moral dangers of single women meant that the earlier they attained adulthood – mainly through marriage – the better. For both men and women, a strong desire to control youth led medieval society to cede early responsibilities to the young in the hope that they would more quickly conform to adult values. This was the idea behind the youth organisations that took various forms across Europe as adult society tried to find new ways of socialising and protecting the young. Governing bodies, religious authorities and parents appear to have been at one in wanting to control the adolescent's development.

Most of the available descriptions of the medieval young comes from those who had left their youth behind. Indeed, the idea of a group dynamic with common attributes – usually sex, drinking and gambling – is one voiced more by adult writers than by youth itself. This casts a particular shadow over the literature; it is one often tinged with regret, either that youth has passed or that it was experienced at all. There is François Villon's literary *Testament*, full of a thirty-year-old's nostalgic look back at a period where he spent too much, loved too much, studied too little. There is also Richard Hatton's actual testament of 1509, where he left his books to King's College, Cambridge, as a recompense for all his careless and bad behaviour in his 'adolescentia'.[123] Youths themselves were perhaps too busy living life to reflect on it.

Notes

1 In Spanish, Italian and French the term 'adolescence' and its equivalents (meaning a stage of life or growing up) starts to be recorded at the end of the thirteenth century, while 'adolescent' and its equivalents (a young person) followed a little later. For discussions of Italian terms for youth see Taddei, 'Puerizia', p. 22. For England, where the terms date to the late fourteenth and fifteenth centuries, see *Middle English Dictionary*, s.v. 'adolescence' and 'adolescenci'. See also Brereton and Ferrier (eds), *Le ménagier de Paris*, p. 1 (lines 30–1).

2 Lindsay (ed.), *Isidori Hispalensis episcopi*, vol. 2, book XI.ii, lines 4–5; Seymour (ed.), *On the properties of things*, vol 1, pp. 291–3.

3 Levi and Schmitt (eds), *A history of young people*, vol. 1, p. 5.

4 For a discussion on German terminology see Schultz, *The knowledge of childhood*, pp. 24–8. For the slipperiness of the English use of 'youth' see Dove, *The perfect age*, p. 135.

5 Gillis, *Youth and history*, p. 2.

6 Trexler, *Public life*, pp. 370–1; Rocke, *Forbidden friendships*, p. 203; Rossiaud, *Medieval prostitution*, p. 105; and see the chapter by Duby 'Youth in aristocratic society', in Duby, *The chivalrous society*, pp. 112–22.

7 Post, 'Ages of menarche and menopause'.

8 Petrarch, *Letters of old age*, vol. 1, p. 230.

9 Lumby (ed.), *Ratis raving*, lines 1276–7.

10 Pastoureau, 'Emblems of youth', p. 227; Burrow, *The ages of man*, pp. 165–7. See also Jaritz, '"Young, rich and beautiful"', pp. 61–9.

11 Phillips, 'Maidenhood', pp. 6, 11; Phillips, *Medieval maidens*, pp. 43–51.

12 Rossiaud, 'Prostitution, youth and society', p. 21.

13 Piponier and Mane, *Dress in the Middle Ages*, p. 107.

14 *The Canterbury tales: General prologue*, lines 75, 89–93, in Benson (ed.), *The Riverside Chaucer*, p. 24.

15 Newton, *The dress of the Venetians*, p. 33; Sears, *The ages of man*.

16 Braunstein, 'Towards intimacy', pp. 560, 580.

17 Sebregondi, 'Clothes and teenagers', p. 35; Kaeuper and Kennedy (eds), *The book of chivalry of Geoffroi de Charny*, pp. 190–1.

18 Hanawalt, *Growing up*, p. 118; Schwinges, 'Student education, student life', p. 226; Cobban, *The medieval English universities*, pp. 371–2.

19 Crouzet-Pavan, 'A flower of evil', p. 185 and n. 44; Newton, *The dress of the Venetians*, pp. 37–8.

20 Owst, *Literature and pulpit*, pp. 393–404; Killerby, *Sumptuary law*, ch. 6.

21 Kaeuper and Kennedy (eds), *The book of chivalry of Geoffroi de Charny*, pp. 192–3.

22 Scott, *A visual history of costume*, nos 101 and 108.

23 Pastoureau, 'Emblems of youth', p. 233.

24 *The Canterbury tales: The cook's tale*, line 4,369, in Benson (ed.), *The Riverside Chaucer*, p. 85; Sebregondi, 'Clothes and teenagers', pp. 34–5.

25 Folts, 'Senescence and renascence', p. 224. Chaucer's squire is also described as having curly hair as if pressed by a 'curler': *The Canterbury tales: General prologue*, line 81, in Benson (ed.), *The Riverside Chaucer*, p. 24.

26 Chamberlayne, 'Crowns and virgins', pp. 61–2; Phillips, 'Maidenhood', p. 8; Scott, *A visual history of costume*, no. 108.

27 The heretical Cathars in southern France were believed to know good and evil at the age of twelve; the inquisition rounded up all those who were twelve or over: Le Roy Ladurie, *Montaillou*, p. 216.

28 Orme, *From childhood to chivalry*, p. 39.

29 Griffiths, *Youth and authority*, p. 18; Crouzet-Pavan, 'A flower of evil', p. 172; Taddei, 'Puerizia', p. 21.

30 E.g. Gwilym's 'The birch hat', in Thomas (trans.) *Dafydd ap Gwilym. His poems*, no. 59, lines 19–22; *The Canterbury tales: General prologue*, line 80, in Benson (ed.), *The Riverside Chaucer*, p. 24.

31 Burrow, *The ages of man*, p. 192; Shahar, *Childhood*, pp. 16–17.

32 Rocke, *Forbidden friendships*, p. 113; Folts, 'Senescence and renascence', p. 221; Gabriel, *Student life*, p. 106.

33 Moorman, *A history of the Franciscan order*, pp. 107–10.

34 Phillips (ed.), *Enrique IV*, p. 91.

35 Rocke, *Forbidden friendships*, pp. 88, 96, ch. 6.

36 Ruggiero, *The boundaries of eros*, p. 160.

37 Rocke, *Forbidden friendships*, p. 87; Brown, *Pastor and laity*, p. 222.

38 Cadden, *Meanings of sex difference*, pp. 174–5.

39 Bennett, 'Ventriloquisms', p. 193; Karras, 'Sex and the singlewoman', p. 133.

40 Ruggiero, *The boundaries of eros*, p. 152.

41 Bynum, *Holy feast*, p. 224.

42 Geremek, *The margins of society*, pp. 151–3.

43 Harris (ed.), *The Coventry leet book*, p. 545.

44 Brant, *Ship of fools*, no. 27, pp. 124–5.

45 Arnade, *Realms of ritual*, pp. 50–1.

46 Nicholas, *Domestic*, pp. 142–3.

47 Hanawalt, *'Of good and ill repute'*, pp. 190–4; McIntosh, *Autonomy and community*, pp. 250–61.

48 Hanawalt, *Growing up*, p. 125.
49 Rossiaud, *Medieval prostitution*, pp. 12–13, 20–1; Rossiaud, 'Prostitution, youth and society', p. 11.
50 Crouzet-Pavan, 'A flower of evil', pp. 188–90.
51 *Ibid.*, p. 190.
52 *Ibid.*, p. 186; Hanawalt, *'Of good and ill repute'*, pp. 179, 190–1; Herlihy, 'Some psychological and social roots', pp. 129–54.
53 Dean's 2001 study *Crime in medieval Europe* argues against the strong historiographical trend to see the later Middle Ages as a period of growing lawlessness. Youth does not feature strongly in his analysis: pp. 47–54. For Wales see Martin (ed.), *Registrum epistolarum Fratris Johannis Peckham*, pp. 776–7.
54 Chaney (ed.), *The poems of François Villon*, e.g. verse xxvi; Thomas Hoccleve, *'My compleinte' and other poems: La male regle*, line 65, p. 66. See too Owst, *Literature and pulpit*, p. 461.
55 Herlihy, 'Some psychological and social roots', p. 152.
56 Otis, *Prostitution*, pp. 108 and 116.
57 Chojnacki, *Women and men*, pp. 227–9.
58 Schultz, 'Medieval adolescence', pp. 521–6; Cuesta, 'Notes on family relationships', pp. 205–8; Jeay, 'Sexuality and family', pp. 328–45.
59 Trexler, *Public life*, p. 423.
60 Owst, *Literature and pulpit*, p. 461. And see ch. 4 above.
61 Alberti, *I libri*, p. 44; Crouzet-Pavan, 'A flower of evil', p. 181.
62 Rossiaud, *Medieval prostitution*, pp. 19–20.
63 Phillips, 'Maidenhood', p. 10; Voaden and Volf, 'Visions of my youth', p. 673; Bynum, *Holy feast*, ch. 7.
64 Orme, *From childhood to chivalry*, pp. 6, 182, 185–90; Demaitre, *Doctor Bernard de Gordon*, p. 12.
65 Shahar, *Childhood*, p. 211.
66 Deschamps, 'Le lay de vaillance', in *Oeuvres complètes*, vol. 2, p. 222.
67 Orme, *From childhood to chivalry*, p. 191; Housley, 'One man and his wars', pp. 27–8.
68 Burrow, *The ages of man*, p. 171.
69 Chojnacki, *Women and men*, pp. 174, 231; Grubb, *Provincial families*, p. 89.
70 Christine de Pisan, *Treasure*, pp. 190–4.
71 Orme, *From childhood to chivalry*, p. 56.
72 Harris, *English aristocratic women*, p. 39.
73 Le Roy Ladurie, *Montaillou*, p. 215.
74 Bennett, *Women in the medieval English countryside*, pp. 75–89.
75 Goldberg, 'Marriage, migration and servanthood', p. 5; Howell, *Land, family and inheritance*, p. 227; Kowaleski, 'Singlewomen', pp. 46–50.
76 Klapisch-Zuber, *Women, family and ritual*, pp. 173–4; Romano, *Housecraft*, pp. 155–6; Herlihy, 'The population of Verona', p. 101.
77 Brodman, *Charity and welfare*, pp. 121, 123. Goldberg, *Women, work and life cycle*, p. 334; Goldberg, 'What was a servant?', p. 16; Grubb, *Provincial families*, p. 97; Lorcin, *Vivre et mourir*, ch. 4, section c; Klapisch-Zuber, *Women, family and ritual*, p. 174; Romano, *Housecraft*, pp. 156–7.

78 Gavitt, *Charity and children*, p. 20; Ruggiero, *The boundaries of eros*, pp. 40–1, 150–1; Hanawalt, 'Violence in the domestic milieu', pp. 212–14; Phillips, *Medieval maidens*, pp. 131–2.

79 Goldberg, 'Masters and men', p. 57; Davies (ed.), *The Merchant Taylors' Company*, p. 34; Karras, *From boys to men*, p. 120; Hanawalt, *'Of good and ill repute'*, p. 192.

80 Michaud-Frejaville, 'Bons et loyaux services', p. 186; Reyerson, 'The adolescent apprentice/worker', pp. 354–5; Reyerson, 'Women in business', p. 120.

81 Fleming, *Women in late medieval Bristol*, pp. 10–11; Epstein, *Genoa*, p. 109; Davies, 'The tailors of London', p. 192; Nicholas, 'Child and adolescent labour', p. 1113; Goldberg, 'Masters and men'.

82 Shaw, *The creation of a community*, p. 100; Michaud-Frejaville, 'Bons et loyaux services', p. 187.

83 Davies, 'The tailors of London', p. 184; Mitterauer, *A history of youth*, p. 70; Reyerson, 'The adolescent apprentice/worker', p. 355.

84 Brucker (ed.), *Two memoirs of Renaissance Florence*, p. 108.

85 Herlihy and Klapisch-Zuber, *Les Toscans*, pp. 573–4.

86 Epstein, *Wage labor*, p. 107; Epstein, *Genoa*, pp. 275–7, table 13; Nicholas, 'Child and adolescent labour', pp. 1111–2; Davies, 'The tailors of London', pp. 106–7; Brodman, *Charity and welfare*, p. 200, fn. 81.

87 Michaud, 'Apprentissage', pp. 22–4; Epstein, *Wage labor*, pp. 106–7; Geremek, *Le salariat*, p. 31.

88 Thrupp, *The merchant class*, pp. 158, 193; Hanawalt, *Growing up*, pp. 82, 113; Klapisch-Zuber, *Women, family and ritual*, pp. 107–8; Nicholas, 'Child and adolescent labour', p. 1131; Hanawalt, *'Of good and ill repute'*, p. 191; Reyerson, 'The adolescent apprentice/worker', p. 355. See too Michaud-Frejaville, 'Bons et loyaux services', p. 193.

89 Herlihy and Klapisch-Zuber, *Tuscans*, p. 137; Klapisch-Zuber, *Women, family and ritual*, p. 108; Epstein, *Wage labor*, p. 105.

90 Thrupp, *The merchant class*, pp. 205–6; Davies, 'The tailors of London', p. 143; Yarborough, 'Apprentices', p. 68.

91 Michaud, 'Apprentissage', pp. 14–15.

92 Michaud-Frejville, 'Bons et loyaux services', pp. 189–90; Nicholas, 'Child and adolescent labour', p. 1109.

93 Wölffin, *The art of Albrecht Dürer*, pp. 23–4; Epstein, *Wage labor*, p. 106.

94 Reyerson, 'Women in business', p. 120; in Orleans over sixty per cent of apprentices lived over thirty kilometres away: Michaud-Frejaville, 'Bons et loyaux services', pp. 197–8, table ix.

95 Davies, 'The tailors of London', pp. 189, 267, and see the helpful map in Davies (ed.), *The Merchant Taylors' Company*, p. 33; Yarborough, 'Apprentices', p. 68.

96 Trigg (ed.), *Wynnere and Wastoure*, lines 7–9, p. 3; Karras, *From boys to men*, p. 119.

97 Epstein, *Wage labor*, p. 111; Thrupp, *The merchant class*, p. 192; Goldberg, 'Masters and men', p. 59; Hanawalt, *Growing up*, p. 134.

98 Davies, 'The tailors of London', p. 194.

99 Orme, *From childhood to chivalry*, p. 71.

100 Rashdall, *The universities*, vol. 3, pp. 352–3; Cobban, *The medieval English universities*, p. 353; Cobban, *English university life*, p. 20; Schwinges, 'Student education, student life', p. 184; Verger, 'The universities', pp. 78–9.

101 Rashdall, *The universities*, vol. 3, pp. 376–81.

102 Brodman, *Charity and welfare*, p. 16.

103 Cobban, *English university life*, pp. 24–5.

104 Thorndike (ed. and trans.), *University records*, p. 332; Cobban, *The medieval English universities*, pp. 345, 361; Orme, *From childhood to chivalry*, p. 78; Karras, *From boys to men*, p. 73.

105 Labarge, 'Gerontocomia', p. 210; Orme, *From childhood to chivalry*, p. 117; Hanawalt, 'Of good and ill repute', p. 180; Riddy, 'Mother knows best', pp. 68–86; Fulton, 'The boy stripped bare'.

106 Geremek, *The margins of society*, pp. 259–62.

107 Arnade, *Realms of ritual*, pp. 72–4.

108 Barron, 'London 1300–1540', p. 429; Rosser, 'Urban culture', p. 359.

109 Orme, *Medieval children*, pp. 221–3; French, *The people of the parish*, p. 127; Rubin, 'Small groups', p. 141; Hanawalt, *The ties that bound*, p. 193; Duffy, *The stripping of the altars*, p. 151.

110 Trexler, *Dependence in context*, pp. 266, 269–70, 272, 279; Eisenbichler, *The boys of the archangel Raphael*, pp. 4–28, 168; Crouzet-Pavan, 'A flower of evil', pp. 212–13; Terpstra, *Lay confraternities*, p. 21.

111 Davies, 'The reasons of misrule'; Rossiaud, 'Prostitution, youth and society', pp. 13–15; Mitterauer, *A history of youth*, pp. 163–4.

112 *Ibid.*, p. 153.

113 Karras, *From boys to men*, p. 143; Geremek, *The margins of society*, p. 287; Le Roy Ladurie, *Montaillou*, p. 216.

114 Pastoureau, 'Emblems of youth', p. 237.

115 Goldberg, 'Masters and men', p. 64.

116 Orme, *Medieval children*, p. 183; Crouzet-Pavan, 'A flower of evil', pp. 206–7.

117 Voaden and Volf, 'Visions of my youth', p. 674.

118 Goldberg (ed.), *Women in England*, pp. 88–90.

119 For the objections see Hanawalt, *Growing up*, pp. 11–12; Ben-Amos, *Adolescence*, ch. 8; Mitterauer, *A history of youth*, pp. 115, 131, 236.

120 Griffiths, *Youth and authority*, pp. 121–2.

121 *Ibid.*, p. 23; Orme, *From childhood to chivalry*, p. 5.

122 Freeman, *François Villon*, p. 204; Trexler, *Dependence in context*, p. 279; Crouzet-Pavan, 'A flower of evil', p. 174; Geremek, *The margins of society*, p. 286; Otis, *Prostitution*, p. 108.

123 Bainbridge, *Guilds in the medieval countryside*, p. 85.

6

Adulthood

ADULTS traditionally populate all society's positions of political and social authority. In medieval Europe no one under twelve could have an official role in government. Decisions on going to war, taxation, the law, the economy, religious belief and cultural direction were all made by mature men (and to some extent women). As a result, 'adulthood' confirmed its pre-eminence in the life cycle not simply by what it could do, but by being a state to aspire to. Children and adolescents, in medieval society as today, were sometimes impatient of delays in their coming of age, while parents and ruling bodies brought children up with the goal of making them worthy adults.

Paradoxically, the adult's predominance in history has meant that 'adulthood' receives little attention in both medieval and modern discussions of the life cycle. As Michael Goodich has noted, writers on the ages of man only vaguely described a middle age between youth and old age.[1] Studies have tended to consider medieval adulthood either as the end of the story (the culmination of the growing-up phases) or, increasingly, via a gendered perspective in discussions of manhood. The lack of attention is understandable, for what the achievement of adulthood ultimately meant was the full integration of an individual into society. Adults were the norm against which children, adolescents and the elderly were judged. Those age groups were singled out in medieval society precisely because of their differences and marginality; conversely few writers reflected upon those in the dominant age category. Nevertheless, as the explosion of work on masculinity and heterosexuality in the late twentieth century demonstrated, there are no natural or unproblematic norms in society. Adulthood is culturally conditioned, a social category, and its attributes and meanings have changed over time and across cultures. It is the purpose of this chapter to investigate what the achievement of maturity meant in the later medieval period, the entrance points to this phase, and the experience of adulthood.

Qualities

As previous chapters have indicated, the achievement of maturity was a gradual process. Society controlled the boundaries of adulthood by allowing individuals access to rights and responsibilities in small steps linked to their chronological age. Access was accelerated around the age of twelve to fourteen as a person became legally able to marry, to join a village tithing (if male), to inherit property (if held by a non-military tenure) or to be liable for taxation. Despite this clustering, however, there was no single age of majority. Legal adulthood depended on locality and gender, with individual towns and villages setting their own age of majority; in Ghent it was fifteen for boys and twelve for girls. Other responsibilities were only allowed in the late teens and early twenties: the minimum age for inheriting land held by military tenure was twenty-one. Even those in their mid-twenties could endure a degree of dependence: in Vicenza, under the influence of Roman law, no one under twenty-five could appear in court without a guardian.[2]

The variety of ages underlines the point that culture played a more important role than biology in determining when a person achieved full adulthood. In setting minimum legal ages, medieval society linked chronological age with capability, responsibility and the acquisition of knowledge. In England, the burgess's son was deemed of age when he could count, measure cloth and conduct his father's business: it was usually between twelve and sixteen. According to the English jurist Bracton a woman (holding in socage tenure) reached full age 'whenever she can and knows how to order her house and do the things that belong to the arrangement and management of the house'.[3] Such wording allowed for broad interpretation and indicates that legal ages were often more guidelines than directives. There are many examples of individual parents and guardians setting their own minimum ages beyond the legal requirements, particularly regarding inheritance. In her will of 1482, the Norfolk gentlewoman Margaret Paston stipulated that her grandson John Calle would receive her £20 bequest only when 'he cometh to the age of xxiiij [twenty four] yer'.[4] Similarly in 1474, Agnesina da Mula Loredan, a Venetian patrician woman, named her children as her beneficiaries, but decreed that none would receive their bequests 'until they became their own masters'. For her that meant her sons at twenty and her daughters at sixteen.[5] The noticeable gender difference reflected ideas concerning a woman's earlier maturity, and a desire for women's early marriage (discussed below). Nor did medieval society automatically grant majority at the minimum age; discretion was used. In Ghent, formal emancipation only occurred when the clan determined that a person was mature and wise enough to justify it; some achieved it only in their twenties or even thirties.[6] In London, the mayor, chamberlain and alderman made their own judgements regarding when an heir in the city's care could inherit. For example John Drew, a grocer of London, came of age in 1420, but the mayor and alderman of the city stated that he appeared 'not as yet of discretion to have the whole [estate] entrusted to him'. He would be given the remainder only 'when he appeared to have better control of himself'.[7]

Adulthood entailed the individual achieving something, be it self-control, discretion or sufficient knowledge. This is reflected in the word 'adult' itself, which is derived from the past participle of the Latin word for growing up (*adolescere*) and means literally 'grown up'. The word was not in common use during the later Middle Ages, but it did begin to make the transition to vernacular languages during the fourteenth century. In Italy, *adulto* entered the vernacular thanks to Dante's figurative use of the word in his *Paradiso*, where *adulto* means mature or full-grown. In its application to a grown person, the French *adulte* is first recorded in the later fourteenth century, and the Spanish equivalent in the fifteenth century, with an English version in the sixteenth.[8] More common words used to describe maturity emphasise the sense of completion. English terms include 'ripe age', 'mature age' and 'full age'; Italian terms include *uomeno fatto* (full or grown man). In addition, the transition from being a dependent into having or helping dependents was reflected in the term most commonly used in learned Latin discussions: *iuventus*. According to Isidore of Seville, the term derived from *iuvare*, meaning 'to help', and later writers followed suit: Dante observed in his *Convivio* that maturity was 'that age that can be helpful'. It is noteworthy that in German the original meaning of the word used for legal majority – *Mündigkeit* – was the ability to protect oneself and others.[9] Alternatively a person was now called simply a man or woman, indicating that he or she had reached full sexual and social identity. In the English morality play *Mundus and infans*, when the adolescent 'Lust and Liking' reaches twenty-one, his name changes and 'Manhood mighty shall be thy name'.[10]

Adulthood, therefore, marked the end of the developmental process; integration within society had taken place. In this regard, it was sometimes visualised as a plateau and characterised as a stable, static period. In contrast to changeable, malleable youth, adults were now considered 'set' in their ways. For the fifteenth-century humanist Matteo Palmieri, thirty-five-year olds had made the decision as to which fork in the road they would travel down; there was now no point of return. For some, this meant that there was little chance of changing for the better. Bernardino of Siena cursed sodomy as a practice rarely abandoned after the early thirties: 'the devil blinds him so badly that if he passes thirty three years of age it's nearly impossible for him to reform'.[11] But the thrust of the more common discourse was to see adulthood in positive terms. The mature complexion, cooling down from the passions of youth, was described as earthy and fruitful; manhood was characterised by rationality, sobriety, responsibility and strength.[12] Such qualities derived from adulthood's position as the midpoint of life: it had all the advantages of youth and old age – physical excellence and a rational outlook – but none of their excesses and defects. In Giles of Rome's *De regimine principum* this stage is described (according to the fourteenth-century Middle English translation of John Trevisa) as 'mene bytwene bothe'.[13]

This idea of balance, of a moral mean, underscored the sense of maturity as the apex of a person's life. In philosophical, literary and legal texts 'perfect age' came to be used as a synonym for mature adulthood. In *Ratis raving*, the fifth age, between thirty and fifty, 'ringis the perfeccioune of resone and discreccioune'. It is the age that can endure most work, can live with great honour and worship, and sees no deterioration 'fore thai ar gud at athir ende'.[14] For Dante, maturity, covering the ages between twenty-five and forty-five, was 'truly the highest point of our life' and a 'perfect age'. This idea of a prime of life could also be applied to specific individuals. Christine de Pizan described her husband as having died in his prime at the age of thirty-four.[15]

As examples have already hinted, the early thirties was the most common choice for the age of perfection. The Bible exercised a strong influence here. Not only was thirty-five the midpoint in the allotted three score years and ten, but there were clear associations with the life of Christ: he was baptised at thirty and died at thirty-three – never facing bodily decay – and shortly afterwards arose from the dead. As a result the Church preached that at the end of the world souls would likewise rise up at the age of thirty-three. In addition, like many other cultures, medieval Europe believed in a Fountain of Youth. Its waters had fantastical properties that would restore health, protect against sickness, and promise immortality. Illuminated depictions of this fountain show old, grizzled and bearded men entering the waters and springing out young without their wrinkles, beards and walking sticks. Yet not any age would do, and thirty-two and thirty-three were considered the most perfect and illness-free ages. In the land of Prester John, for instance, where pure Christianity was said to be preserved, dying no longer happened once a youth had drunk healing waters three times; ageing stopped at the age of thirty-two. Nevertheless, the plateau of middle life did stretch into the forties. For example, those taking the 'medicine' detailed in the Middle English *Book of quinte essence*, would obtain the state and strength of a forty-year-old.[16]

The concepts of the prime of life and perfect age were applied mainly to men and emphasise 'manly' qualities of physical strength, and full control over oneself and others. Mary Dove, Jessica Cooke and Kim Phillips have all shown the gender bias of these ideas and argued that women reached their perfect age earlier, during their youth or maidenhood. This reflected the emphasis placed on physical beauty rather than rational qualities in the stages of a female's life cycle. Nevertheless, there is some evidence that middle life could bring benefits for women too. In the *Danse Macabre of women* the figure of Madame Duchess bemoans the visit of Death because:

> I am not yet thirty
> Alas, when I am just beginning
> To know what a good life really is …
> Wealthy people die thus, in mid life[17]

The mature woman's body was also considered to have advantages over the young woman's in a few instances. The physician Michele Savanorola recommended that wet-nurses be mature women between thirty-two and thirty-five years of age, perhaps even up to forty, as their milk was of superior quality to that of younger women.[18] Philosophers influenced by Aristotle's work on the generation of animals argued that the young and the elderly were more likely to produce females, while it was the mature who produced strong males. By the late thirteenth century Engelbert of Admont would even believe that a woman's most perfect age for generation was around thirty-one to thirty-three.[19]

While the change from inexperienced youth to mature adulthood was seen as a positive move, there was recognition that the process itself could be unsettling; reason and sobriety brought with them a considerable amount of soul searching. There existed a literary tradition that saw the early thirties as a period of great spiritual change: it was the stage at which Christ had begun his teaching and St Augustine had converted to Christianity. In the fourteenth and fifteenth centuries several poets chose thirty-five as the starting age for a new journey, the point where they began to take stock of life thus far experienced. Dante embarked on his literary descent into Hell at the age of thirty-five, opening his *Divine comedy* with the line 'in the middle of the journey of our life I came to myself within a dark wood'. Similarly, Christine de Pizan began her semi-autobiographical *Vision* at the point where 'I had already finished half of my pilgrimage'.[20] Both were 'interior' journeys. For Christine it was an attempt to find meaning in her own life, in the throes of widowhood, and to understand the wider predicament of France, in the throes of political turmoil. Self-reflection was similarly encouraged by the Church, which warned adults against using their new age status to accumulate worldly power to the detriment of their souls. A number of English morality plays recounted the new sins that came with the onset of adulthood – pride, greed, envy – which were revealed to the individual through the emergence of conscience.[21] The move to maturity also brought with it a distinct sense of ending: the final passing of youth and its follies. Among poets, the change often focused on love. Froissart described himself waking from his dream of love in *Le joli buisson de jonece* to find himself at thirty-five, with the first signs of age and the realisation that the time for love making had passed. Some clearly saw the ending of youthful love in positive terms. At forty-three, Charles d'Orléans had accepted the onset of his middle age, for he could 'simply rest after the turbulence of youth, seeking the comfort in the quieter pleasures of mature years'.[22] Yet hitting thirty could also bring on a 'mid-life' crisis. Villon's *Testament* documents the unsettling transition which began 'In my thirtieth year of my life, when I swallowed all my shame'. His poem shows the irreversible break with youth, a stage in his life he could now know only through nostalgia. He presents himself in a kind of limbo: no longer foolish, but not yet wise.[23] In adulthood, life became more complicated. If youth had seen individuals make journeys to seek experience and 'find' themselves, adulthood was a stage where people had to face those selves and find out what they had made of them.

Marriage

While behavioural and physical qualities frequently lay behind definitions of maturity, there were a number of 'events' that marked the progression to adulthood. Of these, the closest to a universal rite of passage was marriage. In a few European languages, the words for husband and wife are synonymous with those for adult man and adult woman (in German, *Frau* and *Mann*).[24] For both men and women marriage was a transformative experience. It brought a new status, ushered in new obligations and privileges, and reconfigured their social and sexual roles. As such, it could render adult status to individuals who would otherwise remain dependants. The Great Council of Venice in 1299 stated that a female of thirteen or under was not legally a woman unless married, while a male under twenty could claim to be a man only if he was married. Similarly, in Ghent, marriage could release a man from wardship: a document written in 1390 referred to an individual as 'his own man, since he has married'.[25]

Legally and symbolically, marriage was considered an indication of responsibility and stability. For men, this was when their wandering days as a knight, scholar, apprentice or journeyman came to an end, as did too many nights out on the town. In a festival in Saint-Germain (Paris) in 1462, a sergeant arrested one reveller on the grounds that he was married and therefore should be at home with his wife.[26] Becoming a husband was also a necessary qualification for achieving full public and political adulthood. In English villages, married men were given offices (as jurors, reeves, aletasters) withheld from their single friends and neighbours. In fifteenth-century Florence attempts were made to bar unmarried men from office, while in Lucca (1454) no man could take up public office between the ages of twenty-seven and fifty unless he was married. For Anthony Molho such rulings reflect the Florentine belief that any man not prepared to marry and produce legitimate offspring should not be allowed to take on political responsibilities. Catherine Killerby, on the other hand, sees the Lucca ruling as an attempt to boost the number of married men.[27] Both reasons, nonetheless, link marriage and public standing in the life of the adult male.

For most young women, marriage was the goal that had been presented to them throughout their childhood. Advice literature like the Middle English poem *How the good wife taught her daughter* asserted that 'if thou have a doughter of age, Pute here sone to maryage'.[28] Marriage also had a greater legal and social impact on women than it had on men. A wife's position depended almost entirely on her husband's rank, wealth and power, and he had full legal rights over any property she brought to the marriage. Her legal identity was subsumed into that of her husband's and she became a *femme coverte*. In theory this meant that she could not write a will, sign a contract, initiate or defend a legal case, or own goods and chattels in her own name, rights she might well have enjoyed as a single woman. Finally, a husband had full power over her person, which could potentially see him dictating her movements and physically punishing her for disobeying. While marriage was a significant turning point in a woman's life cycle, it did not signal a new sense of independence, merely a different kind of dependence. Nevertheless, she was not without some responsibility, and this chapter will indicate the new powers obtained as wife and mother.

Not everyone married in the later Middle Ages, or wanted to do so. The clergy and those in religious orders were excluded from marriage by their vows of celibacy. Chapter 5 drew attention to pious young women who fought against marriage and wanted a chaste life.[29] In addition there was a strong current of anti-matrimonial discourse that listed the tribulations of a married life. Wives were overwhelmingly the focus of clerical vitriol and bourgeois satires: they were quarrelsome, demanding, jealous and promiscuous. The *Quinze joies de mariage* (written some time between 1372 and 1461) describes marriage as a trap and a prison for husbands where 'iron doors are slammed shut behind him and secured with heavy crossbars'.[30] Practical obstacles also stood in the way of marriage. As detailed below, poor financial resources, the lack of suitable partners and family strategies limiting children's opportunities all contributed to the existence of significant numbers of young, single people in northern European towns. Whether from choice or necessity, single women comprised over forty per cent of the adult female population in Coventry, Reims and Zurich, and around a third in the German city of Freiborg.[31] However, the proportion who were never married is more difficult to ascertain, and, despite the numbers, most of society recognised that marriage was naturally the next and key stage of the life cycle. To be a perpetual single woman (outside the cloister) was to be unfulfilled. In Middle High German texts an unmarried woman was still called a *kint* (a child, but more specifically a virgin) however old she was, as if signifying that she had not moved on to the next life stage.[32] The majority of people married, with proportions high among the elite and urban patriciate of southern Europe. In Prato in 1372, nearly ninety-nine per cent of women aged between fifteen and thirty were either married or widowed.[33]

If the expectation was to be married, at what point did the pressure to take a partner begin? Among the higher echelons of society, a betrothal could have been arranged for a son or daughter in later childhood, as family strategies dictated an early alliance.[34] However, canon law decreed that the legal minimum ages of marriage were twelve for girls and fourteen for boys. At these ages individuals were believed to have the rational ability to give consent. Some civic authorities added their support to the minimum ages. The statutes of the commune of Pistoia forbade the marriage of girls before their twelfth year, while in Ghent, the marriage of under-age girls required the magistrate's approval.[35] Both examples, nonetheless, suggest that marriages below those ages were not unknown. While law did play a part, the timing of marriage depended more commonly on a range of factors including gender, status, location, birth order and wealth.

In general, women felt the pressure to marry earlier than men and were groomed in the hope of receiving early proposals. In some areas, and among certain social groups, the pressure was to marry the girl soon after puberty. In the village of Montaillou, the family and friends of Béatrice de Planissoles's daughter began to select a husband for her as soon as she started menstruating.[36] Young brides would mean maximising the child-bearing years, while men, like Chaucer's character January, may well have preferred young girls who could be moulded like 'warm wex' to a husband's wishes.[37] In addition, young single women were viewed as a moral threat. This was particularly the case in Italy, where early marriages were seen as imperative to reduce the chances of a girl's – and thereby her family's – reputation being sullied.[38] Evidence from central and northern Italy and southern France suggests that teen marriages were the norm in southern Europe. The value placed on youth can be seen in the diminishing chances of future marriage once the girl had reached her twenties. While for a fifteen-year-old Tuscan girl there was an eighty-eight per cent chance of marriage, the figure dropped to under seventy per cent when she reached twenty, and only thirty-three per cent when she was twenty-five. If a woman reached thirty-five without marrying then her chance of being wed was just one in ten.[39]

Early marriages were a particular feature of Europe's royalty and aristocracy. A study of German nobility between 1300 and 1520 reveals brides of between twelve and fifteen years of age. Similarly, Barbara Harris has estimated that the majority of aristocratic women living in England between 1450 and 1550 were married between the ages of thirteen and sixteen.[40] At this level of society, the pressures to produce an heir, secure land or a politically useful alliance could lead to marriages below the canonical ages. In 1447, Elizabeth, daughter of Sir Thomas Clifford, was only six when she was married to Robert Plumpton, and had to be carried to the chapel for the ceremony. Her daughter, Margaret (an heiress), was even younger, marrying at the age of four in 1463.[41] While such young cases were exceptional, youth was clearly a premium. It was also among Europe's elite that men tended to marry early in their lives. For England, studies of marriages within ducal families (1330–1479) and members of Parliament (1386–1421) show the mean age of marriage to have been around twenty-two. Should they be heirs, they too could experience childhood betrothals: Warwick the Kingmaker, the eldest son of Richard, . Earl of Salisbury (d.1460), was married aged eight.[42]

Yet there were sections of European society for whom marriage was a relatively late affair. Men in general rarely married before their twenties, and in southern European towns the average age was closer to thirty. In fifteenth-century Florence, only around fifteen per cent of men married before their twentieth birthday and not half would be wed by thirty-five. Unlike their sisters', however, their prospects of future marriage were still healthy at forty: a bachelor had a one-in-four chance of marrying at that age (although not all would wed). This reflects a strong cultural preference in northern Italy for late marriages among men. In the fifteenth century, Maffeo Vegio believed men should wait until they were thirty-six, when their bodies would be strong and they were better able to produce healthy children. Michele Savonarola cited the authorities of Albertus Magnus and Aristotle, who preferred thirty and thirty-seven respectively as the ages of marriage.[43] It will be recalled that this was the period considered man's age of perfection. The delay meant that Florentine and Venetian men were usually much older than their wives, perhaps by as much as ten to fifteen years among wealthy couples.[44] While a large age gap does not necessarily suggest a mismatched couple, it did increase the chance that the husband would die long before his wife, and before his children had fully grown.

Certain groups of women also came to marriage later in life. Not all fifteenth-century Italian towns were like Florence. Information from Vicenza and Verona suggest that fewer than half of local women there were married before their twentieth birthday.[45] More examples of later female marriages are found in northern Europe, where there is evidence for what has been termed the 'European marriage pattern': a late age of first marriage (at least the early twenties), a small difference between the ages of the groom and bride (termed a 'companionate marriage') and a significant percentage of women who never marry. Examples from fifteenth-century Douai and Dijon suggest a first marriage in the early twenties for women, and in the mid- to late twenties for men; the age difference was therefore slight.[46] Research into English marriage patterns shows similar signs of later and more companionate marriages, with examples found in the manor of Coltishall (Norfolk), Kibworth Harcourt, the Lincolnshire fenlands and the city of York.[47] All the examples are drawn from working women and men, particularly where a period of service or apprenticeship delayed their participation in the marriage market. This also increased the likelihood that they would never marry, and marriage rates were generally much lower in northern Europe than in the south.[48]

Gender, class and locality were important variables in determining one's marital timetable, but the deciding factor was most often economic. The business of marriage in late medieval Europe invariably involved some form of financial transaction, whether provided by the couple or their families. Settlements were made at all levels of society, with examples found among the peasants of England and the slaves of Catalonia.[49] It was common across Europe for the family of the bride to provide a dowry, which was usually a cash settlement. This could be a considerable outlay for parents. When Frederick of Königsberg, an archiepiscopal ministerial of southern Styria, provided a dowry for a daughter in 1312, the figure was ten times as much as it would cost him six years later to place two daughters in a Dominican convent.[50] Nevertheless, in German-speaking areas the dowry price seems to have been fixed by custom and did not experience the escalation in costs seen in northern Italian states in the fourteenth and fifteenth centuries. Between the mid-fourteenth century and the early sixteenth century noble dowries in Venice rose by 350 per cent.[51] The situation in Italy was borne out of competition, with families wanting to maximise the chances of their daughters achieving a noble partner. In Florence there appears to have been a crude correlation between the size of a dowry and the timing of the marriage.[52] The Florentine government responded to escalating costs in the city by establishing a dowry fund, the *monte della doti*, whereby fathers invested a deposit that would mature with interest in either seven or fifteen years. Elsewhere and for those lower down in society, charity was the main hope. Bequests to poor virgins are found in numerous European wills and appear to have increased during the late fourteenth century and fifteenth century. Yet the numbers they reached were generally small. Charitable institutions too had to find ways of managing scarce resources. The confraternity of San Nicolás (Catalonia) distributed application forms, and investigated the candidates' characters, before placing a short list into a draw. Preference was given to those women whose childbearing years had nearly run out.[53]

Limited resources particularly affected younger members of the family, who had to wait considerably longer for a partner and watch their prospects dwindle. For young patrician girls in Italy, soaring dowry inflation could place marriage beyond reach. Family strategies could equally limit the opportunities for young men. In the Veneto, where the custom of partible inheritance held, families attempted to curtail the number of sons marrying to avoid the division of the patrimony.[54] More stringently, in eleven noble families of south-western Germany, only around half of all sons and daughters married in the fifteenth century: counts and barons generally allowed only one son per generation to marry.[55] Saving on family resources also meant that even sons of royalty could suffer delays in marriage. The younger sons of Henry IV of England – John, Duke of Bedford, and Humphrey, Duke of Gloucester – did not marry until after the deaths of both their father and their elder brother, Henry V.[56]

Among working families, the wife's ability to contribute the family's income through spinning, brewing or harvesting was influential. Martha Howell argues that the late age of marriage among women in fifteenth-century Douai was linked to the expectation that they would show themselves able to contribute fully to the household economy.[57] Among working men, the timing of marriage was linked to their ability to support themselves and others. For some, it was a forlorn hope: the shepherds in Montaillou saw themselves as too poor to get married.[58] Prevailing economic conditions played a part in determining the age of marriage. In the immediate post-plague era the number of marriages increased and the age of marriage lowered. Information from various Florentine *ricordi* indicates that the average age of first marriage for men fell from thirty to twenty-four between 1350 and 1400. The reasons appear to have been linked to the reduction in population and the easier economic conditions. Zvi Razi has argued that peasants in Halesowen married at younger ages after the Black Death than they had done before because more land became available during the years 1350–1400 and peasant incomes rose. In a similar vein Mavis Mate believes that it was the contracting economic opportunities of the mid- to late fifteenth century that resulted in deferred marriages. In contrast, it appears that improving conditions in fifteenth-century Venice and Florence saw the age of first marriages creep back to over thirty.[59]

The age at which marriage took place affected the degree of choice that an individual had in her or his partner and wedding date. While the Church (as will be discussed below) emphasised individual choice, the structures of society acted against it being automatically and widely exercised. Interference could come from various directions. Under-age heirs holding by military tenure were likely to have their marriages arranged or sold by their overlords. In 1444 Margaret Beaufort was only a year old when her father died and her wardship and marriage were sold to the Earl of Suffolk. She was married six years later to the earl's seven-year-old son. When that union was dissolved, Margaret's wardship was sold to Jasper and Edmund Tudor; she was married to Edmund when she was twelve.[60] For those holding by unfree status, lords had the potential to prohibit or force dependants into marriages. In the Black Forest in 1344, the manor on the monastic estate at Weitenau still claimed the right to force every girl from fourteen and every male householder over the age of eighteen or twenty into marrying the lord's choice.[61] How much this power was exercised is open to debate, however. For England, there is some question over whether seigniorial lords in the later Middle Ages used these fines to interfere in people's lives or simply as a convenient tax. Elaine Clark, for example, shows Norfolk peasants vetoing selected spouses and sees the lord's power as having been drastically reduced by the end of the thirteenth century.[62]

The greatest interference, however, would come from families and guardians, who saw marriage as a matter of negotiation. It was an opportunity to make alliances and a major route to social advancement. In towns and villages across Europe, local laws and customs supported parental power in the arrangement of marriages. In most Italian cities, laws demanded parental consent for the marriages of daughters under certain ages. For example, parental consent was required for daughters up to the age of fifteen (in Vercelli), sixteen (Ascoli), eighteen (Padua), twenty (Brescia, Pisa, Vicenza) and twenty-five (Piacenza and Perugia). While clearly placing limits on the decisions of the young, the laws were also in place to prevent daughters staying 'on the shelf' for too long. In Treviso, women above twenty were allowed to contract marriages without consent in order to counter the careless behaviour of parents who had allowed their daughters to reach such an age unwed. Nevertheless, should daughters marry of their own volition below those ages penalties were incurred, which grew harsher during the fifteenth century. A new law against secret marriages in Padua 1420 penalised a woman with the loss of her dowry and thirty days' imprisonment on bread and water.[63]

Most areas in the rest of Europe had legal penalties for marriages without parental or familial consent. According to Welsh law, a daughter who married secretly could not expect a marriage portion from her father, nor would he pay the *amobr* or 'virginity fine' that was due upon marriage. In Cologne, sons and daughters under twenty who married without permission could lose their rights.[64] Force was also in evidence. The fifteenth-century case of Elizabeth Paston, from the well-known Norfolk family, is frequently highlighted to show the extremes to which a mother could go to force her daughter to obey. When the nineteen-year-old Elizabeth opposed her parents' wishes over a proposed marriage to a fifty-year-old widower, her mother is said to have kept her imprisoned and beaten her several times so that her head was broken in two or three places. While the degree of force worried other family members, there was little that society could or would do to prevent such parental coercion. Any redress was left to the married son or daughter later in life, as requests for annulments in fifteenth-century Ireland indicate. In Armagh, Catherine McKesky requested that her marriage be annulled on the grounds that she had been severely beaten to the ground by her parents and forced to marry John Cusack.[65]

Nevertheless, young men and women were not simply pawns in family marriage strategies, and the significance of individual consent was not lost on Europe's young.[66] Greater freedom in choosing a partner appears to have been closely correlated to an individual's general independence from parents and from family and seigniorial supervision (although it should not be assumed that parents and offspring were always at loggerheads). In northern Europe, the young who had moved away from home to enter service or apprenticeship had achieved some emotional and economic independence, and would make decisions some distance away from their parents. In fifteenth-century London servants or apprentices had the opportunity to find partners during festivals, on market days or in the local tavern.[67] Individual choice appears to have been exercised in the country-side too, although the evidence can be equivocal. In rural England, a number of young brides paid their own marriage fines ('merchets'), which may indicate their greater say in arranging their own marriages, although the small payments may simply reflect the bride's contribution in a greater family expenditure. Peasants appear to have been capable of personal preference in those cases where alliances were unlikely to bring in significant resources for the family.[68] In Italy, the rising age in first marriages during the fifteenth century may hint at growing individual consent.[69] Finally, there are the voices of those whose personal choices are heard in the clandestine unions that ended up in ecclesiastical courts across Europe. Peter Waryn of Drogheda (near Dublin) married Jenet Monteyne secretly in 1454 because he feared the union would anger family and friends.[70] Yet the fear had evidently not stopped the wedding from occurring. It would be inappropriate therefore to see medieval marriages as merely cold, arranged affairs. Marriages could be based on love; it was not merely the stuff of romances, although it is important to remember that the idea of falling in love and marrying was a key storyline in chivalric tales. For several writers, love rather than money or politics was promoted as the prerequisite for marriage. In William Langland's *Piers Plowman*, for example, Wit tries to persuade people to marry 'For no landes, but for love, loke ye be wedded'.[71] For those of strong heart, weak family ties or few resources, love could direct life choices.

The wedding

Marrying in late medieval Europe was a process that marked the establishment of a new social and spiritual union. At the heart of the ceremony lay an exchange of vows. By the fourteenth century, the Christian Church had achieved some success in dictating that a legally constituted marriage in Western Europe rested on a declaration of consent, freely given by both parties. Preferably, the commitment was expressed in the present tense (*verba de praesenti*) as 'I take you'. Alternatively, vows could be expressed in the future tense (the *verba de futura*) as 'I will take you' and followed by sexual intercourse. In England, parts of France and German-speaking areas, importance was attached to the actual saying of the words, while in southern Europe consent was likely to be recorded in written documents. Even relatively poor people in southern France and Italy employed the service of a notary to draw up one or a series of contracts.[72] As the vows were made, the couple showed their mutual commitment through the touching of hands. In northern Europe, the important action was the joining together of the right hands, or hand clasping. In southern Europe, the moment when the ring was placed on the bride's finger – known as the 'ring day' – served to indicate the exact point of marriage. The point is illustrated in Domenico Ghirlandaio's *Marriage of the virgin* (c.1485–90) at Santa Maria Novella, Florence, in which Joseph places a ring on Mary's finger in the presence of a priest at the church door.[73]

This was the essence of the marriage rite, and to the Church legally nothing else mattered. Parents might withhold dowries and ask civic authorities to imprison rebellious offspring, but canon law decreed that the wishes of the family, the presence of witnesses, a public ceremony and indeed the attendance of a priest were irrelevant to establishing the validity of the union. While the Church might want weddings to be public ceremonies overseen by a priest, it tolerated a wide range of local rites and secular practices. Across Europe, marital customs remained a complex fusion of Roman, Germanic and Christian elements, not to mention the Gaelic and Celtic forms evident in Ireland and Wales. Some marriages were quite casual affairs. In London in 1472, William Forster and Ellen Grey discussed their marriage contract at the Greyhound tavern in East Cheap.[74] On other occasions, vows were made under trees, in gardens, in kitchens and in beds. As a result marriage ceremonies differed considerably across Europe.

The Church had a lesser role to play in marriage than in baptism and funeral ceremonies. In contrast with Jewish culture, marriages did not take place in sacred time and were forbidden in the holy seasons of Advent, Lent and Easter.[75] In Italy, neither church nor priest was necessary for the marriage to happen: the ring day usually took place in the bride's home, with the ceremony recorded by the notary.[76] The priest does appear to have had a more important role in northern Europe; in 1403 the Bishop of Magdeburg excommunicated laymen who married couples at home. The desire for a priestly presence partly related to the wish to be blessed, and in Germany and Scandinavia this extended to blessing the couple's bed and bridal chamber. The Church also had an important role to play in publicising the marriage in order to check its viability. In England and France, the banns would be read in the local church on three successive Sundays for the wider public to raise objections. Like the baptismal group, the wedding party would meet at the church door, where the marriage contract would be read out and the ceremony would take place. In German-speaking lands there are examples of specially constructed doors inside the church for the marital ceremony.[77]

There were several ritual stages as marriage negotiations moved from a private arrangement to a public acknowledgement. The first formalities could begin long before the actual wedding day as the two parties discussed the pre-nuptial settlement and the transference of family assets. In Italy, this might also involve a match-maker (*trattadore*) or a marriage broker. The financial arrangements could dictate the timetable of marriage and the transference of bride from her natal family to the conjugal household. In Florence in 1429, Cosa Guasconi married Paolo Niccolini, but she continued to live with her own family until 1433, at which point she was taken to Paolo's house with much feasting. The reason lay in the small instalments of the dowry Paolo was receiving and his desire to have the bulk of the money before his wife came to live with him.[78]

While pomp, people and public places were not essential to a marriage, this does not mean that weddings were prosaic. Even casual settings could be marked with some forms of ritual. Among English peasants clandestine marriages took place in front of witnesses, and there are references to a ring being placed on the bride's finger.[79] Being a bride was considered the apex of a woman's life cycle. In the manuscript illuminations accompanying the *Danse Macabre of women*, the bride is depicted as the most beautiful woman and is given the lines 'On the very day I desired / To have a special joy in my life'.[80] For others too weddings were social occasions, with opportunities for gift giving, dressing up and eating well. For the elite, conspicuous consumption was the order of the day: in 1317 £2 worth of coinage showered over the heads of Richard, son of the Earl of Arundel, and his new bride. The wedding feast celebrated the new union, and conduct books contain rich recipes for wedding parties.[81] That marriages lower down the social scale could be similarly lavish is indicated by the attempts of town governments in Italy and France to curb expenditure by issuing sumptuary legislation. The focus was usually on the number of people attending the wedding, what Jacques Heers calls 'the luxury of assembly', and the limiting of extravagant feasts. Fears were raised concerning public disorder, and there were deep worries, particularly in Italy, that escalating marital costs were preventing people from marrying. In Lucca, wedding celebrations appear to have lasted for three days before the ring day and three days afterwards. Statute restrictions hint at the extent of the festivities. There are references to tricks being played on the couple; there were restrictions on the numbers of trumpets, kettledrums and tambourines; jesters and buffoons were banned; no bran, sheets of paper, snow, sawdust or seeds were to be thrown at the bride and groom; and gift giving was either prohibited or allowed only in moderate amounts.[82]

The ceremony usually ended in the marriage bed, and for some the wedding would mark the transition to adult sexuality. Consummation was not obligatory for a legal marriage, but it was considered essential for the social function of the union. Canon law bound each partner to fulfil the 'conjugal debt', that is, to agree to a partner's sexual demands even if unwilling. Local village laws underlined the need, although not in a way the Church would have approved: in Lower Saxony wives were allowed to have sex outside marriage if the husband was unable to fulfil his marital duties.[83] At the higher echelons of society where land, property and titles would be passed down the patrimonial line, significant emphasis was placed on the virgin bride. Literature sometimes drew attention to this particular rite of passage. One of the fifteenth-century Burgundian stories *Les cent nouvelles nouvelles* considers the 'first night fears' of a fifteen-year-old on her wedding night. She has to be told by her mother what to do, but the girl cannot go through with it at first.[84] Such fears were probably experienced less by women lower down in society. There appears a difference too in the attitudes found in cities like Paris, where the loss of virginity could lead to compensation payments, and those in poorer, rural areas like Cerisy where virginity was not so highly prized.[85] For men, there was a greater probability that sexual maturity had been reached long before the wedding night. Medieval society appears to have had little faith that boys would remain virgins for long: St Vincent of Ferrer (1350–1419) believed that all boys had lost their virginity by fifteen.[86] As Chapter 5 indicated, studies suggest that medieval male youth aggressively linked sex and the achievement of manhood.

The marriage experience cannot be generalised. There were bad partnerships filled with scorn and violence that confirmed the worst of the anti-marriage texts. While cruelty was a cause for separation and severe beatings of wives were subject to legal punishment, society upheld the right for a husband to strike a wife if there was deemed to be 'just cause'.[87] In Montaillou, Guillemette Clergue was afraid of her husband and the beatings she received. As her male neighbour Bélibaste stated: 'a man is worth nothing if he is not his wife's master'.[88] Conversely, a husband who allowed himself to be ruled by his wife was treated with contempt. In fourteenth-century Senlis (northern France) wife-beaten husbands were forced to ride through the village on a donkey as an added humiliation.[89] But there were also unions where love and companionship grew in a supportive atmosphere. It needs stressing that late medieval society did believe that love and affection were possible within marriage. Wives were presented as a positive force for maintaining peace and harmony, not to mention a tidy, well-kept home.[90] During the fifteenth century, German and English poets proclaimed the value of marital love, promoting the marriage partner as a friend and lover. Oswald von Wolkenstein (1376/77–1445) extolled the benefits of marriage to both men and women and openly confessed his love and loyalty to his wife.[91] As Chapter 8 will show, a number of couples took this commitment to the grave and demonstrated their feelings in wills and memorials.

Parenthood

Whatever the feelings generated between spouses before and during marriage, the alliance was never primarily about securing a long-term partner. Its main purpose was to produce children. As Leon Battista Alberti declared, 'one takes a wife, in fact, mainly to have children with her'.[92] Children were expected: in fourteenth-century Ghent, childless marriages were prone to separation.[93] The birth of a child was a significant turning point in a person's life. It brought new responsibilities and threw into relief the adult roles of carer and provider. For a man, fatherhood proved his potency, while placing him 'in the genealogical chain' by providing him with an heir or heiress.[94] For a woman, becoming a mother was fulfilling her main role in life. For Christine de Pizan, children were 'the greatest haven, security and ornament that she can have'.[95] Pregnancy and childbirth were both shows of female strength commanding respect and events requiring sympathy. Late medieval Danish sermons preached that husbands were to be considerate to their pregnant wives; late medieval German cities, like Augsburg and Nuremberg, offered special legal protection and support to pregnant and lying-in women.[96] Among the peasantry, customs sometimes granted pregnant women new privileges: the right to pick fruit and grapes when they wanted; the relaxation of hunting and fishing regulations; and, after childbirth, greater firewood rations and fewer work obligations.[97]

The act of giving birth would have been one of the most important rites of passage in a woman's life. It is a fearsome and painful prospect today, but in the Middle Ages the certainty of pain was mixed with the uncertainty of death. The risk is captured in the lines uttered by the unborn 'Infans' in the morality play *Mundus and infans* where he describes himself and his mother at the point of birth: 'In peril of death we stood ... Full oft of death she was adread / When that I should part her from'.[98] Most women survived the ordeal, but it has been suggested that around a fifth of married women in early fifteenth-century Florence died of causes relating to child-bearing.[99] Medieval society was well aware of the trauma; it was compared to the pains of Purgatory or Christ's suffering on the cross.[100] Trust was placed in the earthly skills of the midwife and the spiritual aid invoked by prayer and childbirth rituals. St Margaret offered special protection for mothers in childbirth, and her life might be read over the expectant mother or placed on her stomach. Belts and amulets were also worn: between 1469 and 1482, Duke Wilhelm III of Saxony and his wife Katharine von Brandenstein lent the glass, spoon and girdle of St Elizabeth to several female relatives and queens to aid a safe and speedy delivery.[101] Additional support came from the midwife's helpers, female friends, neighbours and relatives. This support group also formed part of the celebrations after birth. In Scandinavia, the raucous *kvindegilde* saw women upset carts, destroying haystacks or making men dance as part of the post-delivery celebrations.[102]

The process of starting a family could begin immediately after marriage. Margery Kempe describes how 'When þis creatur was xx [20] 3er of age or sumdele more, sche was maryed to a worschepful burgeys and was with chylde with in schort time, as kynde wolde'.[103] Given the early age of some marriages, pregnancies could occur close to the age of puberty. A well-known example is Margaret Beaufort, who was married at twelve and gave birth to her son at thirteen.[104] Nevertheless, recent research has emphasised that medical and theological writings, parents and wider kin voiced a desire to delay conception for at least a few years after puberty. Those who knew their Aristotle or the work of Albertus Magnus read strong arguments against childbearing at a young age: it would lead to weak and imperfect children and prove a great physical and moral danger to the young girl.[105] In Welsh law a girl was not expected to be sexually active before the age of fourteen; English records seem to show a preference for sixteen; and a number of Venetian and Florentine commentators advocated eighteen.[106] In practice, the delay was often greater, although it is not always clear whether this was a planned delay or a period of youthful sterility. In early fifteenth-century Tuscany, despite the popularity of teenage marriages, the mean age of first birth was twenty-one.[107] Even among royalty, where the desire for an heir produced some of the youngest marriages, intercourse did not follow quickly after marriage.[108] Girls may therefore have had time to experience their youth, or get used to marriage, before they became mothers.

How many years on average a medieval woman spent having children is difficult to estimate. As mentioned in Chapter 2, child numbers appear to have been low in the late Middle Ages.[109] One possible reason for this was the use of contraception. There is fragmentary evidence of medieval couples trying to limit the number of children born. Abstinence, oral sex, sodomy, and *coitus interruptus* are mentioned and condemned in Church records. Recipes for preventative medicine were available: one well-known example is that of Montaillou's Béatrice de Planisolles, whose lover gave her a certain herb wrapped up in a linen cloth which was to be worn round her neck during intercourse to prevent conception.[110] Abortions were strongly condemned, and those undertaken would have been performed in secret. As a result cases only come to light when the individuals involved were found out and prosecuted: in 1409 Adelheit of Stutgarden, a midwife, was expelled from Sélestat for supplying abortions.[111]

Nevertheless, while the general trend may suggest small families, the later Middle Ages indicate that a fertile woman could expect to spend several years bearing children. This was particularly so among the elite, where women married at younger ages and the use of wet-nursing helped to maximise fertility. The average fifteenth-century couple produced seven children in the Veneto and six in Tuscany, while among the aristocracy of England during the years 1450–1550 forty per cent of women had five or more children.[112] Behind these averages are cases of very large families and pregnancies following in quick succession. Cassandra Bevilaqua from the Veneto bore eleven children, producing one every seventeen months, just about as frequently as her body would allow. Blanche, wife of James II of Aragon, produced ten children between 1295 and 1310, dying immediately after the tenth birth at the age of twenty-seven.[113] Other women gave birth at less frequent intervals: for those who fed their own children, the practice of breast-feeding to eighteen or twenty months would have allowed greater spacing between births. The period of maximum fertility was in a woman's twenties, with fecundity diminishing during the thirties. However, women could continue conceiving late into life, as demonstrated by urban women living in the wealthiest Florentine households. In 1427, one-third of wealthy urban women aged between thirty-eight and forty-two had given birth recently, while a tenth of those aged between forty-three and forty-seven had new babies.[114]

A final ritual awaited a mother after birth. On the basis of Old Testament law, the late medieval Church promoted the view that childbirth contaminated the female body. Women were not allowed in a church or to touch a holy object for at least forty days after the birth of a son and eighty days after the birth of a daughter. While in practice the length of time could be much shorter, few women would have witnessed their child's baptism. To purify the woman and mark her re-entry into the Christian community the ritual of 'churching' was undertaken. The new mother, veiled, would be brought to the church door, where she would offer her child's chrisom cloth, a gift and a lighted candle. A priest, by blessing the candle, symbolically purified the woman's body and she was permitted entry into the church. Inside, in a position of complete prostration, she was ritually readmitted into the community of the faithful by the singing of Mass and the chanting of Psalm 120. While this process has been judged harshly by later writers for its treatment of the female body, late medieval women saw it in more positive terms. It was an opportunity for thanksgiving, a time of celebration and an important occasion for a new dress and a party. Some royal churchings were very lavish affairs: sixty royal female attendants, as well as numerous priests and scholars, accompanied Elizabeth Woodville, the wife of Henry VI of England, during her churching ceremony in 1465. Among ordinary women too, the ritual was not a solitary experience. Midwives, godmothers, female relatives and neighbours are recorded accompanying the mother to church.[115]

For most women, giving birth defined their twenties and thirties. Not all women produced large families, and some would remain childless, but all lived in a society where regular childbirth was an expected feature of an adult woman's life. Given the relatively low life expectancy of late medieval Europe, it is possible that a woman's entire adulthood might be taken up with childbearing. Modern European women are likely to extend their sympathy to late medieval mothers who experienced the stresses of several pregnancies in quick succession. Yet the ability to produce so many children may have been a source of pride for some women; better that than to have none at all. The normality of being pregnant meant that, for good or ill, women were expected to carry on their duties as a wife, mother and worker until birth. Peasant women continued to work in the fields, while noble women travelled great distances or were with their husbands on military campaign.[116] Even when they aged and had fewer births, the role as mother continued to influence their lives. A reading of the correspondence of the wealthy Florentine widow Alessandra Strozzi makes it seem clear that her major consuming passion was her sons' education, their employment and finally their marriages. She presented herself at all times as a mother struggling to do the best for her children.[117]

Separation and widowhood

Marriage, as the wedding vows declared and the Bible clearly stated, was to be a permanent contract: 'What therefore God hath joined together, let not man put asunder' (Matthew 19:6). The Church, civic authorities, moral writers and indeed society at large discouraged separation. Even when parents disapproved of their offspring's marriage, they did not countenance breaking marriage vows. The majority of people did stay with their spouses, largely for moral and social reasons, but also because, technically, canon law did not recognise divorce. There were two legal alternatives. First, a marriage could be annulled if evidence proved that an impediment existed which invalidated the union. This might be the existence of a pre-contract, a union made under force or a union within a forbidden degree. By the fourteenth century marriages were forbidden within four degrees of kinship; this meant that those descended from the same great-great-grandfather were not able to marry one another. Following a successful annulment, the couple were free to marry again. A second legal procedure was separation, which involved a division of bed and board (*divortium a mensa et thoro*) but did not give the right of remarriage. For women in particular separation was risky as they could be left without home, children or financial support. In Ghent, it was usually the wife who left the family home following separation, and in England there is only limited evidence for alimony.[118] Legal separation could also be a long and complicated procedure as the issues of property were sorted out. The numbers who chose this route were small, as Church court records in England and the Low Countries have revealed. Official records of Brussels in 1448–59 list only eighty-nine separations, fourteen of which were on the grounds of incompatibility alone and seventy-five combined incompatibility with adultery (commonly), physical cruelty (sometimes) and impotence (occasionally).[119] Other couples chose not to go through legal channels, but simply separated and cohabited with others. Given the informal nature of the arrangement it is impossible to know how many chose this option. What can be said is that neither annulment nor separation gave the person a recognised social status in the way that 'divorced' does in twenty-first-century Europe.

Overwhelmingly, the most common cause of separation was death. The length of marriage varied with the life span of the couple, but few would celebrate what modern parlance would call a silver wedding anniversary. For fifteenth-century England it has been estimated that an average peasant marriage lasted around fifteen to twenty years before the death of a partner.[120] With women being generally younger than their husbands, sometimes significantly so, there was a good chance that it would be the wife who survived longer. Evidence suggests that widowhood was a common and probably expected experience for women in late medieval society. Of those married men whose wills were enrolled in the archdeacon's court in London during the years 1393–1415, eighty-eight per cent left wives as executors.[121] For some, widowhood could last for a considerable period of their adult life, longer even than their status as wife. Alessandra Strozzi of Florence was twenty-nine when her husband died in 1435, and she spent over thirty years as a widow.[122] Widowhood for English aristocratic women could be equally long. Over a third of the aristocratic widows from 1450 to 1550 studied by Barbara Harris survived their husbands by more than twenty years.[123]

Widowhood marked a significant turning point that could match, perhaps surpass, the dislocation felt at marriage. For some historians the change was for the better, and they emphasise a woman's newly gained freedoms and opportunities; Michael Sheehan goes as far as to call it a 'rebirth'. No longer was her legal identity 'covered' by a man's, but she could make contract, sue and be sued, own property and make a plea. A widow had a new degree of legal independence and a greater public prominence.[124] Financially too, a widow could enjoy independent economic power. While arrangements differed across Europe, widows could expect some settlement wherever they lived, and husbands' wills suggest that the legacies could be quite generous.[125] In southern Europe, it was common for the dowry to be returned to the widow or at least to her natal household in order to support any children of the union. This was sometimes supplemented: in Catalonia a husband might provide an additional *escreix* that could amount to half of the dowry.[126] In northern Europe, security commonly came in the form of dower, the property settled on a woman during the marriage arrangements. In Germany, the dower was as large, if not larger, than the dowry, and the widow's claims took priority over any other demands – including debts – on the husband's estate. In Welsh law, the wife's entitlement correlated with the length of marriage. If a woman's husband died within the first seven years of marriage then she was entitled to a share of movables, which usually reflected the woman's family status. However, if the marriage had lasted seven years or more, the wife was entitled to half of the movables of the unit. An alternative arrangement can be found in Douai, where the city's customary law made the wife, not the children, the husband's natural heir.[127] All these arrangements could provide a woman with a degree of financial security, and made some very comfortable indeed. In fourteenth-century England, Elizabeth de Burgh was thrice widowed before spending the last forty years of her life as a widow of an estate worth around £3,000 per year. [128]

Widows could be placed in positions of power. It was not uncommon for a wife to be chosen as an executor of an estate, where she would need to manage large amounts of property and wealth. She might also take over a part or all of her husband's business. Wives would have been involved in the family business from the start, be that a trade or the administration of an estate, and would have the necessary qualifications and experience to carry on the work. In England, Emma Huntyngton, on the death of her husband in 1362, was left both the family house and the family shop for the rest of her life, which allowed her to continue working as an apothecary.[129]

Becoming and remaining a widow could also bring new-found respect, particularly from religious writers, who championed widowhood as a spiritual opportunity. Treatises were written by Francesc Eiximenis, a Spanish Fransiscan (c.1388), and Girolamo Savonarola, a Florentine Dominican (c.1491), which urged women to remain widows in order to serve God better; remarriage would simply bring the distractions and temptations of husband and children.[130] At the same time, widowhood was an ambiguous state that worried many medieval commentators, and disapproval appears in a variety of evidence. If the criticisms of widows' dress and behaviour that appear in Castilian chronicles or French romances bear any resemblance to the reality, then it appears that widows were not prepared to retire from society, but were taking advantage of their newly found opportunities and living life to the full. There were perhaps real widows who would have concurred with the widow in Chaucer's *Criseyde*: 'I am myn owene womman, wel at ese'.[131]

However, the ability and desire to use this newly found freedom depended on a number of factors, and it must be emphasised that widowhood brought potential rather than automatic benefits. Medieval women did not always see widowhood as a time of opportunity, but rather as a frightening and bewildering experience. Christine de Pizan enjoyed fame and fortune in her widowhood, yet she described it as 'this pitiless state [which] usually involves much anguish and much troublesome business'. She did not celebrate the freedoms, but warned of the loss of status, the debts and disputes and the abusive language.[132] She may have been thinking of contemporary court cases involving widows at the *parlement* of Paris, where they had been forced to argue for their dower rights.[133] A widow might also need to renegotiate her position within her family, which might involve a new relationship with her children. In England and France, those holding land by military tenure would know that their overlord had rights over any under-age children, especially if heirs, and could place their wardships with another party. In Florence, Roman law dictated that widows became the guardians of their children only if specifically chosen by their husbands. Similarly, in Ghent, a widow could become her child's legal guardian only with the authority of her late husband's clan.[134] Nor did widowhood necessarily usher in a period of independence. In Florence, tradition held that on the night of her husband's funeral, a young bride would make her return (the *tornata*) to her natal family in a move symbolic of a reverse marriage procession. This would be a new stage of dependency, with a denial of her role as mother.[135]

Financially too, life may not have become better, and this would especially be so among those who retained control of their children. Aristocratic and merchant widows would live on an income smaller than that enjoyed with their husbands; they might be forced to retire to a smaller property and find that social invitations dwindled in number. Lower down in society, where there were fewer resources to go round, women would never earn enough money on their own to replace husbands' earnings.[136] As a consequence, widows, as a social group, were considered a case for charity. The Church believed they required protection, and church courts offered redress to those widows who had suffered unfair judgements in secular courts. Charitable organisations, such as the fraternity of Orsanmichele in Florence, distributed a substantial portion of their income to widows.[137]

The quality of perpetual widowhood therefore owed much to the widow's resources, making it a very varied experience. In fourteenth-century Montpellier, widows were the most active women in the town's economy, taking on the role of moneylender. At the same time, widows of humble origins formed the town's largest group of female borrowers, which suggests that they may have had serious financial worries.[138] But it was not all about financial security. Women had been brought up to see wifedom as their goal. Husbands were companions, sexual partners, the heads of the household and protectors. Emotionally, the death of a spouse could be heartbreaking. Even in a society where love was not a prerequisite for marriage, grief at the death of a spouse was socially expected and far from unusual. In the fifteenth-century Catalan novel *Curial e Güelfa*, the widow Guelfa is said to have 'lacked nothing save only a husband'.[139] For some women that might have been everything.

A number of widows swapped their legal freedom for the economic and emotional security of another marriage. Remarriage was not uncommon in late medieval society. The ménagier of Paris, who was much older than his wife, accepted that she was likely to remarry after his death. He was keen that she should learn well the skills of a good wife under his tutelage so as not to shame him in front of her second husband.[140] The percentage of remarriages varied a great deal across Europe, relating to local laws and economic circumstances. In certain sectors of European society rates of remarriage were quite high. Studies of the widows of English peers in the fifteenth century suggest that approximately forty per cent remarried, while Mavis Mate has calculated that around a third of peasant widows of Sussex in the period 1422–80 remarried.[141] Elsewhere, notably in the towns of York and Montpellier, remarriage rates appear to have been much lower, at around a fifth.[142] It is tempting to link the lower rates in towns to the opportunities available to women to manage wealth and property, but it is difficult to gauge the degree of choice a widow enjoyed in the issue of remarriage.[143] The decision would have involved several personal factors. She might be swayed by the number and age of her children, the need for a business partner or the opportunity to catch a richer husband the second or third time round.

But her decision-making ability would also be subject to external pressures. Husbands tried to dictate the situation from beyond the grave: wills from Catalonia, England, Douai, Venice and Genoa show them tying financial settlements to their wives remaining single.[144] Competing family pressures could also be brought to bear on young widows. In Florence, a husband's family would try to keep the widow (and her dowry) in the marital household, while the widow's natal family was more likely to push for remarriage in order to use her and her dowry to create new alliances.[145] There were official pressures too. From the mid-fourteenth century Catalan law began to penalise women who remarried.[146] In urban areas, the guilds could play a strong role in a woman's decision as they tied her marital status to her ability to continue her husband's work. In Denmark, some guilds allowed a woman to carry on her husband's trade only if she remarried within a certain period; others (such as the skindressers and furriers of Malmø) permitted the widow to continue working only if she remained single and retained a good reputation.[147]

The widow was also at the mercy of changing circumstances, and might find it very difficult to remarry. Her age was a key factor: a widow would be in competition with younger women, who were considered naturally more beautiful and to have more years of childbearing ahead of them. Information derived from Florentine diaries indicates that two-thirds of those who became widows under the age of twenty were remarried, but only one-third of widows in their twenties and a mere eleven per cent in their thirties. After forty, with the possibility of producing children now minimal, the chances of remarriage were slim.[148] The odds would be improved with wealth: a widow with a substantial dower or dowry had a considerable advantage over a poor woman with no land or political connections.[149] Yet her relative appeal could be subject to the vagaries of the land market and regional differences. In some areas widows were more attractive during periods of land shortage, but less appealing when other routes to wealth were available. For example, land shortages in early fourteenth-century Halesowen saw the remarriage of widows at sixty-three per cent. In contrast, following the Black Death, when land became more obtainable, the remarriage rate fell to twenty-six per cent.[150] However, changing economic and legal conditions after 1348 did not have uniform results. In Kibworth Harcourt remarriages increased in the later fourteenth century as legal restrictions were relaxed (men were now allowed to pay a fine to marry widows) and widespread labour shortages allowed heirs to establish themselves earlier in life.[151] The prospects for remarriage, therefore, depended on several, often uncertain, variables.

The focus of this section has been on female widowhood because widowers had far less prominence than widows in medieval Europe. Their numbers were fewer, partly because their wives survived them and partly because a husband was far more likely to remarry, even late in life. They would still be able to father children and had accumulated sufficient resources to compete favourably with younger men. In fifteenth-century Florence, over three-quarters of men up to the age of sixty remarried. A similar situation is found in the culturally and economically different climate of late medieval York, where widowers formed only twenty per cent of all male testators.[152] But the absence of widowers in administrative records and fictional literature is not simply a result of low numbers. Indeed, studies have shown that among certain social groups, the prospect of remarriage was not certain for men. James Grubb's research into twenty- three memoir writers of the Veneto has revealed that over half did not remarry, but experienced fifteen years as widowers.[153] Rather, the rarity of the widower in medieval records reflects a society that did not think of defining a man solely by his marital status, and some languages had no male equivalent of the term 'widow' during the period.[154] In contrast to a woman's situation, the death of a spouse did not change a man's legal status, wealth, home, living conditions, work, and access to children. Little wonder therefore that the widower does not appear as a category in the records of charitable organisations.[155]

Household, work and financial independence

Marriage and parenthood signalled that a person was no longer simply a son or daughter – a family dependant – but someone who had started a new social unit and had assumed the role of helping and protecting others. Ideally, a couple established their own separate household, with the husband having authority over all its members. This expanded his legal and political responsibilities because all property was treated legally under his management and he was liable for any crimes committed by the dependants – wife, children, servants – of the household.[156] The financial settlement that came with marriage would also allow a working man to set himself up in business – underlining his move from trainee to experienced worker – or improve his business standing.[157] When in 1393 Gregorio Dati decided to invest 1,000 florins in a silk company, it was his impending marriage that made it possible, as he wrote: 'I did not actually have the money but was about to get married – which I then did – and to receive the dowry which procured me a larger share and more consideration in our company'.[158] At a broader level, the marriage settlement helped a young couple to start their new home. This is reflected in the word most commonly used in German language records for dowry – *heimsteuer* – literary meaning 'home aid' or 'home contribution'.[159] Gifts given at the wedding were aimed at establishing a new home. When Marco Parenti married Caterina Strozzi in 1448 the gifts given would clearly have helped to set up the couple in some comfort: shirts, towels, handkerchiefs, hose, slippers, knives and coral beads plus a wealth of furnishings.[160]

Yet setting up home was a significant financial step, and some couples still required help from their natal families. For those who had married young, financial assistance might be needed from parents to establish the household, especially if the dowry was paid in instalments. In Ghent parents might pledge a landed estate to the new couple, but reserve the right to exploit the property during their lifetimes. The couple would receive an annuity, which would allow parents to monitor the management of the property before full rights were surrendered to them. Some parents also agreed to subsidise the newly married couple during the first few years. When Pieter Daens and Lisbette Van Wondelgem bought a house in 1361, it was her relations who helped to pay for it.[161] By way of contrast, in the Italian city states, married men often continued to live in their father's house, under his authority. In Verona and Vicenza there are examples of men including notaries, wool merchants and physicians marrying before they had secured enough capital to set up a separate household.[162] It may have been some time before they achieved the position of head of the household.

For some, becoming the head of a household relied on securing an inheritance. This might come through an individual's death, a father's retirement or, in some cities (in southern France, northern Italy and Crete), through the process of emancipation where a judicial order released offspring from the parent's power. An emancipated adult had full legal rights and responsibilities, although he would also need to pass the age of majority of twenty-five (according to Roman law) to gain full legal capacity. [163] In Wales youth stretched until the father had died and the boy had achieved his inheritance. Only at his father's death did a male achieve the status of *uchelwr* or *optimas*, be fully identified with his paternal lineage, and become 'the man of the house'.[164]

Another important route to adulthood was the ending of training and the development into a fully working adult. For an apprentice, this rite of passage would be marked by a public admission to citizenship. In Bristol, the ritual was intended to acknowledge that a person had been, in the words of Anne Yarborough, 'accepted into the web of ties and obligations which defined the identity of the urban adult'.[165] The rituals that propelled a Venetian adolescent into the ranks of full nobility began with the Balla d'Oro or Barbarella, a type of lottery system. On reaching eighteen young nobles were entered in the lottery; the winners were allowed to take up hereditary places in the Great Council at the age of twenty instead of the normal twenty-five. The lottery arose from an increasing desire in fifteenth-century Venice to introduce young men into government and hasten their attainment of adulthood. However, in other areas there was concern that 'working' adulthood should be delayed. In London, the Grocers' guild made apprenticeship ten years long and ordered that no one could leave their training until they reached twenty-five or twenty-six. In another context, in fifteenth-century Basle, the city council decided to raise the age at which one could do business from fourteen to twenty, because it thought that boys were far too careless with property.[166] Europe's workforce may have contained a significant proportion of children, but fifteenth-century society appeared to see the early twenties as the most suitable time to take on full working responsibilities.

Once a person had become a full member of society, what else was there to achieve for the late medieval adult? 'Ages of man' literature presented adulthood as a period of stasis before the decline of old age got under way. Many men and women, through work or family, had achieved their potential; perhaps some felt their lives were standing still. But adult life in the Middle Ages was not one of paralysis. For adult men, there were advancements to be made in work: status and power grew in relation to political and economic responsibilities. There were age barriers still to hurdle. Statutes introduced in 1415 meant that a citizen of Florence had to be over thirty years of age to serve in one of its three councils, and over forty-five to be standard-bearer of justice (the commune's highest office). Experience was valued for a wide range of occupations. In Tarascon (Provence) during the period 1370–1400, a citizen had to serve on a council for seventeen years before he could become a mayor. Positions of power in the Middle Ages rarely came before thirty; for those in administrative, political and military occupations, advancement to key positions would only be achieved in the forties.[167]

For women, marriage was not the end of their development. Instead, a woman embarked on what Chojnacki has termed the 'uxorial cycle' as she grew from a young bride to a mother and mature wife, and finally a widow.[168] It was also as a wife that a woman gained access to a wider range of economic and business roles. Her work and financial contribution were acknowledged if not generally rewarded. In fifteenth-century Cologne, Balthasar von Kerpen noted in his will that he had married a second time 'for the sake of his children and also for the sake of his business'.[169] Most often this meant that the wife's work supported that of her husband; marriage could bring an end to the type of labour that a woman had engaged in before betrothal. Nevertheless, a growing body of research has produced examples of wives working independently, being business partners of men other than their husbands and, as widows, presiding over large, economically productive households. What is more difficult to assess is how far single women could achieve adult independence through employment and inheritance. It is the case that single women could gain some financial security. In Ghent, a suit of 1386 included the phrase that a young girl was to be supported 'until she could earn her own bread'.[170] Yet success was not guaranteed. Kittel's comparison of women in Genoa and Douai emphasises the different opportunities for those in southern and northern Europe. In Genoa, single women were at a disadvantage because of the high priority given to marriage and the suspicion under which they were held; their honour was valued more than their employment skills. In contrast, single women in Douai could enjoy a degree of economic independence: they left wills and owned property indicating a relatively secure financial position.[171] Nevertheless, the apprenticeship system and guild regulations were not geared towards training a woman in occupations that could support her and a family. Unless land or a steady income was acquired, single working women would remain dependent on relatives and continue to live in a period of extended adolescence.[172]

Conclusion

In focusing on adulthood, this chapter has considered the dominant age group in society. It was a stage associated with responsibility, authority and fulfilling social roles. There was no one entrance point, as individuals became full members of society at different points in their life span. Marriage, parenthood, inheritance, and the establishment of one's own business or an official governing position were key transitional points, as they had transformative qualities that changed a person's status. He or she was now a householder, husband, wife, father, mother or master craftsman. Marriage in particular opened up a new chapter in a person's life. Some individuals, mainly girls, were married while they were still in the process of developing physically and psychologically. There is evidence that this was taken into account in the treatment of the young, particularly in the delaying of intercourse. Nevertheless, a girl had made a significant step in fulfilling the role society expected of her, which would be confirmed through the birth of the first child.

Maturity would be seen through the fully gendered body; men were defined by their strength and their ability to grow full beards. Yet, in comparison with the rapid physical and social changes of childhood and adolescence, adulthood was characterised by slower development. Body size and appearance would remain relatively constant, if becoming a little more lined as the years progressed. Nor would an individual receive the level of training that youth endured; experience was what mattered. Descriptions of, and attitudes towards, adulthood can assume that once an individual had grown up, the development process stopped. But it is not the case that adulthood was simply one long stretch of sameness, before the descent into old age began. Men advanced their working lives, and all key positions of power were in the hands of mature men. Women, as wives, helped build up family businesses, run estates or work the fields. As widows, they may have come to share some of the characteristics of adult men in terms of legal and social responsibilities. The acquisition and retention of adult status demanded that a person continually demonstrate her or his 'adult' qualities. To be mature meant not just looking grown-up, but being seen as responsible and capable of looking after oneself and others. Any slips in the performance could see an individual temporarily or permanently stripped of her or his adult status. As the next chapter will show, the problem was that as the body aged, it was not always easy to maintain performance.

Notes

1 Goodich, *From birth to old age*, pp. 143–4.
2 Grubb, *Provincial families*, p. 90.
3 Thomas, 'Age and authority', pp. 221–2; Phillips, *Medieval maidens*, p. 32.
4 Norman (ed.), *Paston letters and papers*, vol. 1, p. 388.
5 Chojnacki, *Women and men*, p. 185.
6 Nicholas, *Domestic*, pp. 136–7.
7 Hanawalt, *Growing up*, p. 203.
8 Dante, *The divine comedy: Paradiso*, canto 7, lines 58–60: 'Questo decreto, frate, sta sepulto / a li occhi di ciascuno il cui ingegno / ne la fiamma d'amor non è adulto' (This decree, brother, is buried from the eyes of everyone whose understanding is not matured within love's flame).
9 Lindsay (ed.), *Isidori Hispalensis episcopi*, vol. 2, book XI.i, line 16; *Dante's Il convivio*, p. 218; Mitterauer, *A history of youth*, p. 55; Dove, *The perfect age*, ch. 1.
10 *Mundus and infans*, line 160, in Lester (ed.), *Three late medieval moralities*, p. 118.
11 Bell, *How to do it*, p. 178; Rocke, *Forbidden friendships*, p. 40.
12 *Dante's Il convivio*, pp. 218, 226–7; Seymour (ed.), *On the properties of things*, ch. 13. See too Goodich, *From birth to old age*, p. 144.
13 Dove, *The perfect age*, p. 28; Fowler, Briggs and Remley (eds), *The governance of kings and princes*, p. 148.
14 Lumby (ed.), *Ratis raving*, pp. 65, 69–70.
15 *Dante's Il convivio*, p. 218; Dove, T*he perfect age*, pp. 13, 17; Christine de Pizan, 'Vision', in Blumenfeld-Kosinski and Brownlee (eds), *The selected writings of Christine de Pizan*, p. 187. See also Fowler, Briggs and Remley (eds), *The governance of kings and princes*, p. 243.

16 Pleij, *Dreaming of Cockaigne*, pp. 187–8; Furnivall (ed.), *The book of quinte essence,* book II, line 11, p. 15.

17 Harrison (ed.), *The Danse Macabre of women*, p. 54, lines 9–11, 16.

18 Bell, *How to do it*, p. 129.

19 Biller, *The measure of multitude*, pp. 258 and 347.

20 Dante, *The divine comedy: Inferno*, canto 1, line 1; Blumenfeld-Kosinski and Brownlee (eds), *The selected writings of Christine de Pizan*, p. 175.

21 See the description of Manhood in *Mundus and infans*, especially lines 267–82, in Lester (ed.), *Three late medieval moralities*, p. 124–5.

22 Discussed in Burrows, *The ages of man*, p. 184.

23 Chaney (ed.), *The poems of François Villon: The Testament*, V.V.1–16; Fein, *A reading of Villon's Testament*, pp. 1 and 5.

24 Bennett and Froide (eds), *Singlewomen*, p. 1.

25 Nicholas, *Domestic*, p. 25; Chojnacki, *Women and men*, p. 186.

26 Geremek, *The margins of society*, p. 287, fn. 106.

27 Bennett, *Women in the medieval English countryside*, p. 104; Molho, *Marriage alliance*, p. 7; Killerby, *Sumptuary law*, p. 58. But see Chojnacki, who shows that bachelors formed a significant proportion of office holders in Venice: *Women and men*, p. 252.

28 I have used the edition appearing in Salisbury (ed.), *The trials and joys of marriage*, lines 181–2, p. 222.

29 See p. 106 above and examples found in Bynum, *Holy feast*, p. 222.

30 Examples found in Wilson and Makowski (ed.), *Wykked wyves*, ch. 4; Salisbury (ed.), *The trials and joys of marriage*.

31 Bennett and Froide (eds), *Singlewomen*, p. 46.

32 Schultz, *The knowledge of childhood*, p. 25.

33 Herlihy and Klapisch-Zuber, *Tuscans*, pp. 88, 214; Molho, *Marriage alliance*, pp. 218, 220.

34 Wunder, *He is the sun*, p. 25.

35 Nicholas, *Domestic*, p. 24.

36 Le Roy Ladurie, *Montaillou*, p. 216.

37 *The Canterbury Tales: The merchant's tale*, line 1430, in Benson (ed.), *The Riverside Chaucer*, p. 156.

38 Kirshner, *Pursuing honor*, pp. 9–13.

39 Chojnacki, *Women and men*, p. 373; Herlihy, *Medieval households*, pp. 103–7; Laribière, 'Le marriage à Toulouse', p. 350; Higounet-Nadal, *Périgueux*, p. 282.

40 Herlihy, *Medieval households*, p. 106; Harris, *English aristocratic women*, pp. 18, 56.

41 Stapleton (ed.), *The Plumpton correspondence*, pp. lxiv, lxx.

42 Hollingsworth, 'A demographic study', p. 365; Fleming, *Family and household*, p. 22.

43 Herlihy and Klapisch-Zuber, *Tuscans*, p. 215; Grubb, *Provincial families*, p. 5; Bell, *How to do it*, p. 212; Chojnacki, *Women and men*, p. 378. For France see Higounet-Nadal, *Périgueux*, p. 282; Delmaire, 'Le livre de famille', pp. 305–6.

44 Herlihy and Klapisch-Zuber, *Tuscans*, pp. 210–1.

45 Grubb, *Provincial families*, p. 4; Herlihy, 'The population of Verona', p. 114, table 8.

46 Rossiaud, *Medieval prostitution*, pp. 15, 17. However, note that, as men preferred to marry young brides, the age gap increased in line with the male age of marriage: Howell, *The marriage exchange*, pp. 107, 108.

47 Howell, *Land, family and inheritance*, pp. 222–5; Hallam, 'Age at first marriage'; Goldberg, 'Marriage, migration and servanthood', p. 8.

48 Goldberg, *Women, work and life cycle*, pp. 227–31; Mate, *Daughters*, p. 34.

49 Bennett, *Women in the medieval English countryside*, p. 98; Brodman, *Charity and welfare*, p. 101.

50 Freed, *Noble bondsmen*, pp. 162–4, 178–9.

51 Chojnacki, *Women and men*, p. 97.

52 Kirshner and Molho, 'The dowry fund'; Herlihy and Klapisch-Zuber, *Tuscans*, p. 220.

53 Brodman, *Charity and welfare*, p. 101; Flynn, *Sacred charity*, p. 60.

54 Grubb, *Provincial families*, p. 4.

55 Hurwich, 'Marriage strategy among the German nobility', p. 175.

56 Friedrichs, 'Marriage strategies and younger sons', pp. 54–6.

57 Mate, *Daughters*, p. 28.

58 Herlihy and Klapisch-Zuber, *Tuscans*, pp. 221–2; Le Roy Ladurie, *Montaillou*, pp. 129–30.

59 Razi, *Life*, pp. 56, 60, 63, 135–7; Mate, *Daughters*, p. 48; Benedictow, *The Black Death*, p. 271; Herlihy and Klapisch-Zuber, *Tuscans*, pp. 81, 86–7; Chojnacki, *Women and men*, p. 194–5, table 11.

60 Jones and Underwood, *The king's mother*, pp. 35–9.

61 Rösener, *Peasants*, p. 181.

62 Clark, 'The decision to marry'. For a good summary of the debate and the references therein see Fleming, *Family and household*, p. 30.

63 Dean, 'Fathers and daughters', pp. 89–96.

64 Davies, 'The status of women', p. 104; Ennen, *The medieval woman*, pp. 170, 176. See too Nicholas, *Domestic*, p. 26 and Dillard, *Daughters of the reconquest*, pp. 40–1.

65 Cosgrove, 'Marriage in medieval Ireland', pp. 44–5.

66 Sheehan, *Marriage*, p. 102.

67 Goldberg, *Women, work and life cycle*, pp. 234, 246; McSheffrey (ed.), *Love and marriage*, pp. 15–18.

68 Hanawalt, *The ties that bound*, pp. 200–2; Bennett, *Women in the medieval English countryside*, pp. 88–9, 96; Fleming, *Family and household*, p. 25.

69 Chojnacki, *Women and men*, p. 179.

70 Cosgrove, 'Marriage in medieval Ireland', p. 38.

71 *Piers Plowman*, IX, 177.

72 Gottlieb, *The family in the Western world*, pp. 72–3.

73 Detail of the artwork and the north–south differences can be found in Hall, *The Arnolfini betrothal*, pp. 34–42.

74 McSheffrey (ed.), *Love and marriage*, pp. 45–6.

75 Cohen and Horowitz, 'In search of the sacred', pp. 232–6.
76 d'Avray, 'Marriage ceremonies', pp. 113–15.
77 Bossy, *Christianity in the West*, pp. 21–3.
78 Ginevra Niccolini di Camugliano, *The chronicles of a Florentine family*, pp. 112–14.
79 Hanawalt, *The ties that bound*, p. 203.
80 Harrison (ed.), *The Danse Macabre of women*, p. 112. See too Le Roy Ladurie, *Montaillou*, pp. 181–2.
81 Murray (ed.), *Love, marriage and family*, p. 271; Laribière, 'Le mariage à Toulouse', pp. 356–7; Brereton and Ferrier (eds), *Le ménagier de Paris*, pp. 184–90.
82 Brundage, *Law, sex and Christian society*, p. 440; Heers, *Family clans*, p. 76; Klapisch-Zuber, *Women, family and ritual*, p. 262; Killerby, *Sumptuary law*, pp. 51–66.
83 Rösener, *Peasants*, pp. 182–3.
84 Richards, *Sex*, p. 35
85 Finch, 'Parental authority', p. 197. See too Goldberg, *Women, work and life cycle*, p. 328.
86 Richards, *Sex*, p. 38.
87 Nicholas, *Domestic*, p. 49.
88 Le Roy Ladurie, *Montaillou*, pp. 193–4.
89 Flandrin, *Families in former times*, pp. 124–5.
90 See St Bernadino of Siena, mentioned in Murray (ed.), *Love, marriage and family*, p. 44.
91 Classen, 'Love and marriage in late medieval verse', pp. 163–88.
92 Alberti, *I libri*, pp. 115, 119.
93 Nicholas, *Domestic*, p. 50.
94 Karras, *From boys to men*, p. 16.
95 Christine de Pisan, *Treasure*, p. 67.
96 Jacobsen, 'Pregnancy and childbirth', p. 101; Rublack, 'Pregnancy, childbirth and the female body', pp. 88, 96, 204–5.
97 Rösener, *Peasants*, p. 183.
98 *Mundus and infans*, lines 35, 42–3, in Lester (ed.), *Three late medieval moralities*, pp. 112–13.
99 Herlihy and Klapisch-Zuber, *Tuscans*, p. 277; Grubb, *Provincial families*, p. 36.
100 See e.g. Dante, *Divine comedy: Purgatorio*, canto 20, lines 20–1.
101 Stoertz, 'Suffering and survival', pp. 102–3; Wunder, *He is the sun*, p. 115.
102 Jacobsen, 'Pregnancy and childbirth', p. 106.
103 Meech and Allen (eds), *The book of Margery Kempe*, p. 6.
104 Jones and Underwood, *The king's mother*, pp. 39–40.
105 Biller, *The measure of multitude*, p. 332.
106 Mate, *Daughters*, p. 21; Phillips, *Medieval maidens*, pp. 36–42; Owen, 'Shame and reparation', p. 48; Chojnacki, *Women and men*, p. 373.
107 Emigh, 'Land tenure', p. 626.
108 Parsons, 'Mothers, daughters, marriage, power', pp. 66–7.

109 Above, p. 31. See also the figures in Lynch, *Individuals*, p. 59.

110 Le Roy Ladurie, *Montaillou*, pp. 172–3.

111 Biller, *The measure of multitude*, p. 142 and chs 6–8 in general; Leyser, *Medieval women*, p. 104.

112 Grubb, *Provincial families*, p. 37; Harris, *English aristocratic women*, p. 30.

113 Grubb, *Provincial families*, p. 36; Sablonier, 'The Aragonese royal family', p. 211.

114 Herlihy, *Medieval households*, p. 148, table 6.4.

115 Gibson, 'Blessing from sun and moon', pp. 139–54; Orme, *Medieval children*, pp. 31–3; Leyser, *Medieval women*, p. 130.

116 Labalme, *Beyond their sex*, p. 52.

117 Crabb, 'How typical', p. 48.

118 Nicholas, *Domestic*, p. 36; Fleming, *Family and household*, p. 83.

119 Nicholas, *Domestic*, p. 36. It is striking how little divorce litigation there was in medieval England: Helmholz, *Marriage litigation*, p. 74.

120 McSheffrey (ed.), *Love and marriage*, p. 7; Bennett, *Women in the medieval English countryside*, p. 61.

121 Wood, 'Poor widows', p. 55.

122 Crabb, 'How typical', p. 47.

123 Harris, *English aristocratic women*, p. 128. See also figures in Rosenthal, *Patriarchy*, p. 183.

124 Sheehan, *Marriage*, p. 194; Labarge, 'Three medieval widows', p. 159; Hanawalt, *The ties that bound*, pp. 220–23; Hanawalt, 'The widow's mite', p. 39; Harris, *English aristocratic women*, p. 127.

125 Hanawalt, 'The widow's mite', p. 25; Harris, *English aristocratic women*, pp. 131–2; Piera and Rogers, 'The widow as heroine', p. 324.

126 Piera and Rogers, 'The widow as heroine', p. 323; Klapisch-Zuber, *Women, family and ritual*, p. 121.

127 Freed, *Noble bondsmen*, p. 167; Walters, 'The European context', p. 117; Kittell, 'Testaments of two cities', p. 62, 67–8; Hanawalt, 'The widow's mite', p. 24.

128 Fleming, *Family and household*, p. 91.

129 Leyser, *Medieval women*, p. 178; Hanawalt, 'The widow's mite', p. 26.

130 Piera and Rogers, 'The widow as heroine', pp. 325–6; Bell, *How to do it*, pp. 272–8.

131 *Troilus and Criseyde*, II, 750–5, in Benson (ed.), *The Riverside Chaucer*, p. 499.

132 Christine de Pisan, *Treasure*, pp. 156–7.

133 Miskimin, 'Widows not so merry', pp. 207–19.

134 Crabb, *The Strozzi of Florence*, p. 63; Nicholas, *Domestic*, p. 121.

135 Chabot, 'Lineage strategies', pp. 132–5.

136 Mate, *Daughters*, ch. 5.

137 See ch. 7 below, fn. 81, for references.

138 Reyerson, 'Women in business', pp. 133–7.

139 I have used the English translation: Waley (trans.), *Curial and Guelfa*, p. 4.

140 Brereton and Ferrier (eds), *Le ménagier de Paris*, *passim*.

141 Rosenthal, *Patriarchy*, p. 183; Harris, *English aristocratic women*, p. 162; Mate, *Daughters*, pp. 125–6.

142 Goldberg, *Women, work and life cycle*, p. 267, table 5.9; Reyerson, 'Women in business', p. 133.

143 Rosenthal, *Patriarchy*, p. 213; Barron and Sutton (eds), *Medieval London widows*, p. xxv; Harris, *English aristocratic women*, p. 165.

144 'Piera and Rogers, 'The widow as heroine', p. 324; Howell, 'Fixing movables', p. 23; Chojnacki, *Women and men*, p. 100.

145 Klapisch-Zuber, *Women, family and ritual*, pp. 119–27.

146 Brodman, *Charity and welfare*, p. 109.

147 Jacobsen, 'Pregnancy and childbirth', pp. 14–15.

148 Klapisch-Zuber, *Women, family and ritual*, p. 120.

149 Brundage, 'The merry widow's serious sister', pp. 33–4; Goldberg, *Women, work and life cycle*, p. 273.

150 Razi, *Life*, p. 138.

151 Howell, *Land, family and inheritance*, pp. 34, 43. The differing economies and employment opportunities in York and Sussex also demonstrate different remarriage rates at either end of the fifteenth century: Mate, *Daughters*, p. 132; Goldberg, *Women, work and life cycle*, pp. 266–72; Mate, *Women in medieval English society*, pp. 34–6.

152 Klapisch-Zuber, *Women, family and ritual*, p. 120; Goldberg, *Women, work and life cycle*, p. 268. Cf. Desportes, 'La population de Reims', p. 502.

153 Grubb, *Provincial families*, p. 223, table 1.4.

154 Kittell, 'Testaments of two cities', p. 59.

155 Henderson, 'Women, children and poverty', tables 7.2 and 7.5.

156 Bennett, *Women in the medieval English countryside*, p. 105.

157 Karras, *From boys to men*, p. 145.

158 Brucker (ed.), *Two memoirs of Renaissance Florence*, p. 110.

159 Freed, *Noble bondsmen*, p. 162.

160 Phillips, *The memoir of Marco Parenti*, pp. 39–40.

161 Nicholas, *Domestic*, p. 27.

162 Grubb, *Provincial families*, p. 5.

163 Kuehn, *Emancipation*, p. 22.

164 Charles-Edwards, *Early Irish and Welsh kinship*, p. 176.

165 Yarborough, 'Apprentices', p. 75.

166 Chojnacki, *Women and men*, p. 195; Wunder, *He is the sun*, p. 18; Hanawalt, *Growing up*, p. 203.

167 Herlihy, 'Age, property and career', p. 145; Rossiaud, 'Crises et consolidations', p. 510; Guenée, 'L'âge des personnes authentiques', p. 276.

168 Chojnacki, *Women and men*, pp. 12 and 96.

169 Wensky, 'Women's guilds', p. 631.

170 Nicholas, *Domestic*, p. 96.

171 Kittell, 'Testaments of two cities', pp. 65, 74, 79.

172 Mate, *Daughters*, pp. 37–8; Herlihy, *Opera muliebra*, pp. 177–9.

7

Old age

As time marched on, the prime of life came to an end. The body continued to cool and dry out, acquiring a new set of characteristics. The final stages of the life cycle witnessed the ageing of the individual to the point where he or she would be identified as 'old' or 'aged'. Few would populate these later years, although demographic changes in the fourteenth and early fifteenth centuries increased the proportion of older people in the populations of Western Europe.[1] While 'aged' was a common identifier in late medieval literature, there were no clear markers of the move from adulthood to old age equivalent to the modern indicators of official retirement, pensions and bus passes. There was no shared rite of passage similar to puberty for youth or marriage for adulthood that might help identify the old. Nor were there any clubs specifically for the elderly to complement the youth confraternities of Florence or the youngling guilds of England. At times, older people were not recognised at all: unlike children and youth, they did not have a saint of their own. When and by what criteria, therefore, did a person achieve old age?

Chronological age

In twenty-first-century Britain, chronological age has a key role in defining the entry into senior citizenship. Sixty-five is the official age for retirement and pension entitlement. During the later medieval period, 'sixty' achieved some pre-eminence as a synonym for 'old'. The poet Olivier de la Marche (c.1426–1502) used 'sixty' to describe an old woman whose past beauty had turned to ugliness; in Touraine in 1410, a letter of remission described a woman as old because she was over sixty; and in Norfolk, Margery Kempe described her husband 'in gret age passing thre scor 3er'.[2] At the same time, those in their seventies and eighties had completed their Biblical life span and were unquestionably ancient. The Florentine chronicler Dino Campagni described how the knight Rossa della Tosa 'kept God waiting a long time, for he was more than seventy-five years old'.[3] Nevertheless, while showing that sixty was an age that denoted being 'old' and seventy-five 'very old', none of these views is consciously precise; they reflect a symbolic rather than an official old age. Medieval communities did not promote one universal, legal old age. The only official recognitions came in the form of exemptions from war, taxation and religious obligations, which, while normally given on grounds of various incapacities, also included a minimum age requirement. The age varied with the exemption offered. In Tuscany tax exemptions were granted to those over sixty in the city and over seventy in the countryside. In religious communities, such as that of San Paolo in Florence or the Scuola della Misercordia in Venice, members over fifty-five or sixty gained exemptions from physical obligations like fasting and scourging. For service in less arduous public and administrative positions, seventy was the more usual age of exemption. In England, from the thirteenth century, seventy was the maximum age for jury service.[4]

Despite a few favoured ages, therefore, no single one was universally held to demarcate the boundary to old age. Francesco Petrarch referred to the different opinions expressed in fourteenth-century Europe, some of which said forty-six, some fifty and others sixty.[5] These may in part reflect the view that old age was a process that could be sub-divided into stages. A common practice, favoured by writers like Dante, was to divide it into two: an early stage beginning around forty-five to fifty, usually called *senectus*, and a second stage beginning in the sixties or seventies, called either *decrepitude* or *senium*, which lasted until death: a case of a 'young-old' and an 'old-old'.[6] Not only was the onset of old age considered a gradual process, but it affected different people in different ways; it was an 'individual event'. Arnold of Villanova (d.1311) believed the diversity lay in a person's balance of humours, while the poet Eustace Deschamps highlighted the issue of gender, believing that women were old at thirty and men at fifty.[7] Old age was also a highly subjective concept, as Petrarch noted: 'when you feel that you are old, then and no sooner will you declare your old age'.[8] It is therefore not surprising that some people felt old before tax exemptions acknowledged them to be so. The English poet Thomas Hoccleve saw himself aged at fifty-three, and the printer Caxton considered himself old at fifty. Some like Erasmus favoured an earlier old age; he wrote his *On the discomforts of age* (1506) when he was forty. For him, old age replaced youth 'after the seventh five-year span [thirty-five], and that hardly complete'.[9] In other words, once the ascent to adulthood had been achieved, a person was always teetering on the edge of descent. At what point on the roller-coaster of life the acceleration was felt depended on a variety of factors, from the constitution of the individual to the role he or she played in society.

Qualities

While medieval writers employed chronological age markers, they preferred identifying an old person in terms of appearance, or by mental and physical capabilities. Medieval scientific descriptions focused particularly on physical changes. As the body grew colder and drier, the face wrinkled, the bones buckled, teeth and hair fell out – like autumn leaves – and the person approached the winter of life topped with a cap of snowy-white hair. Metaphorically, the candle of life was growing dimmer and the body was quietening down; the pulse began to beat more softly and at a lower frequency.[10] Medical texts explained this ageing process as natural and inevitable; it was not an illness. Symptoms of old age, such as grey hair and breathing difficulties, were only considered diseases when occurring in adolescents.[11] Nevertheless, science did not gloss over the point that this was an irreversible decline, and the words used to describe ageing were laden with negatives. Its initial stage saw the advancement of physical frailty, followed later by mental incapacity as the memory failed and senility set in. In the final stages the old were described as developing all the negative qualities of childhood – limited wit, bodily weakness and loss of control – but with no hope of improvement. In 1390 the lord of Eksaarde (Ghent) was declared too incompetent to manage his estate because 'he was so aged that he was a child and had no control of his senses'.[12]

Later medieval society may have accepted a greater degree of hardship than does the modern Western world, but its literature does not show people happily resigned to the ageing process. The dominant discourse bemoaned and feared the inevitable corruption. Decline in old age was linked to the approach of death. A fifteenth-century English lyric described the experience of old age in lines akin to the well-known signs of death:

> Oure body wol yche, oure bonys wol ake
> Owre owne flesshe wol be oure foo
> Oure hede, oure handys, þan wol shake
> Owre legges wol trymble whan we goo [13]

Confraternities offering burial services in Zamora (Castile) underlined this link by charging the over-sixties the highest fees: they were evidently seen as having little time left to make the necessary donations.[14] Another common theme in literature was farewell to an active life. When in 1460 Jehan Régnier composed a poem for his wife on the effects of old age (he was sixty-eight) he mourned 'the good times past', which would never return. Now he was condemned to suffer a runny nose, no teeth and trembling hands and to seek comfort in the study of astrology.[15] The Spanish bawd Celestina, from Fernando de Rojas's 1499 play of the same name, complained that old age was 'all regrets and grudges, one continuous anguish and incurable sore … it's next-door neighbour to death'. She, as others, shared the sentiments of the old woman in the *Danse Macabre of women* who, while recalling a decade troubled by illness and gout, declared, 'I see nothing good in old age'.[16] Medical texts may not have called old age an illness, but writers like Christine de Pizan still held the opinion that 'there is no worse disease than old age'.[17]

For men, old age attacked their manhood, with its associations of independence, strength and mastery of men and women. Margery Kempe's incapacitated elderly husband had 'turnyd childisch aʒen and lakkyd reson', relinquishing his role as adult and head of the household; he was now a burden. Deschamps was probably not alone in forlornly recounting that 'my penis has become a soft tail, which serves only for passing water'. The impotent old man failing to satisfy his young wife is a common theme of European vernacular literature, featuring in the German poetry of Oswald von Wolkenstein and the Tuscan tales of Boccaccio's *Decameron*.[18] While manhood suffered from the ageing process, it was for women that physical changes gave the clearest indication of advancing age. The menopause, which was theoretically assumed to occur at fifty, marked a turning point in the lives of women, both physically and symbolically.[19] Modern medical knowledge suggests that the decrease in oestrogen, combined with a woman's thinner bone density, would have made her prone to brittle bone disease. Arguably more serious was the medieval medical interpretation of the menopause. The cessation of monthly blood flows not only marked the end of a woman's reproductive capabilities, but seemed to suggest that the woman was now storing up all the poisonous humours she had hitherto expelled. This stigmatisation of the female body contributed to the view of the evil, poisonous old woman, which by the end of the Middle Ages would connect her with sorcery and witchcraft.[20] In Italy and Spain, folklore linking old women with evil was dramatically played out in the custom of sawing in half an effigy of an old woman, which the villagers believed would help ward off death.[21]

The stereotype of the old woman was depicted with a cruelty not witnessed in relation to old men. With a woman's life cycle so closely linked to her appearance and biological function, and the ideal of feminine beauty so much associated with youth, the onset of old age reduced her in the eyes of society. As already mentioned, late medieval society believed that women aged more quickly than men because their youthful appearance faded sooner. Chaucer's January summed up this attitude in *The merchant's tale*, where he wanted to marry no woman of thirty or more as such women were 'old boef'. Boccaccio in his *Il Corbaccio* (*c*.1355) described the sagging body of the old woman with misshapen breasts that droop down to the navel 'empty and wrinkled like a deflated bladder'. A century later in Paris, Villon put an equally unpleasant description of the useless female body in the mouth of the Belle Heaulmière, one of the striking characters of his *Testament*. This once beautiful young woman now describes herself as 'whitehaired ... so poor, so shrivelled, so spare, so lean'. Her forehead is wrinkled, she has a hooked nose, hairy ears, thin lips, crooked shoulders and sagging breasts, and she is covered in liver spots.[22] These are only a few examples of the colourful array of artistic descriptions of the ageing female body found in the later Middle Ages.

The problems were not merely physical, however, and both sexes were vilified on the grounds of their behaviour. A common check-list of the faults deemed 'natural' to the old included greed, inebriation, quick temper, envy and spite. In Giles of Rome's *De regimine principum*, old men are characterised as suspicious, distrusting, fearful and ungenerous; their faults clearly outnumber their positive qualities.[23] These and the numerous literary victims of ageism so far discussed would suggest that the old gained little respect in medieval society. That Christine de Pizan devoted two chapters of her *Treasure of the city of ladies* to discuss how the old and young should treat each other is suggestive. Her passages on 'how young women ought to conduct themselves towards their elders' imply that the young were in the habit of being disrespectful and mocking towards the old. Georges Minois has argued that these attitudes became more acute in the century and a half following the Black Death as the growing prominence of the old in society fuelled resentment. There was certainly a sense of unfairness in the young dying while older people remained alive. Llywelyn ap Gutun (writing in Welsh *c*.1480) sighed at a situation where 'Young men are carried off / God leaves an old man for a long time'.[24] But was old age really so bad?

Someone who dreaded the onset of old age was Petrarch, who stated that 'having embraced fleeting youth, I was clinging to it with great effort'. Nevertheless, he found it not as bad as he had expected: 'I discovered old age to be as fruitful as youth was flowery'. In his letters of old age (written during his late fifties and sixties), Petrarch came to promote the positive qualities of being aged. He argued that the learning process continued into old age, and he cited elderly classical figures who were constantly coming across new things.[25] He was not alone in outlining the positive qualities of old age, and it is important to emphasise that the wise old man (and occasionally woman) was a familiar topos; God (the father) was depicted as an old man. In their works of instruction, both Christine de Pizan and Leon Battista Alberti emphasised the wisdom and experience that comes with age and the lessons the old could teach the young.[26] It had been a major theme of Cicero's *De senectute* ('On old age'), a work which came to enjoy some popularity in France and England in the later Middle Ages. At Caister Castle, Norfolk, William Worcester had translated the book for his ageing master Sir John Fastolf (d.1459), who would have appreciated the view that 'it is in old men that reason and good judgement are found'.[27] A few decades later, in 1480, *De senectute* was published in England by Caxton, whose own preface to the work highlighted Cicero's celebration of the experience and knowledge of old men. This was not the only preface where Caxton tried to appeal to his older readers by flattering their wisdom.[28]

Positive portrayals of the elderly body can also be found. A case in point is the 'olde auncyen man of a hunthrid wintre' in the fourteenth-century English poem *Mum and the sothsegger*. This wise man had a 'faire visaige' and was virtuous, comely, well-proportioned, and with a strong body, although it is fair to say that his vigorous nature is described as 'good for his age'.[29] More significantly, Walter Bower wrote a flattering description of the Scottish king Robert II (d. 1406) in his *Scotichronicon* – the chronicles of the Scots – composed in 1440. The king was described as having 'a very handsome face with a luxuriant beard; he had the attractiveness of a snowy white old age, with lively eyes which always spread good humour, and rather long and ruddy cheeks blooming with every mark of handsome amiability'. While one might have expected Bower to praise the king, it is noteworthy that he used the very distinctive features of old age to underpin the king's good qualities.[30]

Nor was old age always compared negatively to youth. Petrarch believed that trust was a characteristic of mature years, not the 'fickle' young.[31] Rather than regretting youth's passing, an individual should be pleased to leave adolescent vices behind. In particular, old age ushered in the opportunity to attain knowledge, repent and counsel others. The Scottish poet Robert Henryson wrote in his 'In praise of age' that he would not want to be young again, as 'the more of age, the nerar hevynnis blis'.[32] Advice offered to the old invariably stressed detachment from the world, meditation on the Scriptures and preparation for death. There should be little distraction: medical authorities linked the cooling of the body with the waning of sexual desire. Marsilio Ficino in his *Book of life* commented how 'With Saturn, the old finally escape from the Venusy stuff that takes away so much of the life of youths'.[33] To religious authorities, this was a positive development as it marked a new opportunity for spiritual renewal: the body could no longer be mastered, but it no longer proved a distraction. In other words, old age was an age of relief. In his *Convivio* Dante eschews the negative descriptions of the ageing man and poetically describes a peaceful ending, comparing the old man to an ancient mariner who is gently lowering his sails on seeing the land ahead, and is slowly coming into harbour.[34]

Yet the reality, as Petrarch found, did not always match the image. He believed that he should be capable of overcoming the erotic impulses he had experienced as a young man, and looked forward to an old age free of lust. But in his *Secretum* he admitted that, so far, he had failed to suppress sexual feelings.[35] He was not alone in suffering this crisis, and society was not kind to the old who fell victim to an adolescent quality, even when they were kings. When Edward III of England fell for Alice Perrers, chroniclers commented on how he had succumbed to a weakness more common to youths, and that it was a disease with which old men (having less heat) had greater difficulty in curing.[36] As Chapter 6 indicated, it was not uncommon, particularly in southern Europe, for a husband to be considerably older than his wife. The marriage of an old man to a young woman could face opposition from young men, who used the rowdy *charivari* to show their grievance at the removal of yet another young woman from the pool of possible brides. In literature the lusty old man became a stock figure of fun. Chaucer's January is a man over sixty when he marries the teenage May. January's lustfulness is caricatured to emphasise the ridiculous behaviour of an ageing man whose scrawny neck wobbles while he tries to make love. It is yet another example to show that acting out of line with one's age group often brought more condemnation than did its natural faults. Women too received their greatest criticisms in pretending to be younger than their age. John Bromyard was only one of a number of writers who criticised 'ancient hags' who 'paint and deck themselves as fair young maidens'.[37] In other words men should not *act* as though younger than they were; women should not try to *look* younger. Medieval society did not appreciate individuals growing old disgracefully.

As with other age groups, a measure of ambiguity is found in medieval attitudes towards the aged. On the one hand, negative images of the old predominate in late medieval literature. Being old could not compete with the prime of life. Manhood meant strength, power and the ability to help others; being elderly meant physical weakness, focusing on oneself and approaching death. Nevertheless, much of the surviving literary evidence comes from poetry and romance tales where an old character is introduced precisely to play a stereotype, to illustrate the passage of time, and to remind people of their mortality. Images could be equivocal. Chaucer's Reeve might be described as lean, mean and choleric, but his actions show him to be wise and wealthy. Criticism and praise were often two sides of the same coin, as the old could instruct the young with words of wisdom, while physically reminding them of the decay to come. More positively, Cicero's benign picture of old age was still believed to have currency on fifteenth-century society. How the old themselves acted or were treated in relation to these images is the subject of the next sections.

Work

With the introduction of state pensions in the twentieth-century Britain, old age became associated with retirement, and a clear distinction is drawn between the working, active young and the inactive old. As shown above, images in the later Middle Ages linked the old to incapacity, but were they similarly considered inactive? This appears to have been far from the case, and work continued to define a person as the years advanced. Among the aristocracy, men held official positions late in life. Joel Rosenthal's study of 267 English peers active in 1351–1451 indicates that twenty-seven per cent were at least sixty, with ten per cent over seventy. Nor did age necessarily force noblemen out of demanding, physical roles. Despite the literary image of the youthful knight, older men continued to be militarily active. John Talbot was captain of the fleet and lieutenant in Aquitaine at sixty-four and was shot through the heart at sixty-five while leading an attack on the French in 1453; John Hawkwood, the famous *condottiere*, was still taking part in tournaments in Bologna in 1392 when he was seventy-two; and the Duke of Norfolk died fighting at Bosworth Field in 1485, aged seventy-five.[38]

Away from the battlefield, both male and female landholders could retain a central role in old age. In southern Europe, an ageing parent held on to the position of head of the household for as long as possible, perhaps presiding over a property that had grown in size and wealth over the years. A similar situation is found lower down in society: the Florentine *catasto* of 1427 suggests that very few peasants retired and passed their holdings on to their sons; they even appear to have become richer as they grew older.[39] In peasant communities in general, security in old age relied on labouring late in life. Coroners' rolls of fourteenth-century England reveal that numerous individuals described as 'old' were active at the time of their death. Accidents occurred while elderly women were collecting fruit, climbing up ladders to get straw, getting water from wells or gleaning at harvest. Much of this work was similar to the tasks assigned to children, and there may well have been a reallocation of responsibilities as a person aged. This appears to have been the case for former servants in Venice: unable to perform the necessary hard labour, they scraped a living by selling food-stuffs, washing and keeping vigil over corpses, and selling candles.[40] For good or ill, there was no sense that the able-bodied old were exempt from working.

More positively, longevity could bring men to the pinnacle of their careers. This was especially so for merchants or professionals whose business and wealth rested on years of experience. The well-known Prato merchant Francesco Datini (b.1335) expanded his business after the age of fifty and built up companies in Prato, Florence, Pisa, Genoa, Barcelona, Valencia and Majorca. In Périgueux men over sixty were among the most influential of the area. Hélie Bernabé became a goldsmith in 1323 at twenty-five and continued to work and fulfil his civic duties until his nineties. His son Arnaud was also long-lived (dying in 1436 at about ninety) and continued his civic duties into his seventies and eighties: between 1387 and 1420 he was elected mayor ten times.[41] Nor did age prevent artistic endeavours, although they might require spectacles: Charles d'Orléans relied on his 'lunectes' to magnify the words he was reading. A number of Welsh poets wrote late into their lives, their old age reflected in their verse. Iolo Goch (*c.*1320–*c.*1398) wrote of his need for a horse when his advancing years made it difficult for him to walk and was grateful to the patron who provided it. Moreover, the writers of Western Europe's history and chronicles were overwhelmingly men over fifty.[42]

For certain positions, the wisdom that came with age brought new opportunities. The Church favoured age because of the supposed spiritual and moral maturity that came with it. Of 672 English chantry priests in the early sixteenth century studied by Kathleen Wood-Legh, twenty-eight per cent were over sixty.[43] The age preference was led from the top. The average age of popes elected between 1415 and 1550 was fifty-four. They included Pope John XXII, who was elected in 1316 at seventy-two and died when he was ninety.[44] It was in Venice, however, that the value placed on old age resulted in what Robert Finlay has described as rule by a gerontocracy. In the second half of the fourteenth century the Venetian Republic was governed by the *vecchi*, or old men, headed by the doge; during 1400–1600 the average age of the doges at election was seventy-two. The highest offices were closed to younger men. A patrician could only enter the Council of Ten, the special commission for state security, at forty, but it was rare for election to occur before fifty. Domenico Morosini 'the wise', for example, entered politics in 1472 at fifty-five after a career as a merchant. He remained active for the next thirty-seven years, becoming the city's oldest patrician in 1507 at the age of eighty-nine and attending the senate until his death in 1509. Politically, therefore, one could be young in Venice at fifty, and some intergenerational tension arose from the age distribution. In 1500 Antonio Grimani requested that his trial for incompetence be moved from the Great Council to the senate because he wanted to be judged by elders rather than youngsters, though the latter were only young by Venetian standards.[45]

Wisdom and experience also brought new responsibilities to the less wealthy elderly of Europe's towns and villages. The emphasis placed on oral testimonies made the more mature useful in a range of court cases. Often drawing on memories implanted in childhood, the aged were principal witnesses in cases relating to land disputes, proofs of age, local customs and canonisation of saints.[46] It is clear that in practice the elderly were not hampered by the popular image of failing mental faculties. While older women were not usually called to be witnesses in these instances, there were several new roles open to them, albeit ones with little or no prestige. On the streets of Paris and in many literary pages, old women appear to have been favoured as go-betweens.[47] As 'wise women' they were called upon in medical cases where a physical examination of the body was required. This might be to ascertain whether a young woman had recently given birth and was the mother of an abandoned baby; or if a woman condemned to execution was pregnant; or whether a man had rightly been accused of impotence. The ageing body of the old woman, so often vilified for the perceived loss of sexual attraction, could be seen as an advantage in certain circumstances. She could become a housekeeper or guardian of a young bride, the nurse of young male children, or a carer in a local hospital. At St Giles's hospital, Norwich, it was stipulated that the four nursing sisters were to be aged around fifty on appointment. This may have been to ensure that the women would not distract the priests with thoughts of lust. Another possibility is that the hospital was influenced by the medical view that menstruating women were a danger to the sick and could contaminate the Eucharist. With fifty being the commonly assumed age for the menopause, these older women would have lost that particular stigma. On the other hand, there were more positive reasons for choosing older women: they were valued for their greater experience, reliability, knowledge and commitment. Experience was required for the nurses of the Hôtel Dieu, Paris, where senior positions were given only to those who had already worked for thirty to forty years.[48] Nursing the sick and undertaking the hospital's spiritual and charitable obligations demanded women capable of hard manual labour: again the image of the weak old woman is undermined by the practice. As care-givers, they also reversed the more common picture of the elderly as recipients of care. In these ways older women may well have gained some authority and regard. It is their ability to earn respect that has led Emmanuel Le Roy Ladurie to argue that it was better to be an old woman than an old man in fourteenth-century Montaillou.[49]

Medieval society assumed that people would carry on working for as long as they could, often in the jobs that had defined their adult lives. Reaching sixty or sixty-five was not necessarily a milestone in a working career. While such people might look old and might well be considered in decline in other areas of their life, they were not defined by inactivity and continued to participate in the labour market. For some older members of society, particularly those working in areas demanding tough physical labour, there was probably a move to lighter work to reflect growing weaknesses. What difference this shift made is difficult to assess; a loss of income or status had to be weighed up against less painful work. Many may have reached the same conclusion as the ageing Giannozzo in the Alberti household: exhausted after his busy day, he admitted that 'I just can't do as much as I used to'.[50] Meanwhile others retained their hold on the power they had gained in adulthood, and a few even increased their influence and gained new decision-making authority.

'Retirement'

If medieval men and women carried on working late into their lives, was there no role for 'retirement'? Was anyone compelled or did anyone request to leave their work and active life because he or she was perceived or perceived herself or himself to be too old? On the issue of compulsion, certain occupations were vulnerable to enforced retirement on the grounds of being too old for the job. Between 1429 and 1435 some twenty-five coroners in England were forced to leave their positions because they were 'too sick and aged'.[51] Disqualification on the grounds of age was rare, but in Lucca people over fifty-five were barred from election to public office.[52] Some individual employers also retired personnel when age began to affect their work. In the late 1470s King Louis XI of France gave several unsuccessful hints to the Count of Dammartin – in his seventies – that he might want to withdraw from his position in command of the lances. In the end the king had to remove him, tactfully stating that it was 'in order to give you relief and comfort'.[53] In general, however, no government, institution or employer operated a fixed-age retirement policy in the Middle Ages. There appears to have been neither the money nor the inclination to make it law; employers wanted to keep as many people as possible working, for as long as possible. The only concession to old age at a legislative level was in the form of an exemption from certain responsibilities. For example, an English statute of 1503 exempted men of sixty and over from 'fighting in the king's wars', while in Venice and Pisa, citizens over seventy were excused from sitting on certain councils, taking up particular posts and acting as ambassadors abroad.[54]

On the whole, the majority of known retirements appear to have been requested by the retirees themselves and negotiated with their employers. The research of Joel Rosenthal has produced a number of case studies illustrating what he sees as the widespread, though limited, use of retirement in England's late medieval population.[55] In the House of Lords in the late fourteenth and early fifteenth centuries, thirty peers were given permission to excuse themselves, two-thirds of them claiming age-related problems. Bishop Heyworth (d.1447), for example, was excused in 1439 'by reason of his age and infirmities'. Some of these were temporary absences, the result of health problems due to old age that would later improve; other people were clearly close to death. William Booth, who received a life exemption in August 1464, was dead by the end of September. What needs to be stressed is that none of the withdrawals was automatically conceded when a specific age was reached. Those who gained exemption were either being rewarded for past services or had cited an age-related disability; being old was insufficient in itself. The story is similar elsewhere, with many experiencing difficulty in securing their exemption. In London, men claiming to be over seventy and asking for exemption from jury service faced stringent checks, and grants were issued mainly because of disabilities arising from old age: deafness, sciatica and general ill-health. Some urban authorities dragged their feet over retirement, especially during periods of labour shortage. York aldermen in the fifteenth century, who were elected in their mid-forties and were to remain until death, had to make several requests in seeking to get their claims accepted. Other officials in York had to pay for the privilege. In 1476 William Warde, draper, paid £10 to secure his exemption from office holding on account of his 'grete age and sekenisse'.[56]

Another type of retirement operated at the peasant level. With their livelihood dependent on manual labour, peasants had particular worries about the physical problems of old age. There would come a point when they would no longer be able to feed themselves or fulfil the obligations set by the lord of their holding. One option was to release control of the property to offspring, who would then become head of the household. Such complete devolution of power was a risk, and sermons, proverbs and folklore relentlessly warned of the possible repercussions. One popular European-wide tale described a father who had relinquished his property to his son and then lived with him and his daughter-in-law. The son began to resent his father, wishing his death, and gradually the old man was moved out of the house and into a cold porch. One day the old man asked his grandson to fetch a blanket. On hearing of the request, the old man's son merely offered a rough sack, whereupon the grandson told him to cut the sack in half: one part he would give to his grandfather and the other half would be saved for his father. Relinquishing power had marginalised the old man and made him a burden. It was far from a fiction. The village of Montaillou offers pathetic examples of old men dependent on their children, mainly their sons, who had now become masters of the household. One old father could not lend his daughter a mule without first asking his son's permission.[57]

An alternative was a more 'conditional devolution' whereby a person handed over the use and management of land in return for a life-long allowance of food, clothing and shelter, and sometimes of cash. Such arrangements might be forced on an elderly, unproductive individual by a lord, a family or the community, but the majority appear to have been arranged by the elderly themselves.[58] While many of these retirements were informal arrangements not troubling the historical record, a number of official maintenance agreements were written in north-western Europe and can be found in Anjou, the Limousin and towns like Reims.[59] A wealth of evidence is available for England because the contracts were enrolled at the manor courts. A typical example is one from 1411 in which William Swift of Walsham-le-Willows (Suffolk) surrendered to his son,

John, twenty acres of land, meadow and pasture. In return John was to ensure that his parents had lodgings, food and clothing for the rest of their lives, along with an annual livery of eight bushels of wheat and malt. Finally, on the death of each parent, John was to pay for thirty requiem masses and pay his parents' executors 7s.[60]

Elaine Clark sees the contracts reflecting a 'hard, individual bargaining' on the part of the elderly, who were determined to have their own needs met. While it is the case that many of the contracts mention impotency or incompetence as reasons for the retirement, early fifteenth-century East Anglian contracts show that the retirees were far from incapacitated or eager to give up their independence. Joan Pekke, a widow from South Elmham, Suffolk, asked for two rooms in the house now held by her son, to which she wanted 'free entry and exit for herself and her friends for life'. William Notte of Wymondham wanted a horse, saddle and bridle so that he could ride whenever he pleased.[61] By the law and custom of the manors, the elderly also had some protection against abuse of contracts: they expected the manor courts to expel the offspring who failed to abide by the contract. In 1327 at Great Waltham, Essex, Estrilda Nenour came to court, telling of a contract she had made with her daughter Agnes. Estrilda had transferred her holding to her daughter on condition that Agnes provide her with accommodation, food and clothing. However, Agnes and her husband had defaulted on the agreement. The court, in upholding Estrilda's claim, granted her 6s 8d in compensation; Estrilda subsequently made a new contract with another, unrelated, couple.[62]

During the later Middle Ages, therefore, securing retirement was an individual matter. It depended on financial circumstances, occupation, health and personal relationships. These factors would further influence the quality of retired life. For some, it was simply a matter of awaiting death, as in the case of William Booth mentioned above. It is unlikely that many considered that the interval between the end of work and death would be long; few would have considered saving money for it.[63] Those with financial security might have the opportunity to enjoy their leisure time. The successful *condottiere* Bartolomeo Colleone hung up his spurs at sixty-seven and spent the last eight years of his life at his castle of Malaga, refusing the countless job offers that came his way, and spending his time hunting and setting up an irrigation system. English peasants with sufficient resources planted gardens, kept bees or went fishing.[64]

Yet the quality of life did not simply depend on resources. For the first time in their adult lives, men might have to endure a position of enforced dependency and loss of status: they might no longer be heads of households nor be able to perform a full political role in their community. These possibilities were less likely to be a novelty for women, whose adult lives had been marked by dependency and who had rarely been defined by their employment and public roles. What may have been a greater worry for them was that old age could be a lonely experience. In contrast to youth, the old and especially old women appearing in literature – like Celestina – are single figures, never forming part of a group. As discussed in the previous chapter, a significant proportion of women at all levels in Western Europe were widows. Nearly half of the retirement contracts secured by peasants in fourteenth-century East Anglia were made by single, old women. It is noteworthy that following the demographic crisis of the mid-fourteenth century contracts were more often negotiated with non-family members. Clark's study of fourteenth-century East Anglia shows that before 1350 about half of the people concerned negotiated contracts with their children, but after 1350 the proportion was less than a quarter. Richard Smith's broader study of arrangements made in the south-east of England, East Anglia and the south-east midlands shows similar results. Before 1348 nearly two-thirds of contracts involved kin; after 1350 well over two-thirds of contracts were arranged with unrelated parties.[65] Death may have carried off sons and daughters, but the opportunities opened up by the Black Death may have been another explanation. At a time of land availability, low rent and high wages, young people had the opportunity to leave their family home and make their own way in life, perhaps taking up a retirement contract on a non-family holding.[66] Some retirement contracts with offspring may have been an attempt to keep sons at home. Opportunistic young people on the look-out for property and a means to establish themselves may not have been particularly worried about the state of the incumbent's health.[67]

Old age for these northern Europeans could therefore be experienced outside the family group. For few did the decision to retire mean spending more time with the grandchildren. The research of Rosenthal and Orme argues against the development of a strong affectionate bond between grandparent and grandchild in late medieval England. Grandchildren were rarely mentioned in wills and were not showered with gifts. In literature, grandmothers are characterised as resenting their daughters-in-law and as hostile to the grandchildren.[68] Nevertheless, it is significant that a more positive picture of grandparent–grandchild relations is found in southern France and Italy, where retirement was less common at all levels of society. In the Languedoc, among the extended family groups that had sprung up in the years following the Black Death, 'grandfather's bed was sacred, as was his ration of food'.[69] In Florence, Alberti wrote of the joy and comfort that small children brought to 'the old people of the family'; Cosimo de Medici (d.1464) interrupted a business meeting with ambassadors from Lucca to play the bagpipe with one of his grandsons.[70] Friendships and company, rather than resources, may have had the greater impact on the life of the old. The three matriarchs who dominate Le Roy Ladurie's account of the village of Montaillou clearly had a long-lasting friendship, spending their time visiting each other, taking in the sun together and coming to each other's aid.

The discussion so far has considered retirement in relation to the elderly remaining within their own homes. For those with status and money, an alternative was to withdraw entirely from mainstream society and enter a monastery or hospital. Here solitude was a choice, while there were still opportunities for communal activity. Christine de Pizan, for example, after a public literary career that lasted over a quarter of a century, withdrew to a nunnery at the age of fifty-four. For more middling sections of society, one way to gain such security was with a corrody, which gave a person residence in a religious house or hospital in return for a gift of money or land. The beneficiary of the corrody (the corrodian) would receive shelter, food, drink, clothing and sometimes small amounts of cash. This practice was widespread in late medieval England and was used to reward those suffering age-related poverty and physical debility. Of thirty corrodies granted by the archbishops of Canterbury between 1313 and 1414 fourteen were for those designated as old, twelve for reasons of poverty, three for blindness and one for leprosy. Philip de Milton was given a corrody in the mid-fourteenth century because of his faithful service to the archbishop and his 'declining into the feebleness of old age'. He was to enter the hospital of Sts Peter and Paul, Maidstone, Kent, where he would receive the same food and drink ration as the brothers of the hospital.[71] Patrons and business associates of religious houses sometimes chose to retire their servants, or themselves, to a favourite house. King Edward III of England, for example, sent a number of retired servants to Durham Priory. In Venice, founders of hospitals often demanded space for faithful employees who could no longer work. The monastic communities also looked after their own, providing for friends and retired servants. Chaplains and wardens of hospitals in Bury St Edmunds could expect a place in the hospitals when old age and sickness prevented them from carrying on their work.[72] Many other corrodies were bought by individuals for themselves. The corrodians of St Giles hospital, Norwich, had either purchased their accommodation outright or made a personal contribution to the hospital. Places were not cheap, ranging in price from £3 to £40, which secured spacious, private living quarters.[73] Impressive fees are found elsewhere. One woman purchased a corrody from Winchcombe Abbey in 1317 for over £98. In return she was to receive daily two monk's loaves, a small white loaf and two gallons of ale, together with an annual allowance of six pigs, two oxen, twelve cheeses, 100 stockfish, 1,000 herrings and 24s of cloth. It is presumed that she must have had servants with her, which would suggest that even while 'withdrawing' from society, she had not given up the good things of life.[74]

It is examples such as these that have fuelled criticism of corrodies. Reformers berated inmates who had paid for their places and were refusing to follow hospital regulations such as praying for the soul of the founder or interacting with the poorer brethren. Monks were criticised for giving food to corrodians that should have gone to the poor. In Carole Rawcliffe's words, 'charges of greed, short-term opportunism and exploitation abounded'.[75] Wealth drove the poor from hospital beds in fourteenth- and fifteenth-century Germany and the Low Countries too, where townspeople bought life annuities that guaranteed a hospital place in their old age. In Lübeck and Gosslar (Germany), the sick were virtually excluded from hospitals as their beds were taken by the wealthy old, who turned these charitable institutions into retirement homes. Wealth brought choice: in the hospice of Mondon (in the Pays of Vaud in France) one woman requested a room with a view of the lake.[76] Some establishments, like St Jan's hospital in Bruges, became widely known for their rooms for prosperous pensioners who had made generous donations to the hospital. Nevertheless, securing places in hospitals or monasteries did enable victims of life-cycle infirmity to gain security when they could no longer work or fend for themselves. Those who were able to do so could help with the sick and assist with the general running of the community. In this way they remained active and retained a sense of usefulness.

Care and well-being

So far, this chapter has shown that the elderly in medieval society were stereotyped as physically weak, and exemptions from war and administrative responsibilities imply that some old people were given age-related assistance. David Herlihy has also argued that Florentines associated the elderly with 'want and deprivation', and studies have shown that the old formed a significant percentage of medieval England's rural poor. As a result, we might expect to see evidence of official or charitable aid for the aged. But medieval society did not see the old as a social category that should be automatically included among the lists of the needy and provided with regular care and assistance. Widows, orphans, the sick, the poor and the disabled appear to have been the main concerns of the Church, with charitable donations more likely to go to young women needing dowries than to the old. Hospital, guild and almshouse regulations did not consistently single out the old as a specific group in need. Nor do the aged feature in testamentary charity. When the old received help and resources it was usually because – as with the case of retirement – they fell into other categories, such as becoming poor or disabled, and had no one to look after them. Even when help was given, there were no resources, nor any interest from official bodies, to assist the aged in improving their quality of life.[77]

There were no state pensions or universal work benefits in medieval Europe. Those who received pensions belonged to specific employment groups. By the fifteenth century a priest who wished to retire could give up his benefice and receive part of its income as a pension. It was not an automatic right, nor was the pension fixed, but was a matter of negotiation between the outgoing cleric and the new. Nevertheless, Nicholas Orme estimates that around three-quarters of retired clergy in England between 1404 and 1540 gained enough to support themselves; the ideal pension was usually considered to be one-third of the benefice's income. Those unable to make such agreements were those attached to poorer benefices, who would have had to survive below a subsistence level of £4.[78] Local governing bodies sometimes rewarded groups that they felt deserved special benefits. A decree of the Grand Council of Venice in 1362 stated that the proceeds of a brokerage tax on pepper should be conferred on native Venetian marines aged sixty and over because of their old age and incapacity. Guilds in Venice also provided some social insurance for ageing workers in the city's shipbuilding business.[79]

For those requiring physical care, there were few options available. No European central or civic government had a social policy, as is understood by that term in twenty-first century society. The only institutional care was provided by Europe's hospitals and almshouses. As noted above, beds were available for those with resources or a powerful patron, but others were admitted because they had become destitute. The hospital of St Paul's, Norwich, had revenue to maintain fourteen poor men and women who were 'decrepit with age, or languished under incurable diseases'. A few were fortunate because of the work they did. The hospital of Gesù Cristo di Sant'Antonio in Venice was founded specifically for ancient mariners and ex-servicemen; in 1351, Jean le Bon established a retirement home for old knights of the chivalric Order of the Star; and God's House at Ospringe, Kent, was a retirement home for royal servants. Personal standing and moral character mattered. In the late fifteenth century, St Jacob's hospital was founded in Leeuwarden (Netherlands) for 'respectable burghers who are old, ill and impoverished'. For women the key factor was marital status, and they received some attention as widows: a limited number of places were available at Ave Maria College (Paris) and the Orbatello (Florence), while Plumtree's hospital (Nottingham) was specifically meant for poor, elderly widows.[80]

Significantly, all these institutions were founded in the fourteenth and fifteenth centuries, and there is some evidence to suggest that the elderly benefited as late medieval charity became more interested in age-related problems. It should be recalled that it was during this period that foundling hospitals for the under-sevens began to appear. The information is more ambiguous for the elderly, but the following examples may be noted. The Orsanmichele in Florence appears to have changed from its focus on labourers and the unemployed before the Black Death to a post-plague emphasis on widows, orphans and the old. By John Henderson's calculation, only two per cent of men provided with help in 1324–25 had been described as old, yet in 1356 the proportion was over seventeen per cent. By the fifteenth century a number of English almshouses were setting minimum age limits in their statutes, such as that at Higham Ferrers (founded 1423), which stipulated fifty. At the same time some of England's lazar houses were given over to the aged. Such trends were regional. In Iberia and Catalonia there appears little evidence of specific shelters being provided for the old, and the elderly remained dispersed through the hospital system. It is also the case that the numbers cared for in Europe's religious institutions were always small, and while the wealthy and privileged servicemen may have entered hospital while capable of doing some labour, the poorer of society appear to have been admitted only when they became categorised as incapacitated.[81]

For an indeterminate number of the aged, begging provided the only means of support. How much help they received is impossible to assess. In the late fourteenth century a growing distinction was made between the undeserving and the deserving poor. In 1351 a royal ordinance in France recommended that preachers urge people not to give charity to the able-bodied, but only to those who were 'deformed, blind, impotent or to other miserable people'. The old may well have qualified on these grounds, but not by age alone and not if they could work. What might have come to their assistance was the likelihood that the old would not be characterised as lazy and dangerous. As a result, they were usually exempt from laws ordering landless people to accept any work offered to them on pain of imprisonment. In 1351 King Pedro I ordered the people in his kingdom of Murcia (south-eastern Spain) to accept any work, but made exceptions for the sick, the disabled, children under twelve and the 'very old'.[82]

The lack of formal care in the Middle Ages was based largely on the assumption that care began and remained at home. Wives were expected to look after elderly or infirm husbands, husbands provided for wives in their wills, and ultimately welfare depended on the kindness of children (of whatever age they might be). Writing in Florence, Alberti believed that a father should love his children and in return obtain 'a kind of fortress in his old age and a refuge in the weary and feeble years'.[83] Such attitudes were enshrined in the Biblical commandment 'honour thy father and mother', which extended to caring for them when they were sick or old. In Italy some communes made neglecting an elderly parent a punishable offence.[84] As this suggests, the young were not always full of goodwill, and the retirement contracts discussed earlier suggest that they could not always be relied upon to help, or to honour their parents' wishes. For Christine de Pizan, sons were particularly blameworthy in this respect, and one reason why she thought parents should welcome daughters was that they were more likely to care for parents in their old age.[85] Society's main answer to the problem was simply to urge offspring to be more responsible and to issue dire warnings of the consequences of failure to do so. According to one English writer, the reason why plague attacked children more than any other age group was that the young had failed in their duties towards their parents.[86] An alternative piece of advice was to recommend that people prepare for their old age early on. Didactic texts urged people to save money for old age or at least spend moderately. Popular tales like *The romance of the rose* show elderly characters bemoaning their profligate youth that has left them penniless.[87]

Preparations for old age did not simply rest with financial security. Keeping good health (and thereby the ability to work) was a subject upon which medieval society had various opinions. Philosophical discussions on the origins and treatment of old age appear in numerous medical compendia based on Greek and Arabic philosophical texts. A more recent influence was a short work on preserving youth and delaying old age written by Roger Bacon in 1239. It became better known through the borrowings made by Arnold of Villanova (d.1311), a Catalan doctor, philosopher and professor at Montpellier, whose contemporaries at the universities of Montpellier and Padua discussed various questions linked to senescence and the ageing process. A more practical response was the writing of regimens of health, which offered commentaries on diet, fresh air, sleep and exercise. Examples include the personal regimens written for the French king Philip IV (c.1335) and for the Czech king Wenceslaus IV (d.1419).[88] At the end of the fifteenth century works devoted exclusively to the care of the aged, which moved beyond issues of ill-health to providing general advice on improving the quality of life, also began to appear.[89] In chronological order they are: *Liber de vita producenda sive longa* ('The book of life'), written in 1489 by Marsilio Ficino (1433–1499), the humanist physician to the Medici; the *Gerontocomia*, printed in 1489 and written by Gabriele Zerbi (1445–1505), physician and professor of medicine at the university of Padua; and *De senectute conservanda* ('On the preservation of old age') written in 1500 by Burchard Hornecke, physician to Emperor Frederick III.[90] Their production followed the more *ad hoc* regimens produced for particular persons of wealthy means. Zerbi's text was for the fifty-seven-year-old Pope Innocent VIII (1432–1492) and Hornecke's for Archbishop Lorenz of Würzburg. The eliteness of their audience is underlined by their use of Latin. For Ficino at least, his book was unashamedly for 'men who are prudent and temperate. For men of intelligence who are useful either privately or publicly to the human race'. He was emphatically not directing his work at dullards, the lazy, pleasure seekers or immoral or evil people.[91] These clearly had no purpose in living to old age. Hornecke seems to have been less discriminating; he stated that his reason for writing was that 'I may relieve man, if not from all – for this cannot be done by nature – then at least from some discomforts and grave miseries of old age'.[92] The word 'man' may well have been exclusive. Zerbi supported his lack of interest in women by citing Aristotle, who argued that women were merely deformed, weaker men. All the writers appear to have come to the subject in their advancing years: Hornecke was in his late sixties and Ficino was fifty-six. Both were evidently suffering the effects of ageing. As Charles Boer has explained, Ficino wrote to Pico della Mirandola stating how in writing the book 'he was not thinking so much about how to retard the onset of his own old age, but merely to hold on to what he had left'.[93]

With no advances in geriatric medicine in the Middle Ages, most texts focused on preventative measures, offering support rather than cure for age-related illnesses. Lying behind the advice was the view (discussed in Chapter 2) that ageing was the result of the body's natural cooling, drying and wasting. This process explained age-related problems like asthma, spinal deformities, dementia and baldness, and made the aged body unable to cope with the more drastic medical treatments like bleeding. Improving health and extending life were considered possible with a diet and life style that focused on restoring the body's vital qualities and avoiding any unnecessary loss. All texts therefore emphasised moderation, which was also in keeping with cultural ideas of the respectable old. Any excessive behaviour was ruled out, including drunkenness, extreme emotions (like anger) and too much sleep. Immoderate sex was particularly discouraged as an exertion that would lead to the loss of vital fluid. Advice extended to the general environment, with suggestions about places to live where the air was neither too damp nor cold: a spot, said Ficino, where one could get the mid-day sun. The old needed to wear more clothes than the young, and to have their bodies stimulated with gentle exercise or massaged to keep them supple. Mental stimulation was equally required with an emphasis placed on bright colours, sweet fragrances, puzzle-solving and stimulating conversation. The comparison with the upbringing of children is marked. By far the greatest attention was given to food and drink, which were to be taken little and often. Wine was a clear favourite because it was believed to rejuvenate the heart, aid sleep and digestion, and bring warmth to the old body. Long lists of appropriate foods were suggested, and special combinations were offered that would delay the onset of grey hair and wrinkles. Zerbi suggested washing the hair in fresh water mixed with herbs such as bitter apple, or cucumber, nutmeg flower, borax and the bile of a bull.[94]

Other recommendations offered new injections of manliness and youthfulness. The powers of snake flesh were praised as the viper was said to give power and force (*vi*) back to man (*vir*). Body heat and fluids could be replaced with the help of the young. Zerbi suggested that old men keep 'in constant embrace a girl who is close to menarche' because her youthful warmth would cure both indigestion and insomnia. Ficino, on the other hand, believed the ageing human should be invigorated with 'youthful fluid', either a young girl's milk or the blood of a willing adolescent. Pope Innocent VIII (d.1492) did not, apparently, find such proposals obnoxious and is said to have downed the blood of three boys for rejuvenation.[95] Such practices may give an impression of an ignorant, barbaric Middle Ages. Yet there is an underlying logic here, and, while the method of taking the blood is alien to the modern world, the theory of blood transfusion is relatively close. These examples further reflect the medieval cult of youth. While death could not be cheated, there was a strong and ambitious desire not only to delay the ageing process, but to reverse it. Recipes for miracle drugs circulated, such as the 'quinte essence' or 'man's heaven', which was believed to restore strength to feeble men and preserve the body.[96] Classical romances and legends, such as the popular *Alexandreid* and *Mandeville's travels*, told of magic lakes and fountains that restored youth and beauty. Pilgrims' accounts and guides to the Holy Land pointed out these waters; in 1512 Ponce de León even organised an expedition to discover the springs of youth. Such was society's concerns about the ageing process that the Church propagated the belief that a person would not age on the days on which he or she heard Mass. Yet it is important to note that while longevity was desired, it was to be experienced in health and not in an enfeebled state. Literary characters like the old man in Chaucer's *Pardoner's tale* preferred to die rather than endure a long life suffering the effects of an old body.[97]

Conclusion

With old age, the wheel of life had taken a downward turn. Surviving literature suggests that it was rarely greeted with pleasure in medieval Europe and there was a desire to delay its onset. Compared with other stages of the life cycle there appeared less to celebrate in achieving old age. There were none of the positive attributes of youth – supple body, quick reactions, beauty – nor the strength and social power of adulthood. Whereas childhood and youth were characterised by the acquisition of new skills and being permitted to use them, old age was perceived as the gradual process of relinquishing particular activities – sex, work, power – and becoming more contemplative. It was as they lost independence and the ability to care for themselves and others that the aged lost their status as full adults. The numerous elderly characters that people medieval European literature are often unsightly; they are there to be pitied or ridiculed or to serve as a foil for younger and more central characters. This image and age discrimination appear to cut across geography, class and gender. Older peasants and women suffered more literary cruelty than did knights and men, but age had a greater role to play in distinguishing a person than it did during adulthood; to be 'old' could define all of them. Attitudes, of course, were not all negative, and the elderly were considered wise and knowledgeable, particularly when imparting moral advice. Nevertheless, the image of the respectable, sedentary old person whose thoughts were on the soul might serve to circumscribe behaviour.

The realities of advanced age could be debilitating. This was a period before the advent of dentures and successful medicines and ointments to sooth age-related problems, and few below the elite owned spectacles. For those afflicted with age-related illnesses, formal care was scarce, and medieval society little considered the aged as a social group in need of help. Unlike children, whose young age prompted society to help them in various ways, those achieving more advanced years did not automatically qualify for assistance. Changes in late medieval society did see the introduction of more 'age-conscious' care in the hospitals. Nevertheless, aid was overwhelmingly secured at an individual level and by those with land to negotiate, or powerful patrons to approach, or those in selective, valued occupations. The norm was to continue working for as long as possible. This might bring reward, and the emphasis medieval society placed on experience meant that the government and decision making of many towns and villages were often in the hands of men in their sixties or older. While looking old, they had not socially lost their adult status. Others, however, through incapacity, were forced to make role changes, undertaking less prestigious jobs than in their prime; some were forced to beg. While this could make life harsh and probably shorter, it reflects the general attitude that being old did not necessarily label an individual in need, or without value to society. It was individual capacity that mattered.

Notes

1 See Chapter 2 above.
2 Minois, *History of old age*, p. 231; Shahar, *Growing old*, p. 28; Meech and Allen (eds), *The book of Margery Kempe*, p. 179.
3 Bornstein (trans.), *Dino Compagni's chronicle of Florence*, p. 99.
4 Herlihy and Klapisch-Zuber, *Tuscans*, pp. 163–4; Weissman, *Ritual brotherhood*, pp. 133–4; Shahar, *Growing old*, pp. 26–7, 31; Thomas, 'Age and authority', p. 237.
5 Petrarch, *Letters of old age*, vol. 1, p. 265.
6 Shahar summarises the various schema in *Growing old*, pp. 15–17.
7 *Ibid.*, p. 12; Huizinga, *The autumn of the Middle Ages*, p. 34.
8 Petrarch, *Letters of old age*, vol. 1, p. 265.
9 Although Erasmus did suffer from bad health throughout his adulthood: Rosenthal, *Old age*, p. 96; Gilbert, 'When did a man in the Renaissance grow old?', p. 12.
10 Grmk, *On ageing*, p. 25.
11 *Ibid.*, p. 6.
12 Nicholas, *Domestic*, p. 110.
13 Brown (ed.), *Religious lyrics*, no. 148. See also Jones, 'The signs of old age', p. 771.
14 Flynn, *Sacred charity*, p. 38.
15 Minois, *History of old age*, p. 238.
16 de Rojas, *La Celestina,* Act 4, scene 2; Harrison (ed.), *The Danse Macabre of women*, p. 94, line 9.

17 Christine de Pisan, *Treasure*, p. 166.
18 Meech and Allen (eds), *The book of Margery Kempe*, pp. 179–81; Jones, 'The signs of old age', p. 774; Boccaccio, *The Decameron*, II.10, pp. 158–9; Shahar, 'The old body', p. 169; Deschamps, 'Regrets d'un vieillard', in *Oeuvres complètes*, vol. 6, pp. 225–30; de Beauvoir, *Old age*, pp. 160–1.
19 Although it fell within a range of thirty-five to sixty, depending on the size and health of the individual: Post, 'Ages at menarche and menopause'.
20 Jacquart and Thomasset, *Sexuality and medicine*, p. 75; Lemay (ed.), *Women's secrets*, p. 129.
21 Minois, *History of old age*, p. 174.
22 *The Canterbury tales: The merchant's tale*, lines 1,420–22, in Benson (ed.), *The Riverside Chaucer*, p. 156; Boccaccio is quoted in Blamires (ed.), *Woman defamed*, p. 175; Chaney (ed.), *The poems of François Villon: The testament*, pp. 57–8.
23 There were six criticisms compared with four positive qualities: Fowler, Briggs and Remley (eds), *The governance of kings and princes*, pp. 144–52.
24 Johnston (trans. and ed.), *Galar Y Beirdd*, p. 95.
25 Folts, 'Senescence and renascence', p. 264; Petrarch, *Letters of old age*, vol. 1, p. 24.
26 Alberti, *I libri*, pp. 39–42; Christine de Pisan, *Treasure*, pp. 165–6.
27 Cicero, *De senectute*, p. 79.
28 Blake (ed.), *Caxton's own prose*, no. 79 and no. 86.
29 Dean (ed.), *Richard the Redeless: Mum and the sothsegger*, lines 956–62.
30 Bower, *Scotichronicon*, pp. 64–5.
31 Petrarch, *Letters of old age*, vol. 1, p. 187.
32 Kindrick (ed.), *The poems of Robert Henryson*, pp. 237–8.
33 Boer (trans.), *Marsilio Ficino's Book of life*, p. 51.
34 *Dante Il convivio*, p. 232.
35 Folts, 'Senescence and renascence', pp. 210, 222.
36 E.g. the anonymous St Albans chronicler for the year 1376: 'Sed illius morbid longe difficilior est curatio senis quam juvenis propter diversas causas, senilis scilicet frigoris et juvenilis caloris': *Chronicon Angliae*, pp. 103–4.
37 *The Canterbury tales: The merchant's tale*, lines 1,820–57, in Benson (ed.), *The Riverside Chaucer*, p. 161; Owst, *Literature and pulpit*, p. 396. See too Christine de Pisan, *Treasure*, p. 163.
38 Minois, *History of old age*, p. 188; Rosenthal, *Old age*, pp. 123, 130.
39 Herlihy, 'Age, property and career', pp. 154–5.
40 Hanawalt, *The ties that bound*, p. 237; Romano, *Housecraft*, p. 179; Herlihy, *Opera muliebra*, p. 155.
41 Origo, *The merchant of Prato*; Minois, *History of old age*, p. 233; Higounet-Nadal, *Périgueux*, pp. 312–13, 317–24.
42 Shahar, *Growing old*, p. 122; Champion (ed.), *Charles d'Orléans: poésies*, XCV, lines 8–11; Johnston (ed.), *Iolo Goch: Poems*, pp. 52–6; Guenée, 'L'âge des personnes authentiques', pp. 266–79. I am grateful to Dr Cynfael Lake for drawing my attention to the poem by Iolo Goch.
43 Wood-Legh, *Perpetual chantries*, p. 232. Cf. the ages of office holding among Durham monks: Piper, 'The monks of Durham', pp. 54–60.

44 Gilbert, 'When did a man in the Renaissance grow old?', p. 31.
45 Finlay, 'The Venetian Republic'.
46 Shahar, *Growing old*, p. 83; Rosenthal, *Old age*, chs 2–3.
47 Geremek, *The margins of society*, p. 286.
48 Rawcliffe, *Medicine for the soul*, pp. 21, 169–71.
49 Le Roy Ladurie, *Montaillou*, p. 216.
50 Alberti, *I libri*, p. 157.
51 Rosenthal, *Old age*, p. 105; Rosenthal, 'Retirement', p. 176.
52 Shahar, 'Old age', p. 54.
53 Kendall, *Louis XI*, pp. 431–2.
54 Shahar, *Growing old*, p. 26.
55 Rosenthal, 'Retirement', p. 174; Rosenthal, *Old age*, p. 100.
56 Rosenthal, *Old age*, pp. 106–7; Kermode, 'Urban decline?', p. 192; Attreed (ed.), *The York household books*, vol. 1, p. 61.
57 Shahar, *Growing old*, pp. 93–4; Le Roy Ladurie, *Montaillou*, p. 217. In England the old members of the household were sometimes labelled 'serviens' along with other dependent adults: Howell, *Land, family and inheritance*, p. 260.
58 Clark, 'The quest for security', p. 191.
59 Minois, *History of old age*, p. 218.
60 Clark, 'The quest for security', p. 193.
61 Clark, 'Some aspects', pp. 312, 318.
62 Smith, 'The manorial court', p. 54.
63 Pelling and Smith (eds), *Life, death and the elderly*, p. 24.
64 Minois, *History of old age*, p. 246; Clark, 'Some aspects', pp. 317–18.
65 Clark, 'Some aspects', p. 315; Smith, 'The manorial court', p. 52.
66 Dyer, 'Changes in the size of peasant holdings', p. 289.
67 Clark, 'The quest for security', p. 195 and n. 16.
68 Rosenthal, 'Three-generation families', pp. 232–3; Rosenthal, 'When did you last see your grandfather?', pp. 223–44; Orme, *Medieval children*, p. 55.
69 Le Roy Ladurie, *The peasants of Languedoc*, pp. 31–2.
70 Alberti, *I libri*, pp. 50, 116; Haas, *The Renaissance man and his children*, p. 141; Alexandre-Bidon and Lett, *Children*, p. 67.
71 Harper, 'A note on corrodies', pp. 97 and 101.
72 Romano, *Housecraft*, p. 179; Harvey, *Living and dying*, p. 186; Harper-Bill (ed.), *Charters of the medieval hospitals of Bury St Edmunds*, nos 1–2, 56, 59, 224–51.
73 Rawcliffe, *Medicine for the soul*, p. 173.
74 Hilton, *A medieval society*, p. 112.
75 Rawcliffe, *Medicine for the soul*, p. 172.
76 Mollat, *The poor in the Middle Ages*, pp. 270–1, p. 309, fn. 3.
77 Herlihy, 'Age, property and career', p. 143; Bennett, *Women in the medieval English countryside*, p. 149 and fn. 22 for further references; Shahar, *Growing old*, pp. 163, 168–70; Rosenthal, *Old age*, pp. 184–6.
78 Orme, 'Sufferings of the clergy', p. 68.
79 Pullan, *Rich and poor*, pp. 214–15; Lane, *Venetian ships*, pp. 76–7.
80 Pullan, *Rich and poor*, p. 208; Demaitre, 'The care and extension of old age', p. 13,

fn. 50; Minois, *History of old age*, pp. 245–6; Rosenthal, *Old age*, p. 186; Geremek, *The margins of society*, p. 182.

81 Trexler, 'A widows' asylum', p. 121; Henderson, 'Women, children and poverty', pp. 172–6, tables 7.2 and 7.5; Dyer, *Standards of living*, p. 244; Orme and Webster, *The English hospital*, p. 112; Clay, *The medieval hospitals*, p. 28; Brodman, *Charity and welfare*, p. 59.

82 Geremek, *The margins of society*, p. 199; Shahar, *Growing old*, pp. 25, 167.

83 Alberti, *I libri*, p. 47.

84 de La Ronciere, 'Tuscan notables', p. 207.

85 Christine de Pizan, *The book of the city of ladies*, pp. 111–12.

86 Horrox (ed.), *The Black Death*, pp. 134–5.

87 Shahar, *Growing old*, p. 93. Dahlberg (trans.), *The romance of the rose*, vol 2, verses 14457–70.

88 Labarge, '*Gerontocomia*', p. 211; Grmk, *On ageing*, p. 58.

89 Demaitre, 'The care and extension of old age', p. 4; Labarge, '*Gerontocomia*', p. 211.

90 Boer (trans.), *Marsilio Ficino's Book of life*; Labarge, '*Gerontocomia*', pp. 209–21; for Hornecke see Demaitre, 'The care and extensions of old age', pp. 3–22.

91 Boer (trans.), *Marsilio Ficino's Book of life*, p. 39.

92 Demaitre, 'The care and extension of old age', p. 22.

93 Boer (trans.), *Marsilio Ficino's Book of life*, introduction, p. xx.

94 *Ibid.*, pp. 46–59.

95 *Ibid.*, pp. 56–7; Demaitre, 'The care and extension of old age', p. 16; Grmk, *On ageing*, p. 45.

96 Furnivall (ed.), *The book of quinte essence*.

97 Grmk, *On ageing*, p. 43; Simmons (ed.), *The lay folk's Mass book*, p. 23.

8

Endings

D EATH naturally marks the end of life. In late medieval descriptions of the ages of man, death followed decrepitude, the final stage of old age. At this point, the circle of life was complete: in the wheel of life depicted in Robert de Lisle's manuscript, death is marked by a tomb, which bears close resemblance to the cradle symbolising the start of life. In other metaphorical descriptions of life, death is journey's end or the sleep at the end of the day. Yet late medieval society was acutely aware that for the majority of people, death would not wait for decrepitude to strike. Death was there from the beginning, as the Danse Macabre literature foretold: 'From the mother's womb, stealthy death is a constant companion / seeking to ensnare us, on our every path'.[1] The onslaught of famine, war and plague in the fourteenth and fifteenth centuries had made death appear unpredictable and indiscriminate. As the old bawd Celestina comments to the young Melibea, 'The lamb goes as quickly to the slaughter as the old sheep, Madam. No one's so old that he can't live one year longer, or so young that he can't die today. So you haven't much advantage over us.'[2]

From this perspective, it is easy to assume that death cast a long shadow over life in late medieval Europe. In addition, much of Western religious belief and culture focused on suffering and death. At the heart of Christianity were the crucifixion and resurrection of Christ, illustrations of which could be found on church walls, in devotional manuscripts and decorating personal religious artefacts from jewellery to portable altars. Preachers urged worshippers to contemplate Christ's dying moments, and to consider their own imminent mortality. Death was a major rite of passage, which marked the transition from mortal life into an afterlife and decided one's destiny. At the moment of death, judgement would be made on the person's soul. Heaven and Hell were possible destinations, but by the fourteenth century Purgatory had become engraved on the consciences of most Europeans. First defined officially by the Council of Lyons (1274), Purgatory allowed for those who had yet to fulfil the penalty for their earthly sins to make satisfaction in the afterlife. Most would remain in this transition stage until the cleansing of their souls was completed, or until the Last Judgement and the Second Coming of Christ.[3]

Death is a fearsome prospect in any age, but late medieval Christendom generated particular reasons to be frightened. Art and visionary literature described Hell and Purgatory in similar terms of excruciating physical and psychological pain. While Purgatory would only be a temporary stage, no one knew how many thousands of years they faced 'cleansing' by being burnt, frozen, and skewered by devils, snakes and toads. Preachers and moral literature used shock tactics to counter complacency and remind their public that the fleeting joys of life would lead to eternal suffering. Images and literature like the 'Dance of Death' and the 'Three Living and Three Dead' were reminders that death came to all and no one knew when it would strike. In the latter story three men (sometimes described as kings) are hunting when they meet three dead men, who warn them that 'what you are, we were, and what we are, you will be'. William Dunbar (c.1460–1513) was one of several poets who employed the refrain, borrowed from the Office of the Dead, 'Timor mortis conturbat me' ('The fear of death disturbs my mind'). The literature and artwork of the period are riddled with the theme of death and its consequences, and many works present death as an enemy, a cruel destroyer. Edelgard Dubruck's reading of late medieval French poetry led her to conclude that 'people of the late middle ages just did not think of death in terms of heavenly bliss'.[4]

Yet throughout history, poets and artists have had a morbid fascination with life's end and tend to dwell on its destructive force. While such voices should not be dismissed, medieval attitudes towards death were far more complex. Christian belief gave meaning to death. It was not an ending, merely a rupture: the soul leaves the body and continues its journey. Visions of the otherworld suggested that souls retained their earthly identity and would remember past experiences and acquaintances. A romantic view is expressed by Carmesina as she laments the death of her beloved Tirant Lo Blanc in the Catalan romance of his deeds: 'After my burial, I shall follow him to Heaven or Hell, where just we were joined in life, so shall we be in death'.[5] Moreover, the separation of body and soul at death was only temporary: eventually they would be resurrected and reunited with a body in perfect age and health. Belief in the existence of Purgatory also meant that the dead were not set adrift or sent into a void, but continued to engage in a reciprocal relationship with the living. Prayers by the living would aid the souls in Purgatory, and the grateful dead would intercede for the living. In this way, the dead were seen as forming an 'age group' with their own rights and responsibilities.[6]

Hope was not uncommon in late medieval society. Positive views of death as the start of a 'new life' are found in Italian writings. In contrast to the doom and gloom of English and French visionary literature, Purgatory in Dante's *Divine comedy* is a place of hope that leads to Heaven. Memoir writers from Verona and Vicenza noted deaths with the lines 'left this life and gained a life which is true life' or 'passed from this mortal to a happier life'. Southern Europe in general did not show the same enthusiasm for illustrating death and the decay of the body.[7] Nevertheless, the distinction between a positive south and a negative north should not be pushed too far. Thoughts of heavenly bliss and resurrection are found in northern religious literature, on epitaphs and even in great doom paintings, which show the dead rising from the grave.[8]

Death promised mixed fortunes, therefore, and this is reflected in the varied responses to the act of dying. Age mattered. Medieval philosophers argued that the death of an old person was easy and natural because there was little heat in the body. It could bring relief from aches, pains and loneliness. In his old age, Francesco Petrarch, who described life as a straight road that one travelled in a single day, was 'already tired of the road, moving almost alone towards the finish line'. Many friends and loved ones had not reached this point, but had been cut off in the morning, and many at midday.[9] In contrast, death in the young was believed to be bitter and painful. Albertus Magnus compared it to an unripe apple that falls from the tree before its time. The reaction to the death of children, as discussed in Chapter 3, was to bemoan the injustice and the lost opportunities.[10] Death in the prime of adulthood could be similarly greeted with dismay. The chronicler of the *Scotichronicon* thought the death of the forty-four-year-old King James I of Scotland in 1437 was premature: 'While the web of his life was still in its early stages, it was the lord's wish to sacrifice him with a shortening of the normal course of life. Before he could grow to the elderly stage, death ran on ahead and snatched him inopportunely, and in premature burial received its prey'.[11]

Those in mid- and later life did not always accept the inevitability of death, as the Church was all too aware.[12] The friends of Francesco Datini, the merchant of Prato, had great difficulty persuading him to prepare for death: his prayers were not focused so much on his soul as on a longer life.[13] To a much greater degree, Louis XI of France spent his last months frantically trying to find a way to lengthen his life. To this end he invited to court San Francesco Paola, founder of the religious order known as the Minims. On meeting him, the king 'knelt before him and begged him to pray to God for him, so that He would deign to prolong his life'. In addition the king donated large sums to shrines and churches, and placed hope in relics. All came to nought, but the king took some persuasion before he acknowledged the inevitability of death and the need to consider his soul.[14] What these two examples reveal is that those around Datini and Louis did not foster their hopes or encourage them to live life to the full as the end neared. They saw it as their duty to remind them of the need to prepare for death. This chapter will discuss the types of arrangements and rituals surrounding a person's last moments on earth, and the planning needed by those wishing to perpetuate the memory of her or his life.

Preparing for death

Most people today would wish death, for themselves and for others, to be a quick and painless affair. Late medieval society would not recognise this death as 'good': it allowed no time for death rites, no time for last-minute preparations. Talismans and charms were carried in the hope of warding off sudden death. One example was the 'letter to Charlemagne', an indulgence allegedly sent in a letter by Pope Leo III to Charlemagne. To those who carried it, it offered virtual blanket protection against evil, disease and sudden death. Similarly, in the years following the Black Death, images of St Christopher, the guardian against sudden death, began to appear more frequently on the walls of English churches.[15]

Individuals wanted time to put their spiritual and earthly life in order. By the later Middle Ages, one important part of the process was making a will. While the mechanisms for drawing up a will differed across Europe – reflecting local practice and customary laws – all shared the aims of ensuring a person's state of grace and facilitating the reallocation of worldly goods among the living.[16] In fourteenth- and fifteenth-century Western Europe, wills were made by a wide cross-section of adult society, including tailors, butchers, bakers, labourers, servants and shepherds. In Douai, even nuns and monks, who were not supposed to own any property and were forbidden to make wills, were finding ways of doing so. It was, however, a gendered process, and across Europe far fewer women than men left wills. Most female testators were widows with power over their dowry, dower or inheritance. Canon law did allow a wife to make a will, as long as she had her husband's consent, but local laws and customs did not always allow it. In England, consent became less customary in the fifteenth century, and here, as in Avignon and Valreas, the number of female testators declined as the century progressed.[17]

In a significant number of cases, wills were death-bed declarations made by people 'sick', 'debilitated' and in a hurry. In Douai such testators appear to have been from the lower echelons of society with little property to protect. The propertied classes, such as the merchants and artisans, tended to prepare for death while still in good health. The typical male testator was a relatively young married father with growing household worries. Concerns for property and inheritance may also have lain behind the will-making of English noblemen between about 1350 and 1485, where the average will was written over a year before death, and there are examples of wills composed over a decade prior to death.[18] Wills were not static documents, however, and alterations and codicils could be made as intentions changed, especially when death neared. The imminence of death prompted Philip V of France to revise his financial bequests upwards and make ever more elaborate arrangements for his burial. In contrast, William Courtney, Archbishop of Canterbury (d.1396), modified his burial plans as he grew humble in the face of death.[19] Testaments would reflect a particular point in a person's life cycle, attuned to the changing nature of her or his family, friends and finances. The demands of those associations, the influence of local clergy and general custom could have played a part in shaping the will; there is a good deal of the formulaic about them.[20] Yet these factors should not be overemphasised to the point at which individual concerns are deemed negligible. Few wrote their wills with the relish and skill of François Villon, whose fictional *Testament* deals out justice and redresses past wrongs in a bid to give meaning to his own life and dictate the direction of others. But even the briefest of documents share what Joel Rosenthal has described as 'an effort to shape the world one could control, not only for the last time but in some ways perhaps for the first time'. This was especially felt by women, who would have had fewer prior opportunities to take command of their identity and 'play God'.[21]

In making a will, primary place was given to religious and devotional concerns. Donations were made to churches, priests and charities; debts and dues were paid; masses and prayers were purchased; requests for burial places and funeral arrangements were listed. They were an opportunity to declare one's faith and to pay recompense. Yet the will was also a worldly document. Parents used them to fulfil their responsibilities to their children, and husbands could provide security for wives, or dictate the lives of their widows. Personal goods were often painstakingly distributed. How and to whom resources were divided varied with the individual, but several studies have suggested that wills reflected the different life experiences and priorities of men and women. In terms of bequests, women from the towns of Douai and York devoted far more attention to personal property than their male contemporaries: women's wills contain large numbers of small requests often of household goods, the items over which they had control. While men looked to lineal relations, women tended to distribute their bequests among a wide circle of friends and neighbours, awarding personal connections and allocating their property unequally between daughters and sons.[22]

Once the hour of death arrived, there were procedures and rituals that were considered essential in order to achieve a good death. While the Church urged individuals to prepare for death throughout their lives, there was a strong belief that death-bed rites had transformative powers; they provided a last heroic stand whereby an individual could save herself or himself from even mortal sin. It was held that in the last hour of life, a great struggle would take place between the angels and devils over rights to a person's soul. This took place while the person was in a weakened state. Bernardino of Siena called dying the 'most cruel, most ferocious' experience, and wrote that the sinner is so attached to the flesh that the separation of body and soul would be excruciating: 'his head pains, his body pains him, his arms pain him, all of his members pain him and his viscera shiver from within'.[23]

Ultimately, it was a battle that the person had to fight alone, but help and encouragement could be given from the sidelines. Saints with special powers at the hour of death, like St Katherine, St Barbara or St Erasmus, could be asked to intercede. More earthly aid was received from those who rushed to the bedsides of friends, family and neighbours. Dying alone was feared: even among the heretics of Montaillou, the dying wanted to be surrounded by family and friends.[24] The last moments on earth could be quite a crowded occasion, which added to the social drama. Shows of grief were welcome: the conspicuous compassion of a figure like Margery Kempe – her 'wepyn and cryin' – was in demand.[25] There was no need to wonder what constituted a good death in the later Middle Ages. A clear steer was provided by the Church, mediated through the pulpit, confession and the knowledge of friends and family. In the fifteenth century advice could also be found in 'guidebooks' known as the *ars moriendi* or the 'art of dying'. Originating in southern Germany, they quickly spread to the rest of Europe and were translated into French, English, Italian and Catalan. Their impact increased with the publication of block-books in which a series of woodcuts strikingly illustrated what to expect during the final hours of life. While they can look fearsome as the devils claw at the bedclothes and hover above, ultimately the works were not intended to frighten or depress, but to assist and encourage. The key to the process was the priest, who would hold up a crucifix, intending to drive away the demons and ask the dying what their sins were and whether they believed in Christ's Passion. Following confession, absolution was granted and – if the person was capable of taking it – the eucharist was given.[26]

Death-bed rituals assisted the process of separation from the world of the living. Through confession and absolution (and indeed the will), the soul was freed from earthly concerns. Administering extreme unction, the last anointing, furthered the separation because popular belief held that anyone who recovered after anointing would be the walking dead: they could not have sexual intercourse, go barefoot or eat meat.[27] At this point, the person entered a period of suspended animation, a liminal stage where death was imminent. Once death had occurred the body was purified by washing – usually undertaken by women – and wound in clean linen: a white sheet symbolising the person's recent confession and absolution. Any alternatives were usually intended to distinguish the person in some way. A baby who died before its mother's churching could be wrapped in its chrisom cloth. Priests and bishops were buried in the vestments of their office, while the aristocracy could be dressed in armour or their richest clothes.[28] In addition there were rituals and customs involved in the laying out the body, informing the neighbourhood, reading the will and appeasing the departing soul.[29]

Death-bed rituals served not only to calm the dying, but to comfort the living. Alessandra Strozzi, on hearing of the death of her son in 1459, wrote, 'I have also been comforted by the knowledge that when he was dying God granted him the opportunity to confess, to receive communion and extreme unction'.[30] By the same token, rites not performed satisfactorily could trouble the living. In Florence, 1406, Giovanni Morelli's nine-year-old son Alberto died. Initially it appeared that everything had been done to ensure that his death had been 'good'. On the day of his death, Alberto was in bed surrounded by weeping relatives; he had time to say numerous prayers and recommend his soul to God and the Virgin; and a month later his death was marked by the saying of commemorative masses. Yet Giovanni struggled to come to terms with his son's death; it haunted both his sleeping and waking hours. As the anniversary of the death approached Giovanni's remorse began to centre on the belief that his son had not had a good death. There had been someone missing at the death-bed – a priest. Giovanni had hung on for too long to fetch him, and had thought at the time that his son's prayers would be sufficient; it should be noted that Alberto was too young to make confession. Giovanni decided to create his own ritual that would take place on the anniversary of his son's death. Dressed simply in a short gown, barefoot, and staring at a painting of the crucified Christ, Giovanni began praying, weeping and kissing and embracing the image, trying to participate in Christ's agony. This period of turmoil was finally rewarded by a vision of his son, accompanied by his special saint, Catherine. Morelli's anniversary ritual therefore appeared to have worked in saving his son's soul and allowing both him and Morelli to rest in peace.[31]

The funeral

The funeral rites marked the stage of transition as the dead person was taken on a one-way journey from the place of the living (usually domestic) to that of the dead (a sacred setting). Like the death-bed rituals, funerals assisted the healing processes associated with loss. They can be seen, as St Augustine believed, as 'rather comforts to the living than helps to the dead'.[32] Nevertheless, late medieval society considered funeral rites necessary for the state of the dead person's soul, and individual needs were met. The funeral and burial were performed as soon after death as possible. Some testators pointedly urged speed. Cardinal Pierre Blau of Avignon wanted to be buried within two or three hours of death.[33] Others are known to have requested a delay of some days following their decease. In England in 1355, Lady Elizabeth de Burgh did not want to be buried until fifteen days after her death. This was partly to allay worries of being buried alive in an age when there was uncertainty over the exact point of death. Time was also needed to make sure that full funeral preparations could be made.[34] The English weather allowed for such postponements, but they were unlikely to have been encouraged in the warmer climes of Italy or Spain. In Florence burial usually occurred within a day of death.[35]

At the heart of the funeral was the church service. Books of hours are useful sources of information for images of the ideal end to life, at least for the elite. They depict the body laid out in the chancel, surrounded by candles and in the presence of the priest, other church personnel and mourners. The key text was the Office of the Dead, which consisted of three parts: vespers would be said over the coffin on the eve of the burial;

Matins and Lauds were sung the next morning. This was followed by a Requiem Mass, which marked the beginning of the living's obligation to the souls of the deceased. It also served to smooth over the social rupture caused by death. The dead were safely installed in the afterlife, and the next of kin were incorporated back into the community. After the celebration of the Mass, absolution took place as the body was blessed and purified with incense and holy water.[36]

While the funeral service had reassuringly standard features, there was opportunity to tailor it to specific needs and desires. Wills can provide information on these preferences, although many people either arranged the ceremony before composing their will or were happy to leave it to their family, guildsmen, executors or custom.[37] The movement of the body from the house to the church could turn into a procession, with candles, chanting and the tolling of bells. The body would be carried to the church in a coffin or on a bier (a wooden stretcher), supported by friends and family or drawn in a cart. In Bury St Edmunds, some testators requested that their godchildren bore their bodies to the church, which directly echoed the occasion when godparents carried their godchildren to the church door at the time of their baptismal ceremony.[38] Such actions were possible of course only if the godchildren had reached adulthood. Children were accorded the same funeral rites as adults, although on a reduced scale. In the Veneto, Silvestro Arnaldi's grandson died at only four days old. A garland was laid on the boy's head, and he was carried to the cathedral by a servant whose arms were uncovered as a mark of mourning. In Brescia the baby daughter of Guiliano Troscoli was placed on a cushion before being carried to the church.[39] Bearers were always men and usually of the same status as the deceased. The evidence from northern Italy suggests that men dominated the public processions to the exclusion of women. In Bologna and Rome women mourned in the house away from the public ceremony; in Verona, women were allowed to join a funeral procession only if the deceased was under seven.[40] The reason may have lain in the view that the unrestrained mourning in private (in which women were key participants) was unsuitable for the more reserved atmosphere of the public ceremony. The Church in particular tried to discourage excessive mourning on the grounds that it suggested a lack of trust in a person's salvation.[41]

As the procession moved towards the church, bystanders would pick out key markers of the dead person's status, relationships and piety. An association with a guild or confraternity would be clearly visible, especially if it had arranged the funeral. One of the main attractions of the guilds was that they virtually guaranteed a decent burial: they could help with expenses and ensure a good attendance. In Zamora (Spain) members of the Misericordia fraternity met at the deceased's house wearing a special funeral garb. They would carry the body, draped with a pall in the colours of the brotherhood, to the burial site.[42]

For those in the higher echelons of society, funerals were an opportunity to demonstrate rank. The use of shields, emblems, flags and banners indicated personal and familial public identity, while the lavishness of the ceremony underlined their political force. When Piero Parenti of Florence arranged his father's funeral in 1497 he aimed for 'a public celebration in keeping with the rank he and I merited'.[43] Competition for social and political power could be played out in Florentine funerals, and not only in the case of the leading men of the family. In 1445 Lucrezia, wife of Luca da Panzono, was buried in Florence with 'as much pomp as possible'.[44] Funerals were also the occasion to broadcast a position only recently attained. Evidence from England suggests that elaborate funerals may have been particularly valued by those families who most needed to assert their presence. In Norfolk in 1466, John Paston's funeral cost £230, around four times the going rate, and was intended to underline his family's relatively recent elevation to gentility.[45] By extension those with a minimal public image – whether because of youth, social status or gender – could have their marginal status underlined in the funeral. In Spain, confraternities carried half as many candles at the funeral of a servant or someone under fourteen as they carried for a full guild member. In England, the peals of the bell-ringers lasted longer for the wealthy and the adult than they did for the poor and the child. In general more was spent on funeral processions for men than for women, more for married women than for single women.[46]

In several symbolic ways, therefore, some sense of the individual was conveyed by funeral rituals. In southern Europe, this was heightened by the visibility of the body during the procession. This gave the person a greater physical presence and became another opportunity to demonstrate status and piety in the funeral clothes. Some chose to wear their best, like Francesco Rinuccini of Florence (d.1381), who was clothed in rich vermillion velvet. Others chose to be buried in a monk's habit as a statement of their piety and allegiance.[47] This was not common practice in northern Europe, where the body was usually enclosed in a coffin or wrapped in a shroud, the face of death hidden from view. The few exceptions were among the elite: the bodies of English and French kings were embalmed and dressed in their full coronation apparel. Among the reasons for this practice was the hope, as expressed in relation to Henry V of

England, that visibility would increase the people's grief and prayers.[48] Where full display was not possible, it became customary to have the figure of the king represented by an effigy made of wood, wax or leather. Such effigies were first used in England at the funeral of Edward II (d.1327), and in France for King Charles VI (d.1422). They sprang partly from practical concerns relating to the condition of the king's body: an effigy would serve to veil the realities of the decomposing body from the gathering onlookers. In addition, an immutable figure made the important political statement, promoted in France, that the royal dignity never dies. Thus the dead played a visible role in the ceremony.[49]

Statements of political and social power require an audience, and the dead would be judged by, and benefit from, the attendance at their funerals. A large number of people would suggest an individual of some social presence, and bring in a substantial number of prayers for the deceased's soul. The advantage of belonging to a guild was that the fraternity would spread the news of death and oblige members to attend funerals. Some confraternities in Spain would pay members to attend the whole ceremony, which would help to compensate for missed work. Quality as well as quantity mattered. Marco Thiene, Count of Quinto (in the Veneto; will dated 1476), wanted his body to be carried by six men from the Gesuati order, all dressed in red cloth that bore the family arms. In front would march sixty 'pauper peasants', thirty dressed in white and thirty in black capes. No important local person was to miss the funeral: all the city's guilds, religious orders, bishop's chaplains and parish priests were to be in attendance at Thiene's expense.[50] Local dignitaries demonstrated the important associations of the individual and his family, while special merit accrued through the attendance of priests and the poor. The latter were seen as a key part of the ceremony because their humble position was believed to make their prayers more efficacious. Mourners were encouraged with promises of a good meal, and funeral feasts were important occasions, marking the reintegration of society. Neighbours and kin could be treated to a fine spread. When Sir Henry Esturmey from southern England died in 1381 his fellow parishioners enjoyed a funeral feast that included sugar, cinnamon, ginger, almonds and cloves.[51] The giving of alms was also a well-known aspect of funerals. In 1437 a belated funeral service was held for the Count of Almagnac, who had died nineteen years previously. The Parisian journal writer, clearly no supporter of the count, described a lavish service of thousands of candles, torches and high-profile guests. But to the journal writer's disgust, 'no alms were distributed, which astonished everyone, for there were four thousand people there who would never have gone near the place if they had known there were to be no alms; they cursed the man they had been praying for'.[52]

While the journal writer had a predilection for large, round figures, the numbers attending a funeral could be considerable. These appear to have increased during the later Middle Ages as funerals in some parts of Europe grew more elaborate. In Avignon, testaments dating from the 1330s onwards increasingly detail funeral arrangements and show a trend for flamboyance and theatricality among a cross-section of society. There are growing numbers of draperies, torches, bells, clergy and especially poor mourners. Other areas of Europe show similar tendencies: funerals grew more spectacular in Lyons and Florence; sumptuary legislation in Vicenza and council ordinances in Verona, Padua and Venice denounced excessive funeral display.[53] For Jacques Chiffoleau the flamboyant funeral in Avignon arose from urbanisation, increasing migration and social mobility in the fourteenth century, which served to separate individuals from familial and ancestral burial places. Their response to this sense of dislocation was to assert their individuality through extravagant funeral ceremonies.[54] Yet this sense of dislocation does not appear to fit the situation in northern Italy. In Florence, funerals emphasised the patrilineage rather than the individual, and families would arrange for kin who died away from the city to be disinterred and brought back to Florence for a second burial. Another possibility is that the growing wealth and competitive nature of towns and cities (and it does appear to have been an urban phenomenon) fuelled display. A more favoured explanation is the growing anxieties in the wake of the Black Death. The coming of the plague had seen funeral rites truncated or not performed, and mass burials occurred. Boccaccio is often quoted for his emotive description of corpses being dragged from houses, being placed on planks of wood instead of biers and carried in a heap to large pits and dropped in. They were 'shown no more consideration than the odd goat would today'. It does appear that in Boccaccio's city of Florence, funeral practices became more elaborate within five years of the first plague, and the rise of ostentatious funerals in the whole of Tuscany and Umbria appears to date from after the Black Death. Plague attacks may also have prompted the production of hundreds of realistic representations of funerals and burials, which appeared in illuminated manuscripts in the years 1375–1500.[55]

Nevertheless, it should not be assumed that everyone who drew attention to their funeral wanted pomp and ceremony. Testament makers across fifteenth-century Europe demonstrate a growing current of humility with their requests for simple funerals. Catherine Felbrigge of Norwich

(1460) chose to 'expressly forbid' (*expresse prohibeo*) large banquets or other useless provisions. Servants' wills in Venice made requests for burial 'without pomp', and James Grubb has argued that in the Veneto 'austerity and self-effacement were closer to the norm'.[56] These requests need to be considered carefully. In Avignon, the merchant Jean 'Bellabocha' asked to be buried without ostentation, yet he still left money for four torches and six poor people to be dressed in black. Similarly, Clare Gittings has pointed out that fifteenth-century English clergy requested funerals without pomp, but the sums they left in their wills suggest a more worldy reality. The Dean of Wells Cathedral in 1443, for example, requested a simple funeral, but left £20 to pay for it.[57] This is not to say that testators were less humble than they made themselves out to be, but the simplicity was relative to the excesses elsewhere. Such austerity usually sprang from a contempt for the body and its worldliness. A few took this view to extreme lengths and in the process created a different kind of spectacle. Philippe de Mézières (d.1405) wanted to have an iron chain placed round his neck at the point of death. His naked body was then to be dragged into the church, tied to a plank and thrown into the grave like carrion.[58]

Burial

Burial physically removed the dead and the process of decay from the eyes of the living. The dead would be carried in a coffin to the place of burial, accompanied by the singing of penitential psalms. The grave site would be marked by a priest through the sprinkling of holy water and the sign of a cross; it was dug while Mass was sung. The body was not usually buried in the coffin, but in a shroud or sometimes naked, and traditionally with the feet pointing east. According to Mirk's *Festial* this was in order 'to ben þe more redy to sene Criste þat comyth oute of þe est to þe dome'. Medieval Europe held strong views on the proper burying of its dead. As mentioned above, horror was expressed at the indignity of plague victims being thrown into mass graves, appearing, in the words of the Florentine chronicler Stefani, to be packed in like layers of a lasagne.[59]

Canon law decreed that people had the right to choose where they were buried, and it appears that fourteenth-century testators grew increasingly eager to state their preferences. In Douai, Tuscany and Umbria, testators in the last quarter of the fourteenth century showed an unprecedented keenness in stipulating their burial site. They also became more specific, indicating their desire to be buried near a particular object (a painting, an altar, a door) or named individuals (spouses, parents).[60] This was the case for both men and women. While canon law was ambiguous on the issue, women did voice their preferences; in Avignon and London they appear to have done so more often than male testators.[61] Some individuals wanted every effort to be made in complying with their wishes. Another advantage of being in a fraternity was that if a person died outside his or her local area, the guild could arrange for the body to be returned. The Holy Trinity fraternity of St Botolph's without Aldersgate, London, would bring home those who had died within a five-mile radius.[62]

Where did most people wish to be buried? A person's choice might be influenced and limited by a number of factors: status, sex, age, family tradition, guild loyalties and personal affection. Crowded spaces and epidemic years could also play their part. Death may be a great leveller, but burial reflected the resources and status of the deceased. The wealthy, through patronage and donations, had access to burial spaces closed from the rest of the population. Monasteries and nunneries were popular choices among the fourteenth- and fifteenth-century English aristocracy, while English cathedrals were usually reserved for bishops, canons and the elite few.[63] Family tradition played a strong role. In fifteenth-century Florence a growing influence on burial choice was the ancestral grave, what Cohn calls the 'lineage grave'. Between 1400 and 1425, eighty-seven per cent of testators who specified a burial space elected an ancestral grave.[64] The language of wills shows the sense of possession with the phrases 'our tomb', or 'the burial space belonging to'. Occupancy was policed, although not always effectively. In 1383 Monna Filippa, the wife of Pollaio Sassetti, was mistakenly placed in the Sassetti family tomb in Santa Maria Novella, Florence. While the error was angrily noted, the family decided to let it pass because she had been a good woman.[65] Among the landed elite of England, there was similarly a strong element of tradition in burial choice, and changes were made only when there was an alteration in family fortunes and power bases.[66]

These are also examples of what Philip Morgan has called a sense of 'place loyalty'.[67] The draw of the parish church was strong, and during the later Middle Ages there was an increasing desire among testators for burial inside the church itself.[68] The clear advantage of a church burial was that a person was in close proximity to where Mass was regularly sung; it also affirmed one's standing in society and improved the chances of the grave retaining an individual identity. In Montaillou the wealthy Mengarde Clergue was buried in the church beneath the altar of the Virgin, whereas most of the village were buried in the graveyard.[69] Not all areas of the church were equal. The most desirable area was the east end and the high altar, which were restricted to the clergy and local worthies. The nave, with its various altars and shrines, was the location for a broader cross-section of society, though still ones with money, such as bakers and drapers. By the end of the fifteenth century, a number of English testators were asking to be buried near the place where they or another person had once sat. In 1463 John Baret of Bury St Edmunds requested burial where 'my lady Shardelowe was wont to sit'. In this way individuals could feel that they would continually hold a place within the community.[70] Rather less communally spirited, some would achieve their desires at the expense of previous incumbents. William Courtney, Archbishop of Canterbury, requested in his first will that he be buried before the cross in Exeter Cathedral, which would mean the removal of the skeletons of three deans who were currently occupying the space.[71]

Lower down in society, it appears that the majority of testators in much of Europe wanted to be buried in their parish churchyards.[72] Cemeteries were not always situated next to churches, but they were invariably close to the centres of settlement. They were not hidden away from everyday life, or spaces confined to the dead. At Exeter the graveyard was in the heart of the city, and its large open space was a place to play ball games, trade and draw water from the well.[73] The central position of cemeteries, however, meant that there was little room to expand, and problems of burial space intensified during plague years. As a result the cemetery was not necessarily a person's final resting place. Once the flesh had decomposed, it was common for the body to be dug up and stored in a charnel house, which was either a free-standing building or in a vault under the church. A celebrated example was the cemetery of the Innocents in Paris. Demand for space was acute because at least twenty parishes had the right to bury their dead there. The charnel houses, located just above the cloister, contained thousands of unmarked bones. For the majority of late medieval society, what mattered was that the body had been buried in consecrated ground, not that there would be a permanent grave.[74]

Did this mean therefore that cemeteries were large, anonymous spaces that were simply, in the words of John Bossy, 'the home of a sector of the population collectivised by the process of dying'?[75] To some extent they inevitably were, but testamentary evidence shows that late medieval parishioners could be very specific about where in a cemetery they would like to be buried. John Coote of Bury St Edmunds (will dated 1502) wanted his grave to be next to the graves of his parents, his children and a priest named John Mosse.[76] There appears to have been a strong desire to retain contact with ties established in life. In Bury St Edmunds, Florence, Douai and Avignon most women who mentioned a burial partner chose their husbands.[77] Husbands in northern Europe were also likely to choose their spouse as their burial partner, while men in southern Europe elected to be buried with their ancestors.[78] A few were buried near guildsmen, publicising their continued loyalties after death.[79] As in the church, some areas of the cemetery were more valued than others – near a charnel house or close to crosses – and the geography of burial space reflected the beliefs and prejudices of society at large.[80] There is evidence from English churchyards to suggest that adult males were far more likely than women to be buried in prestigious places.[81] Not everyone was allowed to be 'incorporated' into society. Those marginalised in life would be so in death: suicides, thieves, excommunicates, heretics and lepers were not to be buried in consecrated ground.[82] Another group of marginals consisted of unbaptised babies. Languishing in Limbo in the afterlife, they were consigned to the periphery of the cemetery. To some commentators this might involve the post-mortem separation of mother and child.[83] The fate seemed too cruel for a number of parents, and there are examples from northern Europe of unbaptised babies being secretly buried in churchyards. In fifteenth-century Marseilles, the couple Jaumette and William were ordered to exhume their still-born son and rebury him in unconsecrated ground. It was perhaps partly to prevent such secret burials that the cemetery of Hereford Cathedral was enclosed in 1398.[84]

Remember me

The shortness and transience of life preoccupied many late medieval writers. 'Where are the snows of years gone by?' asked Villon as he thought of the friends and acquaintances now departed.[85] Death could take not only the person, but the memory of her or his existence. Most people today would like to think that they would be remembered, at least for a time, after their death. In medieval society this desire was inextricably linked with the need to receive prayers, which would quicken the passage through Purgatory.

The Church made sure that everyone was remembered to some degree by providing general prayers for the dead, such as those on All Hallows' Day (1 November). However, these were not considered as effective as prayers and masses directed towards a named individual. It was believed that masses were most needed shortly after the person's death, yet benefits were also to be gained from projecting one's memory further into the future. The easiest way to secure these was to buy them, and a range of options were available to suit all pockets. A person could purchase a specified number of masses, perhaps in a block like the popular 'trentals' (thirty masses), or employ one or more priests to chant for a stipulated period. An alternative was the obit or anniversary, which re-created the funeral rites on the anniversary of death.[86] It was hoped that these commemorative services would draw similar numbers to those at the funeral. In 1429, the obit of Thomas Hungerford (d.1398) was still able to attract ninety-three priests and 363 paupers.[87] For those with fewer finances to spare, guild or confraternity membership would guarantee that prayers would be said for the soul. In England there was also the option of having one's name entered on a bede-roll, a list of names of the benefactors of a church, which would be read out at an annual Requiem and in shortened form every Sunday. This allowed for a continuous presence in the memory of the community. There does appear to have been a general attempt to remember all who desired it. The fifteenth-century bede-roll of All Saints, Bristol, was so long – it extended to 150 folios – that it had to be serialised.[88]

Individuals could make huge demands. Jean de Grailly, captal of Buch, asked for 50,000 masses in 1369.[89] While few would have been able to match such requests, testamentary evidence from areas such as the Lyonnais, Avignon, Douai, the Veneto and Siena reveals an inflationary trend in the number of masses requested during the fourteenth and fifteenth centuries. Between 1300 and 1500 the number of rural testators from the Lyonnais who wanted post-mortem services virtually doubled. Recurrent plague appears to have spurred this upturn in masses, particularly in Tuscany and Umbria.[90] Yet the inflationary tendencies were also driven by the general uncertainty over how many masses would be considered enough. Every little helped, and benefits could be accrued to the soul by regularly jogging someone's memory and prompting a prayer. Testators tried to catch people's (particularly the priest's) eyes by placing their names on items they had bequeathed to the church. Donors' names were engraved on plate, chalices, vestments, windows, church roofs and floor tiles.

There were other means of keeping one's name and existence 'alive'. For those with sufficient resources there was the possibility of investing in a memorial. This might take a number of forms, influenced by cost and regional preferences: tombstones were prevalent in France, brasses in England, engraved copper plaques in Bruges and paintings in Florence.[91] At the cheaper and more ephemeral end of the scale were wooden crosses. A cemetery filled with rows of orderly crosses is depicted in the illuminations made by Jan Van Eyck for the Milan–Turin Book of Hours, commissioned in the early fifteenth century by John of Bavaria.[92] At the top end of the scale, and the preserve of the landed and merchant elite, was the tomb effigy. The extravagant heights that funerary sculpture could reach drew the scorn of satirical literature like Sebastian Brant's *Ship of fools*,[93] but tombs were widely accepted by church and society. Paul Binski has argued that the development of monumental sculpture in the thirteenth century reflected a growing sense of the person, with individuals taking the opportunity to shape their image. This does not mean that the dead person was trying to show herself or himself as a unique being, but indicates what Binski calls 'a socially and culturally constructed entity'. Through various emblems and motifs, a person was able to convey several messages about the social, familial, religious and political associations that forged her or his identity.[94]

With a key purpose being a prompt to prayer, the images appearing on memorials were often designed to express piety and devotion. The majority of tomb effigies show the individuals lying on their backs in a position of prayer or contemplation, and depicted in the perfect body they would inhabit when resurrected. Not everyone was satisfied to demonstrate prayer in such a 'fixed' way, however. In the 1430s Alvaro de Luna, Constable of Castile (d.1453), arranged for a bronze tomb to be built for himself and his wife in their private chapel at Toledo Cathedral. The tombs apparently contained a mechanical device that allowed the figures to move into a kneeling position 'thus creating the illusion that they were attending mass performed at the chapel's altar'.[95]

In contrast to this idealised portrait, a person could choose to make a statement about decay. An innovation of the late fourteenth century was the 'transi tomb', which depicted the dead in the stage of advanced decomposition. It appears an entirely northern phenomenon, and is absent from Spain, Mediterranean France and Italy. The transis therefore appear in areas where the body was generally concealed during funerals. There are further regional differences in the expressions of decay, although the level of gruesomeness remains constant. The emaciated transi was favoured in England; in Austria and Germany the corpse was covered in frogs and snakes; and in France the body was usually riddled with worms. François de la Sarra's tomb in the church of La Sarraz, Switzerland, is a strong contender for the most disturbing. He is depicted with a frog on each eye, two frogs on the mouth and a fifth on the genitals, and his whole body is covered in snakes and worms. Such sophisticated sculpture could be afforded only by the wealthy, and transi tombs were a fashionable choice for northern Europe's elite. There are several possible interpretations of the transi. They were perhaps an attempt to humiliate the body in order to gain salvation, similar to the extreme burial request made by Philippe de Mézières mentioned above. The hope for salvation may be represented in the 'double-decker' tombs that show the decaying body beneath a sculpture of the living body: a case of decay and revival. They could also have an educative purpose, acting as a mirror on men's and women's souls and the need to focus on sin. The cadaver tomb of John Baret in Bury St Edmunds addresses the onlooker directly: 'Ho that wil sadly beholde me with his ie / may se hys owyn merowr and lerne for to die.'[96]

Perhaps ultimately what the transi tombs represented was the difficulty of separating the worldy and the other-worldly. Commissioners of tombs in general did not appear to want to forget their earthly achievements, or at least quell the impulse to make statements about status and associations; they wanted to assert authority beyond the grave. In response to the fragility of life, monuments aimed to preserve the family name, and reaffirm earthly relationships. Some churches were virtually colonised by particular families. The tomb of Sir Reginald Cobham (d.1446) in the chancel at Lingfield church (Surrey) has been positioned in such a way that, in the words of Nigel Saul, it 'virtually blocks the view to the altar'.[97] Such bold, solid markers certainly helped to edge out other competitors for church space and spiritual benefits. In the early fifteenth century, Filippus, Lord of Castellani from the powerful Frescobaldi of Florence, spent 1,000 florins on a tomb for himself and his family, which was to be positioned near the altar of a new chapel in the church of Santo Spirito. The endowment was conditional on there being no coats of arms, other than that of the Frescobaldi, placed on the sepulchre. Any prayers said at the altar were, therefore, safe-guarded for the family.[98] Similar sentiments stimulated the kinship tombs of northern Europe, where the effigies are accompanied by smaller figures representing family members. They express the desire that both living and dead family members, through the generations, should be included in the daily prayers. Gravestones and brasses also began to depict the conjugal family in the later Middle Ages: children increasingly appear on gravestones and brasses during the fifteenth century; husbands and wives are shown together to mark their lifetime relationships. There are gestures of intimacy with hands held and figures turning towards each other. At Careby, Lincolnshire, a knight and his lady are carved lying in bed together: as they were in life, so in death.[99]

In the vast majority of cases, the monuments were not intended to look like the persons concerned. Customers chose from pre-existing stock and from standard patterns. Nevertheless, people were not indifferent as to how their monuments looked. The main concern was to differentiate status by costume, selecting armour for a knight, civilian attire for a burgess and vestments for a priest. Further associations could be signified by coats of arms, insignia or merchants' marks: in London in 1460, the grocer Robert Garstang wanted his executors to place a marble stone over his body on which was marked his name, his sign and the arms of his company.[100] There is also some indication that by the fifteenth century exact representations were being sought. In 1403 the Duke of Orléans wanted 'the likeness of his face and hands, in an attitude of death' to be placed on his tomb.[101] The desire for an authentic picture may have been prompted by the growing practice of making death masks. In Florence, imprints could be made into terracotta, wax or papier-mâché images. In wills from England and northern France, there are requests for sculptured figures that bore resemblance to the dead. Indeed one Douaisian husband demanded that his executors check that the burial sculptures he had ordered for himself and his wife did actually resemble them.[102]

Other images tried to capture something of the spirit of the individual by showing him or her in a 'living' situation. The tombstone of Canon de Villeneuve de Guingamp (d.1417) in the church of St Yves, Paris, shows him reading from a book in front of a large group of attentive students.[103] Two further examples are of those who had died before comparable achievements could be marked. Friedrich von Castell, who died aged five in 1325, was depicted on a gravestone at the church of Rüdenhausen (near Kitzingen, Germany) playing with birds and dogs. The breathtaking tomb of Martín Vázquez de Arce (El Doncel) at Sigüènza Cathedral (Castile), dating from 1493–97, shows the young man perched up on one arm, quietly reading a book of prayers while a page sits at his feet and two squires hold his coat of arms. In depicting both the Doncel and young Friedrich in such active ways, and with actions so typical of their age groups, the monuments appear to underline the tragedy of their premature deaths.[104]

On the other hand, Gómez Manrique wrote that a premature death was better than dying in old age because fame and honour would be greater in those who died before their lives were corrupted.[105] While the deeds of the majority of Europeans would only be known to their nearest and dearest, the political and literary elite hoped that their fame would have wider and longer currency. Deaths of significant individuals resulted in the preaching of a number of sermons at the funeral and commemorative services: they could praise ancestry and wealth, while presenting the dead person's life as a moral example. The sermon preached to mark the death of the Black

Prince in 1376 extolled his power and wisdom, listing his great battle victories, especially Poitiers. Epitaphs became a useful way to ask for prayers while celebrating earthly successes. In St Mary Redcliffe, Bristol, the achievements of William Cannynges (d.1474) that are listed include his tonnage of ten ships and the telling line 'no age nor time can wear out well-woon fame'. Finally writers and readers were aware of literary immortality. The fifteenth-century humanist Aurelio Brandolini wrote, 'Do not Plato and Aristotle … seem to be alive today … whose doctrine and fame fill the whole world?'[106] For a select few, fame could triumph over death.

The end

In the Middle English *Book of vices and virtues* it is written, 'For when þou bygynnyst to lyve, þou bigynnist to dye'.[107] Medieval society recognised that life was short, a temporary occupation of a fleshy body compared with the millennia in the afterlife and eventually as a resurrected soul. Memories could be equally short, and many strove to establish that their time on earth and particularly their time in Purgatory would not be forgotten. Testaments, funeral and burial rituals were used to perpetuate a person's memory, designed to manipulate the way that the dying enter the consciences of the living as never before. It could be argued that endings were more important than beginnings in late medieval society. More attention was paid to the observance and anniversary of a person's death than to her or his birthday. It is obits rather than birth dates that appear regularly in calendars of devotional manuscripts.[108]

Death came to all; it made everyone equal, or so the dances of death proclaimed. Yet people differed in status, gender and age; they had their own families, lived in particular neighbourhoods, joined guilds, established employment and friendship networks. All of these factors made each death and its commemoration different from the next. Some medieval testators were keen to make that difference very noticeable, either by paying for extravagance or by insisting that it was simple. Others had no particular preference and let their families decide.

It may well have come to the same thing in the end. However specific the instructions for burial, once he or she was dead there was little a person could do to see those actions carried out. In Norfolk, John Paston dragged his feet over the memorial for his father. In 1471 his angry mother was embarrassed that five years had passed and still nothing had been done about her husband's tomb. Louis de Mâle, Count of Flanders (d.1384), even left parts of a tomb in storage at his castle in Lille with instructions that his executors should complete it. Yet the tomb failed to materialise for nearly seventy years until his great-grandson Philippe Le Bon took up and revised the project in 1453. Nor were monuments set to last for ever. By the time of the chantry commissions in the 1540s, most of the perpetual chantries that had been founded in Berkshire, Wiltshire and Dorset during the thirteenth and fourteenth centuries had disappeared. As time rolled on and memories faded, old gravestones and monuments were re-cycled. How long a person remained an individuated name is difficult to know. The sheer weight of numbers on some guild books may have meant that as time marched on, the 'older' lost their individuality and became part of the collective dead.[109] These were the practical realities, but medieval people lived and died in the hope that there would not be too long to wait for resurrection and a new cycle of life to begin.

Notes

1   Harrison (ed.), *The Danse Macabre of women*, p. 54; Dove, *The perfect age*, ch. 10.
2   de Rojas, *La Celestina*, Act 4, scene 2.
3   For discussions on Purgatory see Le Goff, *The birth of Purgatory* and Duffy, *The stripping of the altars*, ch. 10.
4   Dubruck, *The theme of death*, p. 98. Dunbar's refrain appears in 'I that in heill and gladnes', Bawcutt (ed.), *William Dunbar*, pp. 105–10. See also Huizinga, *The autumn of the Middle Ages*, ch. 5.
5   Martorell and Galba, *Tirant Lo Blanc*, p. 610.
6   Davis, 'Some tasks and themes', p. 327; Geary, *Living with the dead*, p. 36.
7   Grubb, *Provincial families*, pp. 63, 67–8; Duffy, *The stripping of the altars*, pp. 343–4.
8   Morgan, 'Of worms and war', p. 135; Aberth, *From the brink of the apocalypse*, pp. 256–7.
9   Petrarch, *Letters of old age*, vol. 1, p. 7.
10 Shahar, 'The old body', p. 163; Powell and Fletcher, 'In die sepulture seu trigintali', p. 204.
11 Christine de Pizan's *Vision* in Blumenfeld-Kosinski and Brownlee (eds), *The selected writings of Christine de Pizan*, p. 186; Bower, *Scotichronicon*, vol. 8, book XVI, pp. 303–4.
12 Tristram, 'Old stories longe tyme agoon', pp. 182–3.
13 Origo, *The merchant of Prato*, pp. 341–2.
14 Kinser (ed.), *The memoirs of Philippe de Commynes*, vol. 2, pp. 407–24, quotation at p. 409.
15 A printed version can be found in Horstmann (ed.), *Yorkshire writers*, vol. 1, p. 376; Lindley, 'The Black Death in English art', p. 144.
16 Kittell, 'Testaments of two cities', pp. 50–1; Cohn, 'The place of the dead', p. 25.
17 Chiffoleau, *La comptabilité*, pp. 49–50, 54–60, 65; Howell, 'Fixing movables', pp.

20–1, 26; Grubb, *Provincial families*, p. 81; Lorcin, *Vivre et mourir*, p. 58; Callum, 'And hir name was charite', pp. 183, 185; Cohn, *The cult of remembrance*, pp. 14, 197–9.

18 Howell, 'Fixing movables', pp. 8, 27; Rosenthal, *The purchase of Paradise*, p. 23.

19 Brown, 'The ceremonial of royal succession', pp. 274–5; Dahmus, *William Courtney*, p. 275.

20 For problems with wills see Burgess, 'Late medieval wills', pp. 14–33; Brown, *Popular piety*, pp. 22–3. Testators in Douai and Genoa appear to have been uninfluenced by the officials attending the writing: Kittel, 'Testaments of two cities', p. 54.

21 Rosenthal, *The purchase of Paradise*, p. 81; Gibson, *The theater of devotion*, p. 72; Howell, 'Fixing movables', p. 38.

22 Howell, 'Fixing movables', pp. 36–7; Callum, 'And hir name was charite', p. 185. Cf. Harris, *English aristocratic women*, pp. 167–8.

23 Mormando, 'What happens to us when we die?', pp. 112–13.

24 La Roy Ladurie, *Montaillou*, p. 230.

25 Meech and Allen (eds), *The book of Margery Kempe*, pp. 172–3.

26 Vovelle, *La mort*, pp. 142–6; Mâle, *Religious art*, pp. 348–54; O'Connor, *The art of dying well*; Duffy, *The stripping of the altars*, pp. 315–17; Grubb, *Provincial families*, p. 67; Peacock (ed.), *Instructions for parish priests*, pp. 56–63.

27 Finucane, 'Sacred corpse', p. 42; Aston, 'Death', pp. 208–9.

28 Erbe (ed.), *Mirk's festial*, p. 294. In Montaillou, women played a significant role in preparing the dead: Le Roy Ladurie, *Montaillou*, p. 224. See also Finucane, 'Sacred corpse', p. 44; Daniell, *Death and burial*, p. 44; Orme, *Medieval children*, p. 119; Vivanco, *Death*, pp. 150–1.

29 Bossy, *Christianity in the West*, p. 27; Vovelle, *La mort*, pp. 40–4.

30 Brucker (ed.), *The society of Renaissance Florence*, p. 48.

31 Trexler, *Public life*, pp. 172–85.

32 Gittings, *Death*, p. 170.

33 Chiffoleau, *La compabilité*, p. 123.

34 Gittings, *Death*, pp. 29–30; Finucane, 'Sacred corpse', pp. 41–2; Aston, 'Death', p. 222.

35 Strocchia, *Death and ritual*, p. 45.

36 Wieck, 'The death desired', p. 442; Vovelle, *La mort*, p. 155; Bossy, *Christianity in the West*, p. 28.

37 Cohn, 'The place of the dead', p. 32; Cohn, *The cult of remembrance*, p. 14; Dinn, 'Death and rebirth', pp. 152–3; Vovelle, *La mort*, p. 151; Grubb, *Provincial families*, p. 69.

38 Dinn, 'Death and rebirth', p. 155.

39 Grubb, *Provincial families*, p. 51; Robin (trans and ed.), *Laura Cereta*, p. 159.

40 Grubb, *Provincial families*, p. 82; Strocchia, *Death and ritual*, pp. 10–11; Strocchia, 'Death rites', pp. 126–7.

41 Women were generally believed to be unable to exercise the necessary control: Vivanco, *Death*, p. 165; Horrox, 'Purgatory', p. 106.

42 Flynn, *Sacred charity*, pp. 39, 64–6; Henderson, *Piety and charity*, p. 161; Chiffoleau, *La compabilité*, p. 186.

43 Strocchia, 'Death rites', p. 121.

44 Brucker (ed.), *The society of Renaissance Florence*, p. 45; Strocchia, *Death and ritual*, p. 55.

45 Morgan, 'Of worms and war'; Gittings, *Death*, p. 139.

46 Flynn, *Sacred charity*, p. 66; Daniell, *Death and burial*, pp. 52–3.

47 Cohn, *The cult of remembrance*, p. 124; Strocchia, *Death and ritual*, pp. 39–43.

48 Aston, 'Death', p. 221.

49 Giesey, *The royal funeral ceremony*, pp. 22–4, 79–104; Finucane, 'Sacred corpse', p. 47; Binski, *Medieval death*, pp. 60, 149; Kantorowicz, *The king's two bodies*, pp. 420–3.

50 Grubb, *Provincial families*, pp. 68–9.

51 Daniell, *Death and burial*, p. 52; Gittings, *Death*, p. 28; Heers, *Family clans*, p. 228; Flynn, *Sacred charity*, p. 76; Brown, *Popular piety*, p. 101.

52 Shirley (trans.), *A Parisian journal*, p. 320.

53 Chiffoleau, *La compabilité*, pp. viii, 126–42; Lorcin, *Vivre et mourir*, pp. 141–5; Strocchia, *Death and ritual*, pp. 55–82; Grubb, *Provincial families*, pp. 68–9; Terpstra, *Lay confraternities*, p. 71.

54 Chiffoleau, *La compabilité*, pp. 200–4, 207, 430–2. See too Lorcin, *Vivre et mourir*, pp. 141–5; Harding, 'Burial choice', p. 119.

55 Boccaccio, *The Decameron*, introduction, pp. 11–13; Cohn, *The Black Death transformed*, p. 123; Strocchia, *Death and ritual*, pp. 59, 66; Cohn, 'The place of the dead', pp. 29–33; Horrox, 'Purgatory', p. 105; Fiero, 'Death ritual', pp. 272–3.

56 Tanner, *The Church in medieval Norwich* , pp. 99–100; Romano, *Housecraft*, p. 183; Grubb, *Provincial families*, p. 70. For Castile see Vivanco, *Death*, p. 146.

57 Chiffoleau, *La compabilité*, pp. 142–3; Gittings, *Death*, p. 25.

58 Binski, *Medieval death*, p. 133.

59 Erbe (ed.), *Mirk's Festial*, p. 294; Vovelle, *La mort*, p. 160. For examples of mass graves see Shirley (trans.), *A Parisian journal*, p. 132; Platt, *King Death*, p. 6; Cohn, *The Black Death transformed*, pp. 123–4.

60 Cohn, 'The place of the dead', pp. 26, 28–9. See too London wills, 1380–1520, in Harding, 'Burial choice', p. 122. For a contrasting view see Daniell, *Death and burial*, pp. 97–102.

61 Chiffoleau, *La comptabilité*, p. 183, cites fifty-seven per cent of female testators compared to forty-four per cent of male testators. See also Harding, 'Burial choice', p. 126. For canon law see Ariès, *The hour of our death*, p. 74.

62 Flynn, *Sacred charity*, pp. 66–7; Aston, 'Death', p. 221.

63 Rosenthal, *The purchase of Paradise*, p. 83; Harding, 'Burial choice', p. 124.

64 Cohn, *The cult of remembrance*, p. 35.

65 Brucker (ed.), *The society of Renaissance Florence*, pp. 42–3; Strocchia, *Death and ritual*, p. 70.

66 Daniell, *Death and burial*, p. 92.

67 Morgan, 'Of worms and war', p. 140.

68 Among others see Chiffoleau, *La comptabilité*, pp. 166–7; Brown, *Popular piety*, p. 93.

69 Le Roy Ladurie, *Montaillou*, p. 224; Chiffoleau, *La comptabilité*, pp.168–9.

70 Duffy, *The stripping of the altars*, p. 332; Dinn, 'Monuments', p. 248.

71 Dahmus, *William Courtney*, p. 266.

72 Harding, 'Burial choice', p. 122. See too Deregnaucourt, 'L'élection de sépulture', p. 348.

73 Lepine and Orme, *Death and memory*, pp. 17–18; Chiffoleau, *La compatabilité*, p. 159.

74 Binski, *Medieval death*, p. 55; Mâle, *Religious art*, p. 329.

75 Bossy, *Christianity in the West*, p. 33; Ariès, *Western attitudes*, pp. 22–5.

76 Dinn, 'Monuments', p. 245.

77 Dinn, 'Monuments', p. 253; Chiffoleau, *La comptabilité*, pp. 183–6; Deregnaucourt, 'L'élection de sépulture', pp. 350–1. However contrast these with Grubb, *Provincial families*, p. 82 where he shows that as many women in the Veneto chose to be buried with other kin as with their husbands.

78 Harding, 'Burial choice', p. 127; Deregnaucourt, 'L'élection de sépulture', pp. 350–1. Chiffoleau, *La comptabilité*, p. 192; Grevet 'L'élection de sépulture', p. 357.

79 Lepine and Orme, *Death and memory*, p. 23; Daniell, *Death and burial*, p. 92.

80 Chiffoleau, *La comptabilité*, pp. 162–3.

81 Hadley, *Death in medieval England*, p. 47; Gilchrist, 'Christian bodies', p. 111.

82 Finucane, 'Sacred corpse', p. 56.

83 Erbe (ed.), *Mirk's Festial*, p. 298. The mother herself could be buried in the churchyard, though not in the church (she would remain ritually impure like all women who had not been churched).

84 Orme, *Medieval children*, p. 126; Finucane, 'Sacred corpse', p. 54; Daniell, *Death and burial*, pp. 127–8.

85 Chaney (ed.), *The poems of François Villon: The testament*, p. 37.

86 For a detailed example see Lewis, 'The anniversary service for Blanche, Duchess of Lancaster'.

87 Swanson, *Church and society*, p. 303; Brown, *Popular piety*, p. 101.

88 Duffy, *The stripping of the altars*, pp. 334–5.

89 Swanson, *Religion and devotion*, p. 227.

90 Lorcin, *Vivre et mourir*, pp. 137–8; Chiffoleau, *Comptabilité*, pp. 323–55; and see Cohn, *The cult of remembrance*, pp. 206–11; Grubb, *Provincial families*, p. 78; Cohn, 'The place of the dead', p. 34; Strocchia, *Death and ritual*, p. 58.

91 Vovelle, *La mort*, p. 164.

92 Châtelet, *Early Dutch painting*, p. 38; Vovelle, *La mort*, p. 160.

93 Brant, *Ship of fools*, ch. 85, p. 282.

94 Binski, *Medieval death*, pp. 92–111; Saul, *Death, art and memory*, p. 249.

95 Lenaghan, 'Commemorating', pp. 129–30.

96 Cohen, *Metamorphosis*; Binski, *Medieval death*, pp. 142–6; Morgan, 'Of worms and war', pp. 135–7; Swanson, *Religion and devotion*, pp. 200–1; Camille, *Master of death*, p. 176.

97 Saul, *Death, art and memory*, p. 241.

98 Cohn, *The cult of remembrance*, p. 142, 145; Cohn, 'The place of the dead', pp. 35–7.

99 Coss, *The lady*, pp. 84–97; Saul, *Death, art and memory*, p. 248; Binski, *Medieval death*, p. 106.

100 Harding, 'Burial choice', p. 129.
101 Mâle, *Religious art*, pp. 382–4.
102 Strocchia, *Death and ritual*, pp. 46–8; Cohn, 'The place of the dead', pp. 40, 43; Gittings, *Death*, p. 34.
103 Mâle, *Religious art*, p. 366.
104 Arnold, *Kind und Gesellschaft*, pp. 38–9; Leneghan, 'Commemorating', p. 131.
105 Sieber, 'Gómez Manrique's last poem', p. 160.
106 D'Avray, *Death and the prince, passim;* Barber, *The Black Prince*, pp. 235–6; Burke, 'Death in the Renaissance', p. 61.
107 Francis (ed.), *The book of vices and virtues*, p. 69, lines 18–19.
108 Orme, *Medieval children*, p. 46; Camille, *Master of death*, p. 245.
109 Davies (ed.), *Paston letters and papers*, vol. 1, pp. 359, 602; Morganstern, *Gothic tombs*, p. 140; Saul, *Death, art and memory*, p. 230; Kreider, *English chantries*, pp. 87–9; Brown, *Popular piety*, p. 97; Harding, 'Burial choice', p. 129; Morgan, 'Of worms and war', pp. 132–3.

BIBLIOGRAPHY

Printed primary sources

Alberti, Leon Battista, *I libri della famiglia: the family in Renaissance Florence*, trans. Renée Neu Watkins (Columbia, South Carolina, 1969)

Amt, Emilie (ed.), *Women's lives in medieval Europe: a sourcebook* (London, 1993)

Angela of Foligno's memorial, ed. Cristina Mazzoni and trans. John Cirignano (Cambridge, 1999)

Attreed, Lorraine C. (ed.), *The York household books 1461–1490* (2 vols, Stroud, 1991)

Barbaro, Francesco, 'On wifely duties', in Benjamin G. Kohl and Ronald G. Witt with Elizabeth B. Welles (eds), *The earthly republic: Italian humanists on government and society* (Philadelphia, 1978)

Bataille, Georges (ed.), *The trial of Gilles de Rais*, trans. Richard Robinson (Los Angeles, 1991)

Bawcutt, Priscilla (ed.), *William Dunbar: selected poems* (London and New York, 1996)

Benson, Larry D. (ed.), *The Riverside Chaucer*, 3rd edn (Oxford, 1987)

Blake, N. F. (ed.), *Caxton's own prose* (London, 1973)

Blamires, Alcuin (ed.), *Woman defamed and woman defended: an anthology of medieval texts* (Oxford, 1992)

Blumenfeld-Kosinski, Renate and Kevin Brownlee (eds), *The selected writings of Christine de Pizan* (New York, 1997)

Boccaccio, Giovanni, *The Decameron*, trans. Guido Waldman (Oxford, 1993)

Boer, Charles (trans.), *Marsilio Ficino's Book of life* (Woodstock, Connecticut, 1994)

Bornstein, Daniel E. (trans.), *Dino Compagni's chronicle of Florence* (Philadelphia, 1986)

Bower, Walter, *Scotichronicon*, ed. D. E. R. Watt (Aberdeen, 1987)

Brant, Sebastian, *Ship of fools*, trans. Edwin H. Zeydel (New York, 1944)

Brereton, Georgina E. and Janet M. Ferrier (eds), *Le ménagier de Paris* (Oxford, 1981)

Brown, Carleton (ed.), *Religious lyrics of the fifteenth century* (Oxford, 1939)

Brucker, Gene (ed.), *Two memoirs of Renaissance Florence: the diaries of Buonaccorso Pitti and Gregorio Dati* (New York, 1967)

Brucker, Gene (ed.), *The society of Renaissance Florence: a documentary study* (Toronto, 1998)

Champion, Pierre (ed.), *Charles d'Orléans: poésies* (Paris, 1923)

Chaney, Edward F. (ed.), *The poems of François Villon* (Oxford, 1940)

Christine de Pizan, *The book of the city of ladies*, trans. Earl Jeffrey Richards (New York, 1982)

Christine de Pisan, *The treasure of the city of ladies, or The book of the three virtues*, trans. Sarah Lawson (Harmondsworth, 1985)

Christine de Pizan, *The book of the body politic*, ed. Kate Langdon Forhan (Cambridge, 1994)

Christine de Pizan, *The book of deeds of arms and of chivalry*, ed. Charity Cannon Willard (Philadelphia, 1999)

Cicero, de Senectute, de Amicitia, de Divinatione, trans. William Armistead Falconer (Cambridge, Massachusetts, 1923)

Cobo, Bernabé, *History of the Inca empire*, trans. R. Hamilton (Austin, Texas, 1983)

Dahlberg, Charles (trans.), *The romance of the rose* (Hanover and London, 1971)

Dante Alighieri, *The divine comedy*, trans. Charles S. Singleton (6 vols, Princeton, 1970–75)

Dante's Il convivio (The banquet), trans. Richard H. Lansing (New York, 1990)

Davies, Matthew (ed.), *The Merchant Tailors' Company of London: court minutes 1486–1493* (Stamford, 2000)

Davies, Norman (ed.), *Paston letters and papers of the fifteenth century* (2 vols, Oxford, 1971)

Dean, James M. (ed.), *Richard the Redeless and Mum and the sothsegger* (Kalamazoo, Michigan, 2000)

de Rojas, Fernando, *La Celestina (The Spanish bawd)*, trans. J. M. Cohen (Harmondsworth, 1964)

Deschamps, Eustache, *Oeuvres complètes de Eustache Deschamps*, ed. Le Marquis de Queux de Saint-Hilaire (Paris, 1878–80), vols 2, 6

Dominici, Giovanni, *On the education of children*, trans. A. B. Coté (Washington, DC, 1927)

Dyboski, Roman (ed.), *Songs, carols and other miscellaneous poems from the Balliol MS 354: Richard Hill's commonplace book*, Early English Text Society, e.s., 101 (1907)

Ellis, Roger (ed.), Thomas Hoccleve, *'My compleinte' and other poems* (Exeter, 2001)

Erbe, Theodor (ed.), *Mirk's Festial: a collection of homilies*, Early English Text Society, e.s., 96 (1905)

Evans, Joan (trans. and ed.), *The unconquered hero: a chronicle of the deeds of Don Pero Niño, Count of Buelna* (London, 1928)

Fowler, David C., Charles F. Briggs and Paul G. Remley (eds), *The governance of kings and princes: John Trevisa's Middle English translation of the De regimine principum of Aegidius Romanus* (New York, 1997)

Francis, W. Nelson (ed.), *The book of vices and virtues: a fourteenth century English translation of the Somme le roi of Lorens D'Orleans*, Early English Text Society, o.s., 217 (1942)

Furnivall, Frederick J. (ed.), *The book of quinte essence*, Early English Text Society, o.s., 16 (1889)

Galbraith, V. H. (ed.), *The anonimalle chronicle 1333 to 1381* (Manchester, 1927)

Ginevra Niccolini di Camugliano, *The chronicles of a Florentine family 1200–1470* (London, 1933)

Hardman, Phillipa, *The Heege manuscript: a facsimile of National Library of Scotland MS Advocates 19.3.1* (Leeds, 2000)

Harper-Bill, Christopher (ed.), *Charters of the medieval hospitals of Bury St Edmunds* (Woodbridge, 1994)

Harris, M. D. (ed.), *The Coventry leet book, Early English Text Society*, o.s., 135 (1908)

Harrison, Ann Tukey (ed.), *The Danse Macabre of women: ms. Fr. 995 of the Bibliothèque Nationale* (Kent, Ohio, 1994)

Horrox, Rosemary (ed.), *The Black Death* (Manchester, 1994)

Horstmann, C. (ed.), *Yorkshire writers: Richard Rolle of Hampole, an English father of the Church and his followers* (2 vols, London, 1895)

Hyatte, Reginald (ed.), *Laughter for the devil: the trials of Gilles de Rais, companion-in-arms of Joan of Arc (1440)* (London and Toronto, 1984)

Johnston, Dafydd (trans. and ed.), *Galar Y Beirdd Marwnadau Plant: poets' grief: medieval elegies for children* (Cardiff, 1993)

Johnston, Dafydd (trans. and ed.), *Iolo Goch: poems* (Llandysul, 1993)

Kaeuper, Richard and Elspeth Kennedy (eds), *The book of chivalry of Geoffroi de Charny: text, context and translation* (Philadelphia, 1996)

Kindrick, Robert L. (ed.), *The poems of Robert Henryson* (Kalamazoo, Michigan, 1997)

Kinser, Samuel (ed.), *The memoirs of Philippe de Commynes*, trans. Isabelle Cazeaux (2 vols, Columbia, 1973)

Kirby, J. L. (ed.), *Calendar of inquisitions post mortem*, vol. 18: *1–6 Henry IV: 1399–1405* (London, 1987)

Kline, Daniel T. (ed.), *Medieval literature for children* (New York and London, 2003)

Landucci, Luca, *A Florentine diary from 1450 to 1516*, trans. Alice de Rosen Jervis (London, 1927)

Larrington, Carolyne (ed.), *Women and writing in medieval Europe: a sourcebook* (London, 1995)

Lemay, Helen Rodnite (ed.), *Women's secrets: a translation of Pseudo-Albertus Magnus's De secretis mulierum with commentaries* (New York, 1992)

Lester, G. A. (ed.), *Three late medieval moralities: Mankind, Everyman, Mundus et infans* (London, 1981)

Lindsay, W. M. (ed.), *Isidori Hispalensis episcopi. Etymologiarum sive originum* (2 vols, Oxford, 1911)

Lumby, J. Rawson (ed.), *Ratis raving and other moral religious pieces in prose and verse, Early English Text Society*, o.s., 43 (1870)

Lydgate, John, *Table manners for children, Stans puer ad mensum by John Lydgate*, trans. Nicholas Orme (London, 1990)

McGuire, Brian Patrick (trans.), *Jean Gerson. Early works* (New York, 1998)

McSheffrey, Shannon (ed.), *Love and marriage in late medieval London* (Kalamazoo, Michigan, 1995)

Manzalaoui, M. A. (ed.), *Secreta secretorum: nine English versions, Early English Text Society*, o.s., 276 (1977), vol. 1: text

Martin, Charles Trice (ed.), *Registrum epistolarum Fratris Johannis Peckham archiepiscopi Cantuariensis* (London, 1885)

Martin, G. H. (ed.), *Knighton's chronicle 1337–1396* (Oxford, 1995)

Martorell, Joanot and Martí Joan de Galba, *Tirant Lo Blanc*, trans. David Rosenthal (London, 1984)

Meech, Sanford Brown, and Hope Emily Allen (eds), *The book of Margery Kempe, Early English Text Society*, o.s., 212 (1940)

Middle English dictionary, eds. Hans Kurath and Sherman Kuhn (Ann Arbor, 1952–)

Murray, Jacqueline (ed.), *Love, marriage and family in the Middle Ages: a reader* (Peterborough, Ontario, 2001)

Peacock, Edward (ed.), *Instructions for parish priests by John Myrc*, Early English Text Society, o.s., 31 (1902)

Petrarch, Francesco, *Letters of old age: Rerum senilium libri I–XVIII*, trans. Aldo S. Bernardo, Saul Levin and Reta A. Bernardo (2 vols, Baltimore and London, 1992)

Phébus, Gaston, *The hunting book of Gaston Phébus*, intro. Marcel Thomas and François Arril (Manuscripts in Miniature, 3, London, 1998)

Piers Plowman, ed. Elizabeth Salter and Derek Pearsall (London, 1967)

Ragusa, Isa, and Rosalie B. Green (trans.), *Meditations on the life of Christ: an illustrated manuscript of the fourteenth century* (Princeton, 1961)

Rickert, Edith, *Chaucer's world*, ed. Clair C. Olson and Martin M. Crow (London, 1948)

Robin, Diana (trans. and ed.), *Laura Cereta: collected letters of a Renaissance feminist* (London and Chicago, 1997)

Rowland, Beryl (ed.), *Medieval woman's guide to health: the first English gynaecological handbook* (Kent, Ohio, 1981)

Salisbury, Eve (ed.), *The trials and joys of marriage* (Kalamazoo, Michigan, 2002)

Seymour, M. C. (ed.), *On the properties of things: John Trevisa's translation of Bartholomaeus Anglicus, De proprietatibus rerum: a critical text* (Oxford, 1975)

Sharpe, Reginald R. (ed.), *Calendar of coroners rolls of the city of London AD 1300–1378* (London, 1913)

Shirley, Janet (trans), *A Parisian journal 1405–1449* (Oxford, 1968)

Simmons, Thomas Frederick (ed.), *The lay folk's Mass book*, Early English Text Society, o.s., 71 (1879)

Sneyd, C. A. (ed.), *A relation, or rather a true account, of the island of England c.1500* (Camden Society, o.s., 37, London, 1847)

Stapleton, Thomas (ed.), *The Plumpton correspondence*, with intro. by Keith Dockray (reissued, Gloucester, 1990)

Stargardt, Ute (trans.), *The life of Dorothea von Montau, a fourteenth-century recluse* (Lewiston, 1997)

Thomas, Gwn (trans.), *Dafydd ap Gwilym. His poems* (Cardiff, 2001)

Thompson, Edward Maunde (ed.), *Chronicon Angliae, 1328–1388* (London, 1874)

Thorndike, Lynn (ed. and trans.), *University records and life in the Middle Ages* (New York, 1944)

Trigg, Stephanie (ed.), *Wynnere and Wastoure*, Early English Text Society, o.s., 297 (1990)

Waley, Pamela (trans.), *Curial and Guelfa* (London, 1982)

Whiting, Bartlett Jere (ed.), *Proverbs, sentences and proverbial phrases from English writings mainly before 1500* (Cambridge, Massachusetts, 1968)

Williamson, Maya Bijvoet (trans.), *The memoirs of Helene Kottanner (1439–1440)* (Cambridge, 1998)

Wilson, Katharine M. and Elizabeth M. Makowski (eds), *Wykked wyves and the woes of marriage: misogynous literature from Juvenal to Chaucer* (New York, 1990)

Secondary sources

Aberth, John, *From the brink of the apocalypse: confronting famine, war, plague and death in the later Middle Ages* (New York, 2001)

Alexandre-Bidon, Danièle and Monique Closson, *L'enfant à l'ombre des cathedrales* (Lyon, 1985)

Alexandre-Bidon, Danièle and Didier Lett, *Children in the Middle Ages: fifth–fifteenth centuries*, trans. Jody Gladding (Notre Dame, Indiana, 1999)

Allmand, Christopher, *Henry V* (London, 1992)

Ames-Lewis, Francis, *The intellectual life of the early Renaissance artist* (New Haven and London, 2000)

Archer, Rowena (ed.), *Crown, government and people in the fifteenth century* (Stroud, 1998)

Ariès, Philippe, *Centuries of childhood* (Harmondsworth, 1962)

Ariès, Philippe, *Western attitudes towards death: from the Middle Ages to the present*, trans. P. Ranum (Baltimore and London, 1974)

Ariès, Philippe, *The hour of our death*, trans. Helen Weaver (New York, 1981)

Arnade, Peter J., *Realms of ritual: Burgundian ceremony and civic life in late medieval Ghent* (Ithaca, New York, 1996)

Arnold, Klaus, *Kind und Gesellschaft in Mittelalter und Renaissance* (Paderborn, 1980)

Aston, Margaret, 'Death', in Horrox (ed.), *Fifteenth-century attitudes*

Attreed, Lorraine, 'From Pearl maiden to tower princes: towards a new history of medieval childhood', *Journal of Medieval History*, 8 (1978), 131–43

Bainbridge, Virginia R., *Gilds in the medieval countryside: social and religious changes in Cambridgeshire c.1350–1558* (Woodbridge, 1996)

Banker, James R., 'Mourning a son: childhood and parental love in the consolateria of Giannozzo Manetti', *History of Childhood Quarterly*, 3 (1976), 351–62

Barber, Richard, *The Black Prince* (Stroud, 2003)

Barron, Caroline M., 'The education and training of girls in fifteenth-century London', in Diana E. S. Dunn (ed.), *Courts, counties and the capital in the later Middle Ages* (Stroud, 1996)

Barron, Caroline M., 'London 1300–1540', in Palliser (ed.), *The Cambridge urban history*, vol. 1

Barron, Caroline M. and Ann Sutton (eds), *Medieval London widows, 1300–1500* (London, 1994)

Bassett, Steven (ed.), *Death in towns: urban responses to the dying and the dead, 100–1600* (Leicester, 1992)

Bedell, John, 'Memory and proof of age in England, 1272–1372', *Past and Present*, 162 (1999), 3–27

Beer, Mathias, *Eltern und Kinder des späten Mittelalters in ihren Briefen: Familienleben in der Stadt des Spätmittelalters und der frühen Neuzeit mit besonderer Berücksichtigung Nürnbergs (1400–1550)* (Nürnberg, 1990)

Bell, Rudolph M., *Holy anorexia* (Chicago, 1987)

Bell, Rudolph M., *How to do it: guides to good living for Renaissance Italians* (Chicago, 1999)

Ben-Amos, Ilana Krausman, *Adolescence and youth in early modern England* (New Haven, 1994)

Benedetti, Jean, *Gilles de Rais: the authentic Bluebeard* (London, 1971)

Benedictow, Ole Jørgen, 'The milky way in history: breast feeding, antagonism between the sexes and infant mortality in medieval Norway', *Scandinavian Journal of History*, 10 (1985), 19–53

Benedictow, Ole Jørgen, 'Demography', in Phillip Pulsiano (ed.), *Medieval Scandinavia: an encyclopedia* (New York, 1993)

Benedictow, Ole, *The Black Death 1346–53: the complete history* (Woodbridge, 2004)

Bennett, Judith M., *Women in the medieval English countryside: gender and household in Brigstock before the plague* (Oxford, 1987)

Bennett, Judith M., 'Ventriloquisms: when maidens speak in English songs, c.1300–1550', in Anne L. Klinck and Ann Marie Rasmussen (eds), *Medieval woman's song* (Philadelphia, 2002)

Bennett, Judith M. and Amy M. Froide (eds), *Singlewomen in the European past 1250–1800* (Philadelphia, 1998)

Bennett, Michael, 'Education and advancement', in Horrox (ed.), *Fifteenth-century attitudes*

Biller, P. P. A, 'Marriage patterns and women's lives: a sketch of a pastoral geography', in Goldberg (ed.), *Woman is a worthy wight*

Biller, Peter, *The measure of multitude: population in medieval thought* (Oxford, 2000)

Binski, Paul, *Medieval death: ritual and representation* (London, 1996)

Blockmans, W. P., 'The formation of a political union, 1300–1600', in J. C. H. Blom and E. Lamberts (eds), *History of the Low Countries*, trans. James C. Kennedy (New York, 1999)

Boase, Roger, *The troubadour revival: a study of social change and traditionalism in late medieval Spain* (London, 1978)

Bolton, Jim, '"The world upside down": plague as an agent of economic and social change', in Ormrod and Lindley (eds), *The Black Death in England*

Bossy, John, *Christianity in the West 1400–1700* (Oxford, 1985)

Boswell, John, *The kindness of strangers: the abandonment of children in Western Europe from late antiquity to the Renaissance* (London, 1989)

Braunstein, Philippe, 'Towards intimacy: the fourteenth and fifteenth centuries', in Georges Duby (ed.), *A history of private life*, vol. 2: *Revelations of the medieval world*, trans. Arthur Goldhammer (Cambridge, Massachusetts and London, 1988)

Brissaud, Y.-B. 'L'infanticide à la fin du moyen âge, ses motivations psychologiques et sa répression', *Revue historique de droit français et étranger*, 4th ser., 50 (1972), 229–56

Brodman, James William, *Charity and welfare: hospitals and the poor in medieval Catalonia* (Philadelphia, 1998)

Brooke, Christopher N. L., *The medieval idea of marriage* (Oxford, 1989)

Brown, Andrew D., *Popular piety in late medieval England: the diocese of Salisbury, 1250–1550* (Oxford, 1995)

Brown, D. Catherine, *Pastor and laity in the theology of Jean Gerson* (Cambridge, 1987)

Brown, Elizabeth A., 'The ceremonial of royal succession in Capetian France: the funeral of Philip V', *Speculum*, 55 (1980), 266–93

Brundage, James A., *Law, sex and Christian society in medieval Europe* (Chicago, 1987)

Brundage, James A., 'The merry widow's serious sister: remarriage in classical canon law', in Robert R. Edwards and Vickie Ziegler (eds), *Matrons and marginal women in medieval society* (Woodbridge, 1995)

Bullough, V. L., and C. Campbell, 'Female longevity and diet in the Middle Ages', *Speculum*, 55 (1980), 317–25

Burgess, Clive, 'Late medieval wills and pious convention: testamentary evidence reconsidered', in Michael Hicks (ed.), *Profit, piety and the professions in later medieval England* (Gloucester, 1990)

Burke, Peter, 'Death in the Renaissance 1347–1656', in Jane H. M. Taylor (ed.), *Dies illa. Death in the Middle Ages* (Liverpool, 1984)

Burrow, J. A., *The ages of man: a study in medieval writing and thought* (Oxford, 1986)

Bynum, Caroline Walker, *Holy feast and holy fast: the religious significance of food to medieval women* (Berkeley, California, 1987)

Cadden, Joan, *Meanings of sex difference in the Middle Ages: medicine, science and culture* (Cambridge, 1995)

Camille, Michael, *Master of death: the lifeless art of Pierre Remiet, illuminator* (New Haven and London, 1996)

Carey, Hilary M., *Courting disaster: astrology at the English court and university in the later Middle Ages* (London, 1992)

Carmichael, Ann G., 'The health status of Florentines in the fifteenth century', in Marcel Tetel, Ronald G. Witt and Rona Goffen (eds), *Life and death in fifteenth-century Florence* (London, 1984)

Carmichael, Ann G., *Plague and the poor in Renaissance Florence* (Cambridge, 1986)

Chabot, Isabelle, 'Lineage strategies and the control of widows in Renaissance Florence', in Sandro Cavallo and Lyndan Warner (eds), *Widowhood in medieval and early modern Europe* (Harlow, 1999)

Chamberlayne, Joanna L., 'Crowns and virgins: queenmaking during the Wars of the Roses', in Lewis, Menuge and Phillips (eds), *Young medieval women*

Charles-Edwards, T. M., *Early Irish and Welsh kinship* (Oxford, 1993)

Châtelet, Albert, *Early Dutch painting in the northern Netherlands in the fifteenth century*, trans. Christopher Brown and Anthony Turner (Oxford, 1981)

Chiffoleau, Jacques, *La comptabilité de l'au-delà* (Palais Farnese, Rome, 1980)

Chojnacki, Stanley, *Women and men in Renaissance Venice: twelve essays on patrician society* (Baltimore, 2000)

Christian, W. A., *Apparitions in late medieval and Renaissance Spain* (Princeton, New Jersey, 1981)

Clark, Elaine, 'Some aspects of social security in medieval England', *Journal of Family History*, 7 (1980), 307–20

Clark, Elaine, 'The decision to marry in thirteenth and fourteenth century Norfolk', *Medieval Studies*, 49 (1987), 496–516

Clark, Elaine, 'The quest for security in medieval England', in Sheehan (ed.), *Aging and the aged*

Classen, Albrecht, 'Love and marriage in late medieval verse: Oswald von Wolkenstein, Thomas Hoccleve and Michel Beheim', *Studia Neophilologica*, 62 (1990), 163–88

Clay, Rotha Mary, *The medieval hospitals of England* (London, 1909)

Cobban, Alan B., *The medieval English universities: Oxford and Cambridge to c.1500* (Aldershot, 1988)

Cobban, Alan B., *English university life in the Middle Ages* (London, 1999)

Cohen, Esther and Eliot Horowitz, 'In search of the sacred: Jews, Christians and rituals of marriage in the later Middle Ages', *Journal of Medieval and Renaissance Studies*, 20 (1990), 225–49

Cohen, Kathleen, *Metamorphosis of a death symbol: the transi tomb in the late Middle Ages and the Renaissance* (Berkeley, California, and London, 1973)

Cohn, Samuel K., *The cult of remembrance and the Black Death* (Baltimore, 1992)

Cohn, Samuel K., 'The place of the dead in Flanders and Tuscany: towards a comparative history of the Black Death', in B. Gordon and P. Marshall (eds), *The place of the dead: death and remembrance in late medieval and early modern Europe* (Cambridge, 2000)

Cohn, Samuel K., 'The Black Death: end of a paradigm', *American Historical Review*, 107: 3 (2002), 703–38

Cohn, Samuel K., *The Black Death transformed: disease and culture in early Renaissance Europe* (London, 2002)

Cosgrove, Art, 'Marriage in medieval Ireland', in Art Cosgrove (ed.), *Marriage in Ireland* (Dublin, 1985)

Coss, Peter R., *The lady in medieval England 1000–1500* (Stroud, 1998)

Coulton, G. G., *Infant perdition in the Middle Ages* (Medieval Studies, 16, London, 1922)

Cowgill, Jane, 'Chaucer's missing children', *Essays in Medieval Studies*, 12 (www.luc.edu/publications/medieval)

Crabb, Ann Morton, 'How typical was Alessandra Macinghi Strozzi of fifteenth-century widows?', in Mirrer (ed.), *Upon my husband's death*

Crabb, Ann Morton, *The Strozzi of Florence: widowhood and family solidarity in the Renaissance* (Ann Arbor, 1999)

Crouzet-Pavan, Elisabeth, 'A flower of evil: young men in medieal Italy'. in Levi and Schmitt (eds), *A history of young people*

Cuesta, María Luzdivina, 'Notes on family relationships: medieval Castilian narrative', in Itnyre (ed.), *Medieval family roles*

Dahmus, Joseph, *William Courtney, Archbishop of Canterbury 1381–1396* (University Park, Pennsylvania, and London, 1966),

Daniell, Christopher, *Death and burial in medieval England 1066–1550* (London, 1997)

Davies, M. P., 'The tailors of London and their guild c.1300–1500', unpublished D.Phil. thesis, University of Oxford, 1994

Davies, R. R., 'The status of women and the practice of marriage in late medieval Wales', in Jenkins and Owen (eds), *The Welsh law of women*

Davies, Natalie Zemon, 'Some tasks and themes in the study of popular religion', in

Charles Trinkhaus with Heike Oberman (eds), *The pursuit of holiness in late medieval and Renaissance religion* (Leiden, 1974)

Davies, Natalie Zemon, 'The reasons of misrule: youth groups and charivaris in sixteenth-century France', *Past and Present*, 80 (1971), 41–75

d'Avray, D. L., *Death and the prince: memorial preaching before 1350* (Oxford, 1994)

d'Avray, David, 'Marriage ceremonies and the church in Italy after 1215', in Dean and Lowe (eds), *Marriage in Italy*

Dean, Trevor, 'Fathers and daughters: marriage laws and marriage disputes in Bologna and Italy, 1200–1500', in Dean and Lowe (eds), *Marriage in Italy*

Dean, Trevor, *Crime in medieval Europe 1200–1550* (Harlow, 2001)

Dean, Trevor and J. K. P. Lowe (eds), *Marriage in Italy, 1300–1650* (Cambridge, 1998)

de Beauvoir, Simone, *Old age*, trans. Patrick O'Brien (London, 1970)

de La Ronciere, Charles, 'Tuscan notables on the eve of the Renaissance', in Georges Duby (ed.), *A history of private life*, vol. 2: *Revelations of the medieval world*, trans. Arthur Goldhammer (Cambridge, Massachusetts, 1988)

Delmaire, Bernard, 'Le livre de famille des Le Borgne (Arras 1347–1538): contribution à la démographie historique médiévale', *Revue du Nord*, 65 (1983), 301–26

Demaitre, Luke E., *Doctor Bernard de Gordon: professor and practitioner* (Toronto, 1980)

Demaitre, Luke E., 'The care and extension of old age in medieval medicine', in Sheehan (ed.), *Aging and the aged*

deMause, Lloyd (ed.), *The history of childhood: the evolution of parent–child relationships as a factor in history* (London, 1974)

Denley, Peter, 'Governments and schools in late medieval Italy', in Trevor Dean and Chris Wickham (eds), *City and countryside in late medieval and Renaissance Italy: essays presented to Philip Jones* (London, 1990)

Deregnaucourt, Jean-Pierre, 'L'élection de sépulture d'après les testaments douaisiens (1295–1500)', *Revue du nord*, 65 (1983), 343–52

Desportes, Pierre, 'La population de Reims au XVᵉ siècle', *Le moyen âge*, 4th ser., 21 (1966), 463–509

Dillard, Heath, *Daughters of the reconquest: women in Castillian town society, 1100–1300* (Cambridge, 1984)

Dinn, Robert, 'Baptism, spiritual kinship, and popular religion in late medieval Bury St Edmunds', *Bulletin of the John Rylands University Library of Manchester*, 72: 3 (1990), 93–106.

Dinn, Robert, 'Death and rebirth in late medieval Bury St Edmunds', in Bassett (ed.), *Death in towns*

Dinn, Robert, '"Monuments answerable to men's worth": burial patterns, social status and gender in late medieval Bury St Edmunds', *Journal of Ecclesiastical History*, 46 (1995), 237–55

Dobson, Mary J., *Contours of death and disease in early modern England* (Cambridge, 1997)

Dove, Mary, *The perfect age of man's life* (Cambridge, 1986)

Dubruck, Edelgard E., *The theme of death: French poetry of the Middle Ages and the Renaissance* (The Hague, 1964)

Dubruck, Edelgard E. and Barbara I. Gusick (eds), *Death and dying in the Middle Ages* (New York, 1999)

Duby, Georges, *The chivalrous society*, trans, Cynthia Postan (London, 1977)

Duffy, Eamon, *The stripping of the altars* (London and New Haven, 1992)

Dunstan, G. R., 'The human embryo in the Western moral tradition', in G. R. Dunstan and Mary J. Seller (eds), *The status of the human embryo* (London, 1988)

Dupâquier, Jacques (ed.), *Histoire de la population française*, vol. 1: *Des origines à la renaissance* (Paris, 1995)

Dyer, Christopher, 'Changes in the size of peasant holdings in some west midland villages, 1400–1500', in Richard M. Smith (ed.), *Land, kinship and life-cycle* (Cambridge, 1984)

Dyer, Christopher, *Standards of living in the later Middle Ages: social change in England c.1200–1520* (Cambridge, 1989)

Eisenbichler, Konrad, *The boys of the archangel Raphael: a youth confraternity in Florence, 1411–1785* (Toronto, 1998)

Eisenbichler, Konrad (ed.), *The premodern teenager: youth in society 1150–1650* (Toronto, 2002)

Emigh, Rebecca Jean, 'Land tenure, household structure and age at marriage in fifteenth-century Tuscany', *Journal of Interdisciplinary History*, 27: 4 (1997), 613–31

Ennen, Edith, *The medieval woman*, trans. Edmund Jephcott (Oxford, 1989)

Epstein, Steven, *Wage labor and guilds in medieval Europe* (Chapel Hill, North Carolina, 1991)

Epstein, Steven, *Genoa and the Genoese, 958–1528* (Chapel Hill, North Carolina, 1996)

Farmer, Sharon, *Surviving poverty in medieval Paris: gender, ideology and the daily lives of the poor* (Ithaca, 2002)

Fein, David A., *A reading of Villon's Testament* (Birmingham, Alabama, 1984)

Fiero, Gloria K., 'Death ritual in fifteenth-century manuscript illumination', *Journal of Medieval History*, 10 (1984), 271–94

Fildes, Valerie, *Wet nursing: a history from antiquity to the present* (Oxford, 1988)

Finch, A. J., 'Parental authority and the problem of clandestine marriages in the later Middle Ages', *Law and History Review*, 8 (1990), 189–204

Finlay, Robert, 'The Venetian Republic as a gerontocracy: age and politics in the Renaissance', *Journal of Medieval and Renaissance Studies*, 8 (1978), 157–78

Finucane, Ronald C., 'Sacred corpse, profane carrion: social ideals and death rituals in the later Middle Ages', in Joachim Whaley (ed.), *Mirrors of mortality. Studies in the social history of death* (London, 1981)

Finucane, Ronald C., *The rescue of innocents: endangered children in medieval miracles* (Basingstoke, 1997)

Flandrin, Jean-Louis, *Families in former times: kinship, household and sexuality*, trans. Richard Southern (Cambridge, 1976)

Fleming, Peter, *Family and household in medieval England* (London, 2001)

Fleming, Peter, *Women in late medieval Bristol* (Bristol, 2001)

Flynn, Maureen, *Sacred charity: confraternities and social welfare in Spain, 1400–1700* (London, 1989)

Folts, James D., 'Senescence and renascence: Petrarch's thoughts on growing old', *Journal of Medieval and Renaissance Studies*, 10 (1980), 207-37

Freed, John B., *Noble bondsmen: ministerial marriages in the archdiocese of Salzburg 1100-1343* (Ithaca and London, 1995)

Freeman, M. J., *François Villon in his works: the villain's tale* (Amsterdam, 2000)

French, Katherine L., *The people of the parish: community life in a late medieval English parish* (Philadelphia, 2001)

Friedrichs, Rhoda L., 'Marriage strategies and younger sons in fifteenth-century England', *Medieval Prosopography*, 4 (1993), 53-69

Fulton, Christopher 'The boy stripped bare by his elders: art and adolescence in Renaissance Florence', *Art Journal*, 56: 2 (1997), 31-40

Gabriel, A. L., *Student life in Ave Maria College, medieval Paris* (Notre Dame, Indiana, 1955)

Gauvard, Claude, 'Fear of crime in late medieval France', in Barbara A. Hanawalt and David Wallace (eds), *Medieval crime and social control* (Minneapolis, 1999)

Gavitt, Philip, *Charity and children in Renaissance Florence: the Ospedale degli Innocenti, 1410-1536* (Ann Arbor, 1990)

Geary, Patrick J., *Living with the dead in the Middle Ages* (Ithaca, 1994)

Genicot, L., 'Crisis: from the Middle Ages to modern times', in M. M. Postan (ed.), *The Cambridge economic history of Europe*, vol. 1: *The agrarian life of the Middle Ages* (Cambridge, 1966)

Geremek, Bronislaw, *Le salariat dans l'artisanat Parisien aux xiiie-xve siècles*, trans. Anna Posner and Christiane Klapisch-Zuber (Paris, 1968)

Geremek, Bronislow, *The margins of society in late medieval Paris*, trans. Jean Birrell (Cambridge, 1987)

Gerli, E. Michael (ed.), *Medieval Iberia: an encyclopedia* (New York, 2003)

Gibson, Gail McMurray, *The theater of devotion: East Anglian drama and society in the late Middle Ages* (Chicago, 1989)

Gibson, Gail McMurray, 'Blessing from sun and moon: churching as women's theater', in Barbara A. Hanawalt and David Wallace (eds), *Bodies and disciplines. Intersections and history in fifteenth-century England* (Minneapolis, 1996)

Gibson, Gail McMurray, 'Scene and obscene: seeing and performing late medieval childbirth', *Journal of Medieval and Early Modern History*, 29 (1998), 7-24

Giesey, Ralph E., *The royal funeral ceremony in Renaissance France* (Geneva, 1960)

Gilbert, C., 'When did a man in the Renaissance grow old?', *Studies in the Renaissance*, 14 (1967), 7-32

Gilchrist, Roberta, 'Christian bodies and souls: the archaeology of life and death in later medieval hospitals', in Bassett (ed.), *Death in towns*

Gillis, John R., *Youth and history: tradition and change in European age relations, 1770 –present* (New York and London, 1974)

Gittings, Clare, *Death, ritual and the individual in early modern England* (London, 1984)

Goldberg, P. J. P., 'Marriage, migration and servanthood: the York cause paper evidence', in Goldberg (ed.), *Woman is a worthy wight*

Goldberg, P. J. P., *Women, work and life cycle in a medieval economy: women in York and Yorkshire c.1300-1520* (Oxford, 1992)

Goldberg, P. J. P., 'Masters and men in later medieval England', in D. M. Hadley (ed.), *Masculinity in medieval Europe* (Harlow, 1999)

Goldberg, P. J. P., 'What was a servant?', in Anne Curry and Elizabeth Matthew (eds), *Concepts and patterns of service in the later Middle Ages* (Woodbridge, 2000)

Goldberg, P. J. P. (ed.), *Woman is a worthy wight: women in English society c.1200–1500* (Stroud, 1992)

Goldberg, P. J. P (ed.), *Women in England, c. 1275–1525* (Manchester, 1995)

Goldberg, P. J. P. and Felicity Riddy (eds), *Youth in the Middle Ages* (York, 2004)

Goodich, Michael E., *From birth to old age: the human life cycle in medieval thought, 1250–1350* (Lanham and London, 1989)

Goodich, Michael E., *Violence and miracle in the fourteenth century* (Chicago and London, 1995)

Gordon, Eleanora C., 'Accidents among medieval children as seen from the miracles of six English saints and martyrs', *Medical History*, 35 (1991), 145–63

Gottlieb, Beatrice, *The family in the Western world from the Black Death to the industrial age* (Oxford, 1993)

Grendler, Paul F., *Schooling in Renaissance Italy: literacy and learning, 1300–1600* (Baltimore, Indiana, 1989)

Grmk, Mirko D., *On ageing and old age: basic problems and historic aspects of gerontology* (The Hague, 1958)

Grevet, René, 'L'élection de sépulture d'après les testaments au audomarois de la fin du xvᵉ siècles', *Revue du nord*, 65 (1983), 353–60

Griffiths, Paul, *Youth and authority: formative experiences in England 1560–1640* (Oxford, 1996)

Griffiths, Ralph A., 'The interaction of war and plague in the later Middle Ages', in John Cule (ed.), *Wales and medicine* (London, 1975)

Grössinger, Christa, *Picturing women in late medieval and Renaissance art* (Manchester, 1997)

Grubb, James S., *Provincial families of the Renaissance: private and public life in the Veneto* (Baltimore and London, 1996)

Guenée, Bernard, 'L'âge des personnes authentiques: ceux qui comptent dans la société médiévale sont-ils jeunes ou vieux?', in Françoise Autrand (ed.), *Prosopographie et genèse de l'état moderne* (Paris, 1984)

Guenée, Bernard, *Between Church and State: the lives of four French prelates in the late Middle Ages*, trans. Arthur Goldhammer (Chicago and London, 1991)

Haas, Louis, 'Social connections between parents and godparents in late medieval Yorkshire', *Medieval Prosopography*, 10 (1989), 1–21

Haas, Louis, 'Women and childbearing in medieval Florence', in Itnyre (ed.), *Medieval family roles*

Haas, Louis, *The Renaissance man and his children: childbirth and early childhood in Florence, 1300–1600* (New York, 1998)

Hadley, D. M., *Death in medieval England: an archaeology* (Stroud, 2001)

Hale, J. R., *Renaissance Europe, 1480–1520* (London, 1971)

Hall, Dianne, *Women and the Church in medieval Ireland 1140–1540* (Dublin, 2003)

Hall, Edwin, *The Arnolfini betrothal: medieval marriage and the enigma of Van Eyck's double portrait* (Los Angeles and London, 1994)

Hall, Stuart and Tony Jefferson (eds), *Youth subcultures in post-war Britain* (London, 1975)

Hallam, H. E., 'Age at first marriage and age at death in the Lincolnshire fenland, 1252–1478', *Population Studies*, 39 (1985), 55–69.

Hanawalt, Barbara A., 'Childrearing among the lower classes of late medieval England', *Journal of Interdisciplinary History*, 8 (1977), 1–22

Hanawalt, Barbara A., *Crime and conflict in English communities, 1300–1348* (Cambridge, Massachusetts, 1979)

Hanawalt, Barbara A., *The ties that bound: peasant families in medieval England* (Oxford, 1986)

Hanawalt, Barbara A., 'The widow's mite: provision for medieval London widows', in Mirrer (ed.), *Upon my husband's death*

Hanawalt, Barbara A., *Growing up in medieval London: the experience of childhood in history* (Oxford, 1993)

Hanawalt, Barbara A., *'Of good and ill repute': gender and social control in medieval England* (Oxford, 1998)

Hanawalt, Barbara A., 'Violence in the domestic milieu of late medieval England', in Richard W. Kaeuper (ed.), *Violence in medieval society* (Woodbridge, 2000)

Hanawalt, Barbara A., 'Medievalists and the study of children', *Speculum*, 77 (2002), 440–60

Hanawalt Barbara A. (ed.), *Women and work in pre-industrial Europe* (Bloomington, 1986)

Harding, Vanessa, 'Burial choice and burial location in later medieval London', in Bassett (ed.), *Death in towns*

Hareven, Tamara K., 'The last stage: historical adulthood and old age', in Erik H. Erikson (ed.), *Adulthood* (New York, 1978)

Harper, Richard I., 'A note on corrodies in the fourteenth century', *Albion*, 15 (1983), 95–101

Harris, Barbara J., *English aristocratic women, 1450–1550: marriage and family, property and careers* (Oxford, 2002)

Harvey, Barbara, *Living and dying in England, 1100–1540: the monastic experience* (Oxford, 1993)

Hatcher, John, *Plague, population and the English economy, 1348–1530* (London, 1977)

Hatcher, John, 'Mortality in the fifteenth century: some new evidence', *Economic History Review*, 2nd ser., 39 (1986), 19–38

Heers, Jacques, *Family clans in the Middle Ages: a study of political and social structures in urban areas*, trans. Barry Herbert (Amsterdam, 1977)

Helleiner, Karl F., 'The population of Europe from the Black Death to the eve of the vital revolution', in E. E. Rich and C. H. Wilson (eds), *The Cambridge economic history of Europe*, vol. 4 (Cambridge, 1967)

Helmholz, Richard H., *Marriage litigation in medieval England* (Cambridge, 1974)

Helmholtz, Richard H., 'Infanticide in the province of Canterbury during the fifteenth century', *History of Childhood Quarterly*, 11 (1975), 282–340

Henderson, John, *Piety and charity in late medieval Florence* (Oxford and New York, 1994)

Henderson, John, 'Women, children and poverty in Florence at the time of the Black Death', in John Henderson and Richard Wall (eds), *Poor women and children in the European past* (London, 1994)

Herlihy, David, *Medieval and Renaissance Pistoia: the social history of an Italian town, 1200–1430* (New Haven and London, 1967)

Herlihy, David, 'Some psychological and social roots of violence in the Tuscan cities', in Lauro Martines (ed.), *Violence and civil disorder in Italian cities, 1200–1500* (Berkeley, 1972)

Herlihy, David, 'The population of Verona in the first century of Venetian rule', in J. R. Hale (ed.), *Renaissance Venice* (London, 1973)

Herlihy, David, 'Life expectancies for women in medieval society', in R. T. Morewedge (ed.), *The role of women in the Middle Ages* (London, 1975)

Herlihy, David, *Medieval households* (Cambridge, Massachusetts, 1985)

Herlihy, David, *Opera muliebra: women and work in medieval Europe* (New York, 1990)

Herlihy, David, 'Age, property and career in medieval society', in Sheehan (ed.), *Aging and the aged*

Herlihy, David, *Women, family and society in medieval Europe: historical essays, 1978–1991* (Oxford, 1995)

Herlihy, David, *The Black Death and the transformation of the West*, intro. Samuel K. Cohn (London, 1997)

Herlihy, David and Christiane Klapisch-Zuber, *Les Toscans et leurs familles: une étude du 'catasto' florentin de 1427* (Paris, 1978)

Herlihy, David and Christiane Klapisch-Zuber, *Tuscans and their families: a study of the Florentine catasto of 1427* (New Haven, 1985)

Higounet-Nadal, Arlette, *Périgueux aux xive et xve siècles: études de démographie historique* (Bourdeaux, 1978)

Hilton, R. H., *A medieval society* (London, 1966)

Hollingsworth, T. H., 'A demographic study of the British ducal families', in D. V. Glass and D. E. C. Eversley (eds), *Population history: essays in historical demography* (London, 1965)

Horrox, Rosemary (ed.), *Fifteenth-century attitudes* (Cambridge, 1994)

Horrox, Rosemary, 'Purgatory, prayer and plague: 1150–1380', in Jupp and Gittings (eds), *Death in England*

Houlbrooke, Ralph, *Death, religion and the family in England 1480–1750* (Oxford, 1998)

Housley, Norman, 'One man and his wars: the depiction of warfare by Marshal Boucicaut's biographer', *Journal of Medieval History*, 29 (2003), 27–40

Howell, Cicely, *Land, family and inheritance in transition: Kibworth Harcourt, 1280–1700* (Cambridge, 1983)

Howell, Martha C., 'Fixing movables: gifts by testaments in late medieval Douai', *Past and Present*, 150 (1996), 3–45

Howell, Martha C., *The marriage exchange: property, social place, and gender in cities of the Low Countries, 1300–1550* (Chicago, 1998)

Hsia, R. Po-Chia, *The myth of ritual murder: Jews and magic in Reformation Germany* (London, 1988)

Hughes, Jonathan, 'Stephen Scrope and the circle of Sir John Fastolf: moral and intellectual outlooks', in Christopher Harper-Bill and Ruth Harvey (eds), *Medieval knighthood*, vol. 4 (Woodbridge, 1992)

Huizinga, Johan, *The autumn of the Middle Ages*, trans. Rodney J. Payton and Ulrich Mammitzsch (Chicago, 1996)

Hurwich, Judith J., 'Marriage strategy among the German nobility', *Journal of Interdisciplinary History*, 29: 2 (1998), 169–95

Itnyre, Cathy Jorgensen (ed.), *Medieval family roles: a book of essays* (New York and London, 1996)

Jacobsen, Grete, 'Pregnancy and childbirth in the medieval north: a topology of sources and a preliminary study', *Scandinavian Journal of History*, 9 (1984), 91–111

Jacquart, Danielle and Claude Thomasset, *Sexuality and medicine in the Middle Ages*, trans. Matthew Adamson (Princeton, 1988)

Jaritz, Gerhard, '"Young, rich and beautiful". The visualization of male beauty in the late Middle Ages', in B. Nagy and M. Sebők (eds), '... *the man of many devices, who wandered full many ways': festschrift in honor of János M. Bak* (Budapest, 1999)

Jeay, Margaret, 'Sexuality and family in fifteenth-century France: are literary sources a mask or a mirror?', *Journal of Family History*, 4 (1979), 328–45

Jenkins, Dafydd and Morfydd E. Owen (eds), *The Welsh law of women* (Cardiff, 1980)

Jones, G. F., 'The signs of old age in Oswald von Wolkenstein's "Ich sich und hör"', *Modern Language Notes*, 89: 5 (1974), 797–86

Jones, Michael K. and Malcolm G. Underwood, *The king's mother: Lady Margaret Beaufort, Countess of Richmond and Derby* (Cambridge, 1992)

Jordan, William Chester, *The great famine: northern Europe in the early fourteenth century* (Princeton, 1996)

Jupp, Peter C. and Clare Gittings (eds), *Death in England: an illustrated history* (Manchester, 1999)

Kantorowicz, Ernst H., *The King's two bodies: a study in medieval political theology* (Princeton, 1957)

Karras, Ruth, 'Sex and the singlewoman', in Judith M. Bennett and Amy M. Froide (eds), *Singlewomen in the European past 1250–1800* (Philadelphia, 1998)

Karras, Ruth Mazo, *From boys to men: formations of masculinity in late medieval Europe* (Philadelphia, 2003)

Kellum, Barbara, 'Infanticide in England in the later Middle Ages', *History of Childhood Quarterly*, 1 (1974), 367–88

Kendall, Paul Murray, *Louis XI* (London, 1974)

Kermode, Jennifer I., 'Urban decline? The flight from office in late medieval York', *Economic History Review*, 2nd ser., 35 (1982), 179–98

Kertzer, D. I. and Laslett, P., *Aging in the past. Demography, society and old age* (Berkeley, California, 1995)

Killerby, Catherine Kovesi, *Sumptuary law in Italy 1200–1500* (Oxford, 2003)

King, Margaret L., *The death of the child Valerio Marcello* (Chicago, 1994)

Kirshner, Julius, *Pursuing honor while avoiding sin: the Monte delle Doti of Florence* (Milan, 1978)

Kirshner, Julius and Molho, Anthony, 'The dowry fund and the marriage market in early *quattrocento* Florence', *Journal of Modern History*, 50 (1978), 403–38

Kittell, Ellen E., 'Testaments of two cities: a comparative analysis of the wills of medieval Genoa and Douai', *European Review of History*, 5 (1998), 47–82

Klapisch, Christiane, 'Fiscalité et démographie en Toscane 1427–1430', *Annales économies sociétés civilisations*, 24 (1969), 1313–37

Klapisch-Zuber, Christiane, *Women, family and ritual in Renaissance Italy*, trans. Lydia G. Cochrane (Chicago and London, 1985)

Klapisch-Zuber, Christiane, 'Plague and family life', in Michael Jones (ed.), *The new Cambridge medieval history*, vol. 6: *c.1300–c.1415* (Cambridge, 2000)

Knight, L. Stanley, 'Welsh cathedral schools to 1600 AD', *Y Cymmrodor*, 29 (1919), 93–6

Knight, L. Stanley, 'Welsh schools from AD 1000 to AD 1600', *Archaeologia Cambrensis*, 19 (1919), 1–18, 276–91

Kowaleski, Maryanne, 'Singlewomen in medieval and early modern Europe: the demographic perspective', in Judith M. Bennett and Amy M. Froide (eds), *Singlewomen in the European past, 1250–1800* (Philadelphia, 1999)

Kreider, Alan, *English chantries: the road to dissolution* (Cambridge, Massachussets, 1979)

Krötzl, C., 'Christian parent–child relations in medieval Scandinavia according to Scandinavian miracle collections', *Scandinavian Journal of History*, 14 (1989), 21–37

Kuehn, Thomas, *Emancipation in late medieval Florence* (New Brunswick, New Jersey, 1982)

Labalme, Patricia, *Beyond their sex: learned women in the European past* (New York, 1980)

Labarge, Margaret Wade, '*Gerontocomia*, On the care of the aged: a fifteenth-century Italian guide by Gabrielle Zerbi (1445–1505), in Archer (ed.), *Crown, government and people*

Lane, Frederic Chapin, *Venetian ships and shipbuilders of the Renaissance* (Baltimore and London, 1934)

Laribière, Geneviève, 'Le mariage à Toulouse aux XIVᵉ et XVᵉ siècles', *Annales du Midi*, 79 (1967), 335–61

Law, John Easton, 'Age qualification and the Venetian constitution: the case of the Capello family', *Papers of the British School of Rome*, 39 (1971), 125–37

Le Goff, Jacques, *The birth of Purgatory*, trans. Arthur Goldhammer (Chicago, 1984)

Lenaghan, Patrick, 'Commemorating a real bastard: the chapel of Alvaro de Luna', in Elizabeth Valdez del Alamo with Carol Stamatis Prendergast (eds), *Memory and the medieval tomb* (Aldershot, 2000)

Lepine, David and Nicholas Orme, *Death and memory in medieval Exeter* (Devon and Cornwall Record Society, n.s., 47, Exeter, 2003)

Le Roy Ladurie, Emmanuel, *The peasants of Languedoc*, trans. John Day (Illinois, 1974)

Le Roy Ladurie, Emmanuel, *Montaillou: Cathars and Catholics in a French village, 1294–1324*, trans. Barbara Bray (Harmondsworth, 1980)

Levi, Giovanni and Jean-Claude Schmitt (eds), *A history of young people in the West*, vol. 1, trans. Camille Naish (Cambridge, Massachusetts and London, 1997)

Lewis, Katherine J., Noël James Menuge and Kim M. Phillips (eds), *Young medieval women* (Stroud, 1999)

Lewis, N. B., 'The anniversary service for Blanche, Duchess of Lancaster, 12th September, 1374', *Bulletin of the John Rylands University Library of Manchester*, 21 (1937), 176–92

Leyser, Henrietta, *Medieval women: a social history of women in England 450–1500* (London, 1995)

Lindley, Phillip, 'The Black Death in English art', in Ormrod and Lindley (eds), *The Black Death in England*

Lorcin, Marie-Thérèse, *Vivre et mourir en Lyonnais à la fin du moyen âge* (Paris, 1981)

Loschky, David and Ben D. Childers, 'Early English mortality', *Journal of Interdisciplinary History*, 24: 1 (1993), 85–97

Lynch, Katherine A., *Individuals, families, and communities in Europe, 1200–1800* (Cambridge, 2003)

McIntosh, Marjorie Keniston, *Autonomy and community: the royal manor of Havering, 1200–1500* (Cambridge, 1986)

MacKay, Angus, 'Religion, culture, and ideology on the late medieval Castilian-Granadan frontier', in Robert Bartlett and Angus MacKay (eds), *Medieval frontier societies* (Oxford, 1989)

Mâle, Emile, *Religious art in France: the late Middle Ages*, trans. Marthiel Matthews (Princeton, 1986)

Marcus, Ivan G., *Rituals of childhood: Jewish acculturation on Medieval Europe* (New Haven, 1996)

Mate, Mavis E., *Daughters, wives and widows after the Black Death: women in Sussex, 1350–1535* (Woodbridge, 1998)

Mate, Mavis E., *Women in medieval English society* (Cambridge, 1999)

Michaud, Francine, 'Apprentissage et salariat á Marseille avant la peste noire', *Revue historique*, 291: 1 (1994), 3–36

Michaud-Frejaville, Françoise, 'Bons et loyaux services: les contrats d'apprentissage en Orléanais (1380–1480), *Annales de l'est*, 34 (1982), 139–208

Minois, Georges, *History of old age: from antiquity to the Renaissance*, trans. Sarah Hanbury Tension (Chicago, 1989)

Mirrer, Louise (ed.), *Upon my husband's death: widows in the literature and histories of medieval Europe* (Ann Arbor, 1992)

Miskimin, Harry A., 'Widows not so merry: women and the courts in late medieval France', in Mirrer (ed.), *Upon my husband's death*

Mitterauer, Michael, *A history of youth*, trans. Graeme Dunphy (Oxford, 1992)

Molho, Anthony, *Marriage alliance in late medieval Florence* (Cambridge, Massachusetts, 1994)

Mollat, Michel, *The poor in the Middle Ages: an essay in social history*, trans. Arthur Goldhammer (New Haven, 1986)

Moorman, John R. H., *A history of the Franciscan order from its origins to the year 1517* (Oxford, 1968)

Moran, J. H., *The growth of English schooling 1340–1548* (Princeton, 1985)

Morgan, Philip, 'Of worms and war: 1380–1558', in Jupp and Gittings (eds), *Death in England*

Morganstern, A. A., *Gothic tombs of kinship in France, the Low Countries and England* (University Park, Pennsylvania, 2000)

Mormando, Franco, 'What happens to us when we die? Bernardino of Siena on "the four last things"', in Dubruck and Gusick (eds), *Death and dying*

Morrison, Alan S., Julius Kirshner and Anthony Molho, 'Epidemics in Renaissance Florence', *American Journal of Public Health*, 75 (1985), 528–35

Moss, Douglas, 'Death in fifteenth-century Tottenham', *Local Population Studies*, 37 (1986), 36–44

Newton, Mary Stella, *The dress of the Venetians, 1495–1525* (Aldershot, 1987)

Nicholas, David, *The domestic life of a medieval city: women, children and the family in fourteenth-century Ghent* (Lincoln and London, 1985)

Nicholas, David, 'Childhood in medieval Europe', in Joseph M. Hawes and N. Ray Hiner (eds), *Children in historical and comparative perspective: an international handbook and research guide* (New York, 1991)

Nicholas, David, *Medieval Flanders* (London, 1992)

Nicholas, David, 'Child and adolescent labour in the late medieval city: a Flemish model in regional perspective', *English Historical Review*, 110 (1995), 1103–31

Nicholas, David, *The later medieval city, 1300–1500* (London and New York, 1997)

Nirenberg, D., *Communities of violence: persecution of minorities in the Middle Ages* (Princeton, New Jersey, 1996)

O'Connor, Mary Catherine, *The art of dying well: the development of the ars moriendi* (New York, 1942)

Origo, Iris, *The merchant of Prato* (Harmondsworth, 1957)

Orme, Nicholas, *English schools in the Middle Ages* (London, 1973)

Orme, Nicholas, *From childhood to chivalry: the education of English kings and aristocracy, 1066–1530* (London, 1984)

Orme, Nicholas, 'Sufferings of the clergy: illness and old age in Exeter diocese', in Pelling and Smith (eds), *Life, death and the elderly*

Orme, Nicholas, 'Children and literature in medieval England', *Medium Aevum*, 68 (1999), 218–46

Orme, Nicholas, 'Schools and school-books', in Lotte Hellinga and J. B. Trapp (eds), *The Cambridge history of the book in Britain*, vol. 3: *1400–1557* (Cambridge, 1999)

Orme, Nicholas, *Medieval children* (New Haven and London, 2001)

Orme, Nicholas and Margaret Webster, *The English hospital, 1070–1570* (New Haven, 1995)

Ormrod, W. M. and P. G. Lindley (eds), *The Black Death in England* (Stamford, 1996)

Otis, Leah Lydia, *Prostitution in medieval society: the history of an urban institution in Languedoc* (Chicago and London, 1985)

Otis, Leah Lydia, 'Municipal wetnurses in medieval Montpellier', in Barbara A. Hanawalt (ed.), *Women and work in pre-industrial Europe* (Bloomington, 1986)

Ottaway, Patrick, *Archaeology in British towns from Emperor Claudius to the Black Death* (London, 1992)

Owen, Morfydd E., 'Shame and reparation: woman's place in the kin', in Jenkins and Owen (eds), *The Welsh law of women*

Owst, G. R., *Preaching in medieval England* (Cambridge, 1926)

Owst, G. R., *Literature and pulpit in medieval England* (Cambridge, 1933)

Ozment, Steven, *Ancestors: the loving family in old Europe* (Cambridge, Massachusetts, 2001)

Palliser, D. M. (ed.), *The Cambridge urban history of Britain*, vol. 1: *600–1540* (Cambridge, 2000)

Parsons, John Carmi, 'Mothers, daughters, marriage, power: some Plantagenet evidence', in John Carmi Parsons (ed.), *Medieval queenship* (Stroud, 1994)

Parsons, John Carmi, '"Que nos in infancia lactauit": the impact of childhood care-givers on Plantaganet family relationships in the thirteenth and early fourteenth centuries', in Constance M. Rousseau and Joel T. Rosenthal (eds), *Women, marriage and family in medieval Christendom. Essays in memory of Michael M. Sheehan* (Kalamazoo, 1998)

Pastoureau, Michel, 'Emblems of youth: young people in medieval imagery', in Levi and Schmitt (eds), *A history of young people*

Pelling, Margaret and Richard M. Smith (eds), *Life, death and the elderly: historical perspectives* (London, 1991)

Phillips, Kim M., 'Maidenhood as the perfect age of woman's life', in Lewis, Menuge and Phillips (eds), *Young medieval women*

Phillips, Kim M., *Medieval maidens: young women and gender in England, 1270–1540* (Manchester, 2003)

Phillips, Mark, *The memoir of Marco Parenti: a life in Medici Florence* (London, 1987)

Phillips William D. (ed.), *Enrique IV and the crisis of fifteenth-century Castile*, (Cambridge, Massachusetts, 1978)

Piera, Monserrat, and Donna M. Rogers, 'The widow as heroine: the fifteenth century Catalan chivalresque novel Curial e Güelfa', in Mirrer (ed.), *Upon my husband's death*

Pilcher, Jane, *Age and generation in modern Britain* (Oxford, 1995)

Piper, A. J., 'The monks of Durham and patterns of activity in old age', in Caroline M. Barron and Jenny Stratford (eds), *The Church and learning in later medieval society* (Donington, 2002)

Piponier, Françoise and Perrine, Mane, *Dress in the Middle Ages*, trans. Caroline Beamish (New Haven, Connecticut, 1998)

Platt, Colin, *King Death: the Black Death and its aftermath in late medieval England* (London, 1996)

Pleij, Herman, *Dreaming of Cockaigne: medieval fantasies of the perfect life*, trans. Diane Webb (New York, 2001)

Poos, Lawrence L., *A rural society after the Black Death: Essex, 1350–1525* (Cambridge, 1991)

Post, J. B., 'Ages of menarche and menopause: some medieval authorities', *Population Studies*, 25: 1 (1991), 83–7

Powell, Susan and Alan J. Fletcher, '"In die sepulture seu trigintali": the late medieval funeral and memorial sermon', *Leeds Studies in English*, n.s., 12 (1981), 195–220

Power, Eileen, *Medieval English nunneries, c.1275–1535* (Cambridge, 1922)

Pullan, Brian, *Rich and poor in Renaissance Venice* (Oxford, 1971)

Rashdall, Hastings, *The universities of Europe in the Middle Ages*, vol. 3: *English universities – student life* (Oxford, 1936)

Rawcliffe, Carole, *Medicine and society in later medieval England* (Stroud, 1995)

Rawcliffe, Carole, *Medicine for the soul: the life, death and resurrection of an English Medieval hospital. St Giles's Norwich, c.1249–1550* (Stroud, 1999)

Razi, Zvi, *Life, marriage and death in a medieval parish: economy, society and demography in Halesowen, 1270–1400* (Cambridge, 1980)

Reyerson, Kathryn L., 'Women in business in medieval Montpellier', in Hanawalt (ed.), *Women and work*

Reyerson, Kathryn L., 'The adolescent apprentice/worker in medieval Montpellier', *Journal of Family History*, 17 (1992), 353–70

Richards, Jeffrey, *Sex, dissidence and damnation: minority groups in the Middle Ages* (London, 1991)

Riddy, F., 'Mother knows best: reading social change in a courtesy text', *Speculum*, 71 (1996), 68–86

Rocke, Michael, *Forbidden friendships: homosexuality and male culture in Renaissance Florence* (Oxford, 1996)

Romano, Dennis, *Housecraft and statecraft. Domestic service in Renaissance Venice, 1400–1600* (Baltimore and London, 1996)

Rösener, Werner, *Peasants in the Middle Ages*, trans. Alexander Stützer (Cambridge, 1992)

Rosenthal, Joel T., *The purchase of Paradise: gift giving and the aristocracy, 1307–1485* (London, 1972)

Rosenthal, Joel T., 'Mediaeval longevity: and the secular peerage, 1350–1500', *Population Studies*, 27 (1973), 287–93

Rosenthal, Joel T., 'Retirement and the life cycle in fifteenth-century England', in Sheehan (ed.), *Aging and the aged*

Rosenthal, Joel T., *Patriarchy and families of privilege in fifteenth-century England* (Philadelphia, 1991)

Rosenthal, Joel T., *Old age in late medieval England* (Philadelphia, 1996)

Rosenthal, Joel T., 'Three-generation families: searching for grandpa and grandma in late medieval England', in Itnyre (ed.), *Medieval family roles*

Rosenthal, Joel T., 'When did you last see your grandfather?', in Archer (ed.), *Crown, government and people*

Ross, James Bruce, 'The middle-class child in urban Italy, fourteenth to early sixteenth century', in deMause (ed.), *The history of childhood*

Rosser, Gervase, 'Urban culture and the Church 1300–1540', in Palliser (ed.), *The Cambridge urban history*, vol. 1

Rossiaud, Jacques, 'Prostitution, youth and society in the towns of southwestern France in the fifteenth century', in Robert Forster and Orest Ranum (eds), *Deviants and the abandoned in French society*, trans. Elborg Forster and Patricia M. Ranum (Baltimore and London, 1978)

Rossiaud, Jacques, 'Crises et consolidations, 1330–1530', in Georges Duby (ed.), *Histoire de la France urbaine*, vol. 2 : *La ville médiévale des Carolingiens à la Renaissance* (Paris, 1980)

Rossiaud, Jacques, *Medieval prostitution*, trans. Lydia G. Cochrane (Oxford, 1988)

Rubin, Miri, 'Small groups: identity and solidarity in the late Middle Ages', in Jennifer Kermode (ed.), *Enterprise and individuals in fifteenth-century England* (Stroud, 1991)

Rubin, Miri, *Gentile tales: the narrative assault on late medieval Jews* (New Haven and London, 1999)

Rublack, Ulinka, 'Pregnancy, childbirth and the female body in early modern Germany', *Past and Present*, 150 (1996), 84–110

Ruggiero, Guido, *The boundaries of eros: sex crime and sexuality in Renaissance Venice* (Oxford, 1985)

Russell, Josiah Cox, *British medieval population* (Alberquerque, 1948)

Sablonier, Roger 'The Aragonese royal family around 1300', in Han Medick and David Warren Sabean (eds), *Interest and emotion: essays on the study of family and kinship* (Cambridge, 1984)

Saul, Nigel, *Death, art and memory in medieval England: the Cobham family and their monuments, 1300–1500* (Oxford, 2001)

Sawyer, Birgit and Peter, *Medieval Scandinavia: from conversion to Reformation circa 800–1500* (Minneapolis, 1993)

Schofield, John and Alan Vince, *Medieval towns* (Leicester, 1994)

Schultz, James A., 'Medieval adolescence: the claims of history and the silence of the German narrative', *Speculum*, 66 (1991), 519–39

Schultz, James A., *The knowledge of childhood in the German Middle Ages, 1100–1350* (Philadelphia, 1995)

Schultz, James A., 'Childhood', in John M. Jeep (ed.), *Medieval Germany: an encyclopedia* (New York, 2001)

Schwinges, R. C., 'Student education, student life', in Hilde de Ridder-Symoens (ed.), *A history of the European university*, vol. 1: *Universities in the Middle Ages* (Cambridge, 1991)

Scott, Margaret, *A visual history of costume: the fourteenth and fifteenth centuries* (London, 1986)

Sears, Elizabeth, *The ages of man: medieval interpretations of the life cycle* (Princeton, 1986)

Sebregondi, Ludovica, 'Clothes and teenagers: what young men wore in fifteenth-century Florence', in Eisenbichler (ed.), *The premodern teenager*

Shahar, Shulamith, *Childhood in the Middle Ages* (London, 1990)

Shahar, Shulamith, 'The boy bishop's feast: a case study in Church attitudes towards children in the high and late Middle Ages', in Diana Wood (ed.), *The Church and childhood* (Oxford, 1994)

Shahar, Shulamith, 'The old body in medieval culture', in Sarah Kay and Miri Rubin (eds), *Framing medieval bodies* (Manchester, 1994)

Shahar, Shulamith, *Growing old in the middle ages,* trans. Yael Lotan (London, 1997)

Shahar, Shulamith, 'Old age in the high and late Middle Ages', in Paul Johnson and Pat

Thane (eds), *Old age from antiquity to post-modernity* (London, 1998)

Shaw, David Gary, *The creation of a community: the city of Wells in the Middle Ages* (Oxford, 1993)

Sheehan, Michael M. (ed.), *Aging and the aged in medieval Europe* (Toronto, 1990)

Sheehan, Michael M., *Marriage, family and law in medieval Europe: collected studies*, ed. James K. Farge (Cardiff, 1996)

Sieber, Harry, 'Gómez Manrique's last poem: consolatoria para Doña Juana de Mendoça', in Alan Deyermond and Jeremy Lawrence (eds), *Letters and society in fifteenth-century Spain. Studies presented to P. E. Russell on his eightieth birthday* (Llandysul, 1993)

Smith, Llinos Beverley, 'Proofs of age in medieval Wales', *Bulletin of the Board of Celtic Studies*, 38 (1991), 134–44

Smith, Llinos Beverley, 'Fosterage, adoption and god-parenthood: ritual and fictive kinship in medieval Wales', *Welsh History Review*, 16 (1992), 1–35

Smith, Richard M., 'The people of Tuscany and their families in the fifteenth century: medieval or Mediterranean?', *Journal of Family History*, 6 (1981), 107–28

Smith, Richard M., 'The manorial court and the elderly tenant in late medieval England', in Pelling and Smith (eds), *Life, death and the elderly*

Smith, Robert S., 'Barcelona "bills of mortality" and population, 1457–1590', *Journal of Political Economy*, 54 (1936), 84–93

Stoertz, Fiona Harris, 'Suffering and survival in medieval English childbirth', in Itnyre (ed.), *Medieval family roles*

Strocchia, Sharon T., 'Death rites and the ritual family in Renaissance Florence', in Marcel Tetel, Ronald G. Witt and Rona Goffen (eds), *Life and death in fifteenth-century Florence* (Durham and London, 1989)

Strocchia, Sharon T., *Death and ritual in Renaissance Florence* (Baltimore and London, 1992)

Swanson, R. N., *Church and society in late medieval England* (Oxford, 1989)

Swanson, R. N., *Religion and devotion in Europe, c.1215–c.1515* (Cambridge, 1995)

Taddei, Ilaria, 'Puerizia, adolescenza and giovinezza: images and conceptions of youth in Florentine society during the Renaissance', in Eisenbichler (ed.), *The premodern teenager*

Taglia, Kathryn Ann, 'The cultural construction of childhood: baptism, communion, and confirmation', in Constance M. Rousseau and Joel T. Rosenthal (eds), *Women, marriage and family in Medieval Chistendom: essays in memory of Michael M. Sheehan* (Kalamazoo, 1998)

Tanner, Norman P., *The Church in medieval Norwich, 1370–1532* (Toronto, 1984)

Terpstra, Nicholas, *Lay confraternities and civic religious in Renaissance Bologna* (Cambridge, 1995)

Thomas, Keith, 'Age and authority in early modern England', *Proceedings of the British Academy*, 62 (1976), 205–48

Thrupp, Sylvia, *The merchant class of medieval London, 1300–1500* (Chicago, 1948)

Trexler, Richard C., *Public life in Renaissance Florence* (New York, 1980)

Trexler, Richard C., 'A widows' asylum of the Renaissance: the Orbatello of Florence', in Peter N. Stearns (ed.), *Old age in preindustrial society* (New York, 1982)

Trexler, Richard C., *Dependence in context in Renaissance Florence* (Binghamton, New York, 1994)

Tristram, Philippa, "'Old stories longe tyme agoon": death and the audience of Chaucer's pardoner', in Herman Braet and Werner Verbeke (eds), *Death in the Middle Ages* (Louvain, 1983)

Tucker, M. J., 'The child as beginning and end: fifteenth and sixteenth century English childhood', in in deMause (ed.), *The history of childhood*

Turner, Victor, *The ritual process: structure and anti-structure* (New York, 1969)

Van Gennep, Arnold, *The rites of passage*, trans. Monika B. Vizedom and Gabrielle L. Caffee (London, 1960)

Verger, Jacques, 'The universities', in Michael Jones (ed.), *The new Cambridge medieval history*, vol. 6: *c.1300–c.1415* (Cambridge, 2000)

Vivanco, Laura, *Death in fifteenth-century Castile: ideologies of the elite* (Woodbridge, 2004)

Voaden, Rosalynn and Stephanie Volf, 'Visions of my youth: representations of the childhood of medieval visionaries', *Gender and History*, 12 (2000), 665–84

Vovelle, Michel, *La mort et l'occident de 1300 à nos jours* (Paris, 1983)

Walker, S. S., 'Proof of age of feudal heirs in medieval England', *Medieval Studies*, 35 (1973), 306–23

Walker, Sue Sheridan (ed.), *Wife and widow in medieval England* (Anne Arbor, 1993)

Walters, D. B., 'The European legal context of the Welsh law in matrimonial property', in Jenkins and Owen (eds), *The Welsh law of women*

Ward, Jennifer C., *English noblewomen in the later Middle Ages* (London and New York, 1992)

Webb, Diane M., 'Friends of the family: some miracles for children by Italian friars', in Diana Wood (ed.), *The church and childhood* (Oxford, 1994)

Weinstein, Donald and Rudolph M. Bell, *Saints and society: the two worlds of Western Christendom, 1000–1700* (Chicago, 1982)

Weissman, Ronald F. E., *Ritual brotherhood in Renaissance Florence* (New York, 1982)

Wensky, Margaret, 'Women's guilds in Cologne in the later Middle Ages', *Journal of European Economic History*, 11 (1982), 631–50

Wieck, Roger S., 'The death desired: books of hours and the medieval funeral', in Dubruck and Gusick (eds), *Death and dying*

Wölffin, H., *The art of Albrecht Dürer*, trans. A. and H. Grieve (London, 1971)

Wood, Robert A., 'Poor widows, c. 1393–1415', in Caroline M. Barron and Anne F. Sutton (eds), *Medieval London widows 1300–1500* (London, 1994)

Wood-Legh, K. L., *Perpetual chantries in Britain* (Cambridge, 1965)

Wrigley, E. A. and R. S. Schofield, *The population history of England, 1541–1871: a reconstruction* (London, 1981)

Wunder, Heide, *He is the sun, she is the moon: women in early modern Germany*, trans. Thomas Dunlap (Cambridge, Massachusetts, 1998)

Yarborough, Anne, 'Apprentices as adolescents in sixteenth-century Bristol', *Journal of Social History*, 13 (1979), 67–81

INDEX